Robert Boardman is Professor of Political Science and Director of the Centre for Foreign Policy Studies at Dalhousie University, Nova Scotia. His previous publications include *International Organiz- ation and the Conservation of Nature*, *Britain and the People's Republic of China, 1949–1974*, *Europe, Africa and Lomé III* (co-editor with Panayotis Soldatos and Timothy M. Shaw), *Nuclear Exports and World Politics* (co-editor with James F. Keeley), *Foreign Policy-Making in Communist Countries* (co-editor with Hannes Adomeit) and *The Management of Britain's External Relations* (co-editor with A. J. R. Groom).

PESTICIDES IN WORLD AGRICULTURE

PESTICIDES IN WORLD AGRICULTURE

The Politics of International Regulation

Robert Boardman

Dalhousie University

106402

St. Martin's Press   New York

First published in the United States of America in 1986

Printed in Hong Kong

ISBN 0-312-60285-5

Library of Congress Cataloging-in-Publication Data
Boardman, Robert.
Pesticides in world agriculture.
Bibliography: p.
Includes index.
1. Pesticide residues in food—International
cooperation. 2. Pesticides—Environmental aspects.
3. Environmental policy—International cooperation.
4. Agricultural laws and legislation. I. Title.
HD9000. 9. A1B63 1986   363.1'79   85-27742
ISBN 0-312-60285-5

For Matthew

Contents

Preface

An excursus on the reasons why a book came to be written is usually the part of it best ignored. I owe a special debt of thanks, however, which calls for this peculiar form of self-indulgence. The suggestion that I might tackle a book on the international regulation of pesticides came originally from Dr Geoffrey le Patourel, of the Imperial College Field Station, Silwood Park, during the course of a visit he paid to Nova Scotia in 1979. Far more familiar than I could ever be with the questions that form the core of the study, he has provided valuable insights during my own visits to England in the period since. At the same time as acknowledging this help, I rush to relieve him of any responsibility for the direction the study has actually taken, and for any errors of fact, or of judgement on my part, that will undoubtedly have crept in.

I have tried to do two things. This is, first, an account of some of the main developments and issues involved in the international regulation of pesticides. Inevitably it strays into areas of national regulation at some points, partly in order to identify the contexts of policy processes, but partly also because the approaches of some countries have wider repercussions in the international system. A second objective was to make use of this subject as a means of exploring the phenomena of international regulatory politics in ways that might have a wider applicability, and therefore be of more general interest, to political scientists and students of international relations.

During the research I benefited greatly from the assistance of many people, most of whom, unfortunately, as officials of governments or of the secretariats of international organisations, ought properly to remain anonymous. They include officials of the United States Department of Agriculture, especially of the Agricultural Research Services, Beltsville, Maryland; the Office of Pesticide Programs, Environmental Protection Agency, Washington, DC; and staff of the Congressional Research Service. I was helped considerably by staff of the International Register of Potentially Toxic Chemicals (IRPTC), in the Geneva offices of the United Nations Environment Programme

(UNEP); and officials of the Plant Production and Protection Division, Food and Agriculture Organisation, in Rome. I also made use of the library and documentation services of the World Health Organisation, Geneva, and the UNEP secretariat in Nairobi. I should also like to thank officials of the Commission of the European Communities, Brussels; the staff of the library and documentation centre of the Council of Europe, Strasbourg; and staff of the International Centre of Insect Physiology and Ecology, Nairobi.

I was also assisted by officials of the Ministry of Agriculture and the Ministry of Science, Technology and Environment of the Government of Malaysia, who took the time to review pesticides policy questions with me. I should also like to thank the Socio-Economic Research and General Planning Unit, Prime Minister's Department, for help and for permission to carry out research in Malaysia; staffs of the libraries of the Universiti Pertanian Malaysia, Serdang, and the University of Malaya; officials of the Environmental Protection Society of Malaysia; and, finally, my Nova Scotian colleague, Richard Stubbs, of the Department of Political Science, St Francis Xavier University, who helped make the time in Kuala Lumpur still more useful and enjoyable.

I am particularly grateful to the Director-General and staff of the secretariat of the Groupement International des Associations Nationales de Fabricants de Produits Agrochimiques (GIFAP), in Brussels, for assistance during my visit and for helpful information afterwards. The staff of the library of the Centre for Overseas Pest Research, London, worked with patient and friendly efficiency to provide me with materials on several occasions.

A significant portion of the research was carried out with the support of grants from the Research Development Fund, Dalhousie University, and the Social Sciences and Humanities Research Council of Canada, and I should like to thank both of these.

Thanks are also due to my colleague Tim Shaw, who took an early interest in the study, and proposed the inclusion of the volume in the Macmillan International Political Economy Series being published under his general editorship.

My family put up with the intrusion of this pest into their lives for longer than anyone should be called upon to do. To them as always, a special note of gratitude.

R.B.
Chester Basin

1 Introduction

The chemicals used in modern agriculture, forestry, industry and medicine have demonstrated an impressive potential for generating symbolic politics. The history of chemical politics is littered with the hulks of many past *causes célèbres*: the Seveso explosion in the Icmesa chemical plant in Italy in 1976, which exposed several communities to high concentrations of toxic compounds; Love Canal in the United States, where a number of hazardous materials, some of them carcinogenic, leached to the surface and into family dwellings after having been buried in the 1950s; or the case of Lekkerkerk in the Netherlands. Pesticide chemicals have produced their own patterns of political encounters and regulatory policies, linked to, but often distinct from, those of the extended family network of chemical politics. Some of these chemicals have become staples in the political diet over long periods. The residues of attitudes left behind may then continue to be active. Herbicide politics in many western countries in the 1980s was heir to the DDT politics of the 1960s.

Such issues are not confined to individual countries. Chemicals are international in character. Pesticides, for examples, enter international trade, particularly trade between the advanced industrialised nations. Many are produced with a view to sales in clearly defined export markets. Foods and other commodities may contain potentially dangerous pesticide residues, and these products too cross national borders. If, in such cases, the regulatory systems in the importing country are more stringent than those in the exporting country – as happens routinely with agricultural exports from developing countries to western Europe or North America – then effective regulation of the domestic market may have to be combined with *de facto* trade barriers. Similar regulatory dilemmas apply to the chemicals themselves. Pesticides issues can also be transmitted between countries. Herbicide spraying to control vegetation in olive groves in Corfu in the mid-1980s prompted criticism from environmental groups elsewhere in Europe concerned about the threats this posed to the wild flora of the island.

1

Pesticides derive their stamina in political systems from their dual character. They are valuable because they are lethal. Some groups of compounds emerged out of the search for more effective nerve gases that might be useful on the battlefield. According to some reliable estimates the deaths resulting from the peacetime use of pesticide chemicals may run as high as several thousand a year. Set against such hazards is the sheer destructive power of the multitude of animal and plant species that constitute the actual targets of these chemicals. Not for nothing do the protagonists of chemical strategies of pest control in agriculture quickly resort to the imagery of warfare. Here, it seems, is evidence either of the existence of a malevolent or playfully malicious deity, or of a cosmic struggle for supremacy between humans and insects.

This duality has its sharpest definition in developing countries. Under some conditions up to one-third or a half of a crop may be lost because of attack by pests. Because of economic, administrative or other weaknesses, pesticides may not be used in ways likely to maximise the benefits to be derived from them or to minimise the costs associated with them. Misuse may exacerbate problems of insect resistance to chemicals. Pesticides may thus prove to be a counter-productive instrument of agricultural development. Innocent bystanders, such as fish used as a protein source in rice-growing areas of South-east Asia, may be caught between the chemical weapon and the target. In these circumstances the regulatory problem – even assuming that enforcement can be taken for granted – becomes acute. It would be hypothetically possible, though politically un-profitable, to calculate death and illness rates, whether from malnu-trition or poisoning, likely to be linked with any pest control strategy on a continuum from non-use to maximum use, and to shape policy accordingly. In practice, many of the difficulties of the regulatory approach in developing countries arise from contradictions between possible criteria. Regulatory standards aimed at in some western countries, for example on the question of pesticide residues in foods, may have limited applicability. Agricultural chemicals behave diffe-rently in temperate and tropical climates. In some countries it mat-ters whether wild birds are affected by pesticide use on farms or in forests; in others it does not. In the context of economic development priorities, regulatory frameworks may clash with other goals by deterring foreign investment. Setting up local industries may relieve pressure on foreign exchange reserves; but even if practicable, the option may not be desirable if, because of lack of research capabilities or technical expertise, it entails production of early-generation pesticides noted for their toxicity to man and their persistence in the environment, or unsafe industrial practices.

The subject of this book is the international regulation of pesticides. The phrase has a self-contradictory twist. No regulatory agencies can be found at the international level. Institutions with a variety of regulatory aims abound, but none can be regarded as comparable in its powers with a regulatory agency of a government operating in its domestic environment. International organisations act as forums for bargaining and compromise among states, or else as entities which can in some situations persuade governments to move in certain directions. While much of the discussion in the chapters which follow is about the role of such organisations, the focus is as much on the limitations on their powers to act as on their freedom of manoeuvre in a complex and changing international system. For this reason we must also take into account those policies of governments which themselves have a significant effect on the international politics of pesticides, as well as the chemical companies whose activities generate the regulatory issues which are the main theme of the study. But before we can begin to tackle these questions, a closer look at the nature of these issues is required. What is the pesticides debate about?

Debate may be too complimentary a word. The differing viewpoints have often seemed to come from opposing armed camps. The main contours of the arguments for and against continued, or expanded, pesticide use in agriculture and forestry are well defined. So is the documenting of the facts: that pesticides increase crop yields by attacking pest populations but have costs associated with them in terms of the build-up of resistance on the part of insect or other pests, the persistence of chemicals or their metabolites in soils and ecosystems, and a variety of hazards to users, consumers and others who may inadvertently come into contact with them. A number of different interpretations are possible, however, and proponents of different perspectives have become adept at the art of talking past each other. Those critical of established patterns of pesticide use can be portrayed as affluent townsfolk: well-intentioned, but susceptible to propaganda from anti-farming interests or to the bias of an ignorant or hysterical media coverage.[1] Those, on the other hand, sympathetic to the case that modern agriculture has fundamental and continuing requirements for pest control chemicals may be caricatured as gullibly responsive to statistics manipulated to promote the interests of the chemical industry, such as the figures on world famine and crop loss trends.[2] These kinds of perspectives – admittedly here over-simplified – are important because it is often the myths, in the sense of the broad outlooks through which facts and values are filtered and organised, that shape the politics of pesticides.

One such myth balances on a distinction between chemicals and the natural order. Though clearly grounded in error and misleading in its policy implications, the perceived distinction has real conse-quences. A chemical is a chemical even if it is not an artifice. Further, from a toxicological perspective, substances cannot be regarded as intrinsically hazardous or safe to man. There are degrees of hazard. Or, in the famous formulation by Paracelsus in 1538, 'All things are poison and none without poison. Only the dose determines that a thing is not a poison.' Nature, as well as the laboratory, has an excellent track record in the production of things that are poisonous in small doses. Some plants – tobacco, chrysanthemum, pyrethrum – have been used as a basis for a number of different pesticides, but it would be wrong to assume that such products, by virtue of their botanical origins, have an unassailable superiority over others con-cocted from the tinkerings of chemists. Even the most innocuous-seeming plants may conceal dangers. There are toxic substances in parsnips.[3] Attacking 'chemicals' is nonetheless often a useful way of getting the phenomena of modernity on to political agendas. The large numbers of chemical compounds, not only pesticides, in use in industrial society provide ample scope for the argument that here lie corrosive long-term effects for the lives of its members. Early in 1983 the American Chemical Society's Chemical Abstracts Service regis-tered its six millionth chemical, based on mentions in the literature since 1965. Even the number in common use, though much smaller, is still a substantial 60 000–70 000.[4]

Some initial distinctions can help to clarify some of these ques-tions. Firstly, up to a point it is possible to distinguish between relatively more subjective or objective terminologies and concepts in pesticides debates. One of the culprits here is the word 'pest', and, by derivation, pesticide.[5] A pest is a pest if it is defined as such; the usage is not an offshoot of a scientific classification of species. Not all insects, arachnids, and other groups of species commonly attacked by pesticides deserve the designation. Honey bees are an important non-target species often affected by pesticide use. Spiders have traditionally had an important symbolic role in many cultures. A 1903 report on parts of West Africa described the spider as 'the national hero, the impersonation of the genius of the race. To him are ascribed the qualities most characteristic of the people, or those most to be desired: cunning, sleeplessness, almost immortality, an unlimited capacity for eating, and an equal genius for procuring the necessary supplies.'[6] The relation between insects and plants is not that of a one-way flow of destructive power. The relationship has been described as more that between two co-evolving, competing and often mutually dependent biochemical systems. Some insect influences on plants are essential for them, and not only in the form of pollination. Indeed it has been suggested that 'most insect species, most of the time, have little effect on plant abundance.'[7]

Secondly, the real choices to be made in pest control and pesticide management are inherently difficult and complex ones. Some of the choices presented in debates on these subjects are useful as rhetorical flourishes, but false and simplistic if taken at face value. 'We can either use pesticides and fertilisers at our disposal or starve', as Nobel laureate Norman Borlaug has put it. 'Insects are the only animals giving man a real battle for supremacy', as one textbook on applied entomology sizes up the war.[8] Worms or EDB in your cereal? This was the choice as it appeared in one account of the discovery in the United States in the mid-1980s that ethylene dibromide caused cancer in laboratory animals.[9] Some choices affecting pesticide use are made in practice by consumers in western countries who may refuse to buy discoloured, misshapen or pock-marked fruit and vegetables in supermarkets. Assessing the consequences of a total cessation of pesticide use is a speculative enterprise in which answers may stem more from cherished first principles than from hard evidence. One study from the United States, though, has concluded that there is no indication that major food shortages would occur if all pesticides were to be banned; serious shortages might occur, however, in the case of some fruits and vegatables, including apples, peaches, onions and tomatoes.[10]

Thirdly, it is sometimes useful to adopt the toxicologist's distinction between chronic and acute consequences of exposure to pesticides. A Seveso-type incident may be calamitous, but the problems of toxic chemicals management are not restricted to those of low-frequency, high-cost events. There are also enduring, day-by-day questions, none of which, taken in isolation, may be sufficiently costly to attract sustained political or media attention. At what point this becomes a distinction without a difference is not easy to judge. Parathion had caused hundreds of deaths by the early 1960s, the

World Health Organisation (WHO) stated in a 1962 report.[11] Deaths from accidental or deliberate ingestion of the herbicide paraquat are a regular occurrence in Papua New Guinea, Guyana and some other developing countries.

Fourthly, some costs of pesticide use can be categorised as broadly economic in character and others as more generally ecological in their effects. Again, this is the kind of distinction that cannot be upheld for too long. A quantitative accumulation of ecological effects through food webs, atmospheric transport, or the changing population dynamics of species can clearly at some point entail qualitatively different economic consequences. The impact of pesticide use on rice crops in Spain on fish populations in the Mediterranean is one example. The more general phenomenon of insect resistance is another. Honey production in New York state was seriously curtailed in 1980, in part because of reductions in honey bee populations brought about by pesticide use, in particular two compounds used respectively against the gypsy moth and for protecting sweet corn.[12] In some developing countries, even so, where regulatory criteria tend to be less firmly fixed, difficult choices may have to be made between those consequences of pesticide use which must be brought within the ambit of government regulations, and those which in practice can be ignored.

Finally, a distinction can be made between those costs to human health and safety and the environment which are intrinsic to the chemical structure of certain compounds, and those which arise from the circumstances in which they are used. The distinction has significant regulatory implications. If in practice high rates of illiteracy are the norm among users of a pesticide, then a regulatory focus on the details of labelling and written instructions may be largely inappropriate. If cheap (and cool) protective clothing is not easily available to a farmer or farmworker in a tropical developing country, then advice from agricultural extension officers may have little practical significance. Ways can be found around some of these obstacles. Stenching agents or emetics can be added to weedkillers that are used carelessly (or as raw materials for suicides).[13] General levels of understanding of the nature of pesticides may be slower to change. A productive source of misuse in the Sudan has been the simple classification by users of pesticides, and chemicals generally, as either poison (*sim*) or medicament (*dawa*).[14] Regulatory frameworks usually incorporate evidence acquired from field testing of compounds under conditions of actual use. However, this does not fully resolve the question of principle of where responsibility for hazardous misuse of chemicals should lie; and in practice the bulk of testing for regulatory purposes takes place in the laboratory.

Underlying these and other regulatory dilemmas can often be found lack of agreement among various actors on the procedures which should be followed. A commitment to scientific norms may go only part of the way. In the more controversial cases in western countries in recent years, participants in the regulatory process have been divided on questions of the interpretation of available scientific findings, and also, perhaps more importantly, on the questions of how much enquiry is needed before a conclusion can be reasonably accepted as final, and of the extent to which the regulatory process should concern itself with other kinds of evidence. In other words, *who* should decide, and *how* should they decide?

Discovery of chlorinated dioxins in fish near a chemical plant in Michigan in 1978, for example, led to disagreement about the causal factors involved, not all of which could be attributed to the vested interests of the participants: whether this was a result of practices inside the plant which should be altered, as environmental critics argued, or whether, as the company concerned maintained, such compounds were formed by normal combustion processes.[15] Test laboratories themselves may be deficient. One of the laboratories used by the US Environmental Protection Agency (EPA) in the 1970s was found during the course of a routine investigation to have employed dubious or careless testing methods. The resulting doubt cast on the validity of previous test results in relation to particular pesticides had ramifications not only in the United States, but throughout the international pesticides regulatory system.[16] Prevailing scientific and legal assumptions tend to be uneasy with 'wait-and-see' philosophies. In a major court case in Nova Scotia in 1983, a group of landowners and environmentalists opposed herbicide spraying of forests by a local Swedish-owned pulp and paper company. The provincial Supreme Court heard testimony from a variety of experts in the fields of toxicology, epidemiology, and forest ecology and management. It came to the conclusion that an injunction against use of the chemicals concerned, 2,4-D and 2,4,5-T, could not be justified since it had not been established that known dioxin levels in the compounds were unsafe. The criterion of greater objectivity in the use and interpretation of scientific findings, more particularly, appeared to the court to favour the defendants.[17]

Regulatory politics here is at root the politics of data. The task of a regulatory agency is first that of prising data out of a diffident company. Most of the scientific work done in relation to pesticides is not done out of a disinterested thirst for knowledge. The aim is application and use. Companies want to market saleable products. Information divulged to a regulatory body is less controllable. Chemical companies have an interest, therefore, in labelling as much of their scientific data as possible as commercially sensitive: data which, if released, could erode the competitive edge achieved at considerable expense in the process of research and development. Regulatory bodies may accordingly be at a disadvantage since industrial data on pesticides are often the best data. An agency or international organisation which attempts to evaluate the toxicity of a compound or the hazards associated with it merely on the basis of published scientific data is unlikely to have wide credibility, particularly in industry. Outside the centrally planned economies, then, the model of a regulatory body devising and then enforcing a set of regulatory standards has only a limited validity. These bodies have often been critical of the quality of information coming to them from industry. The point applies with greater force at the international level. Not only, from a company's point of view, are such international organisations inherently more leaky, they may also have as members governments committed to maximum disclosure of information available to them, or governments notoriously less respectful of western definitions of industrial property rights than a firm operating in a science-based industry would prefer.

The regulation of pesticide chemicals thus involves a complex juggling of competing values, criteria and interests. The regulatory setting is frequently circumscribed by imperfect or incomplete information. Increasingly, too, regulatory activity occurs in a broader political context; regulation is not an activity confined to the world of little-known government agencies. In some countries – as in regulatory politics in a variety of environmental areas in the United States during the 1970s – regulatory standards or principles may be relatively short-lived because they are at once subject to renewed debate. The basic rules of the regulatory game may themselves be open to change and reformulation as actors detect in altered procedures or approaches the possibility of regulatory outcomes more sympathetic to their aims.

The international character of pesticides and the pesticides economy adds significantly to these uncertainties. Regulatory politics within western countries have been shaped in part by this external dimension. The larger chemical companies have always been attentive to exports but during the 1960s, and increasingly during the 1970s, many began to assess Third World prospects more seriously. In part this was a means of relieving the pressure from regulatory stringency and circumventing the penalties of industrial maturation which were being experienced as disturbing trends at home. A number of aspects of this shifting focus entered debates on the regulation of hazardous exports. Pressure groups active in environmental and development areas turned increasingly to evidence from developing countries, such as that on the testing of carcinogenic compounds on children in Egypt in the mid-1970s.[18] Groups differed, however, in their general approaches to the requirements of chemicals regulation. Pesticides could be a divisive issue in this kind of pressure group activity because of the clear needs of many developing countries for compounds such as DDT which had become favoured targets of environmentalists' attacks in western countries.[19]

Many of the assumptions that have formed part of the regulatory environment of approaches to pesticides in the industrialised nations may have limited applicability in relation to developing countries. False or adulterated products are likely to be more widespread, and also more potent sources of regulatory concern. In one famous incident in Kenya, a batch of imported agrochemicals turned out on inspection to consist of a bulk delivery of a useless white powder. Product reliability and efficacy form more urgent regulatory objectives than do assessments of environmental costs. Flourishing local black markets or porous national borders can undermine effective regulation in developing countries, as can the constraints of inadequate administrative resources; and where agricultural officials act in a variety of client roles in relation to foreign chemical companies, the vigour with which regulatory activity is undertaken is necessarily weakened. In many developing countries a reservoir of household or farm practices appropriate to an agrochemical economy cannot be assumed. Lack of consumer attention to elementary steps such as the washing and cooking of vegetables – which in any case remove only a proportion of pesticide residues[20] – opens up the possibility of significant hazards. Some collisions can occur between the goals of economic development and environmental health regulation. Local formulation of pesticides, for example, widely practised as a relatively straightforward final stage of production, or advocated as the basis of an expanding agrochemical cottage industry in Third World countries, can in some cases mean little more than the mixing of highly toxic active ingredients with water in discarded beer or medicine bottles. The design of elaborate labelling or storage regulations by governments may have minimal impact on the actual conditions of pesticide handling and use.

These kinds of questions enter international regulatory arenas in a number of different ways. They form a part of debates on strategies and approaches within international aid or technical assistance bodies. Regulatory gaps in developing countries have increasingly found their way on to the agendas of these bodies and a multitude of international technical meetings. Assessments of changing regulatory requirements in western countries, or in settings such as the European Community, have become more attuned to questions of the external impact of regulations: whether, for example, exporting companies should be compelled to inform the governments of consumer countries of the make-up or hazards of imported chemicals. The issue of agrochemical supply, distribution and use is only one of many involved in processes of agricultural development generally, but it remains an important one. Their toxic properties, then, put pesticides at key junctures in wider debates on both agricultural modernisation and environmental protection. The diversity to be found in national regulatory systems is itself a productive source of issues. Chemical companies have been persistent in raising these questions in various ways in international forums, and in spelling out the costs to them of a lack of regulatory uniformity. Much international regulatory activity in the field of pesticides derives, indeed, from concerns expressed by the United States and other western countries in the early 1960s and since about the potential of agrochemicals regulations to act as non-tariff barriers to trade.

The discussion in the following chapters is divided into three main sections. The first of these (Chapters 2-3) looks at the broader context of international relations within which regulatory activity on pesticides takes place, and at the main structures of the international pesticides economy which have a bearing on the issues examined. Three sets of regulatory questions are singled out for more detailed investigation in the next section (Chapters 4-6). These centre respectively on the treatment of issues arising from the residues of pesticides in foods, a subject which has given rise to international technical negotiations over many years in the machinery of the Codex Alimentarius Commission, which was set up in the 1960s by the Food and Agriculture Organisation (FAO) and the World Health Organisation (WHO) with a broad mandate in the area of food standards;

questions of the registration of pesticides for production and sale, and the politics of various harmonising endeavours that have been set in motion through both world and regional inter-governmental organisations; and, thirdly, problems connected with the regulation of the environmental consequences of expanded pesticide use, as these have been tackled by international organisations. The third section (Chapters 7-8) deals more particularly with issues of agricultural development and pesticides, and with the interplay between the various factors that make for regulatory change in developing countries. The ways in which international agencies have been actors in this process are then highlighted in a case study of regulatory politics in Malaysia.

Part I

2 Regulatory Politics and the International Economy

Much of the stuff of international politics can, in one way or another, be described as regulatory phenomena. International arrangements of the kind embodied in the Charter of the United Nations or the General Agreement on Tariffs and Trade (GATT) have as their objective some form of regulation. In these cases the objects, as well as the subjects, of policy are states. Regulation in this sense can be defined as the imposition of negotiated restraints on behaviour. The nature of the international system, however, means that the governing or regulatory framework cannot be taken for granted; where institutions, mechanisms or procedures exist, they lack the enforcement power – though not necessarily the power of persuasion – more usually associated with their national counterparts. A second meaning of the term derives from usages in connection with politics inside countries. Regulation there, particularly as far as the nations of the western industrialised world are concerned, refers us rather to the relations between the state and the economy, or, more specifically between government and business. While it can be deployed in analyses of almost any aspect of state intervention, from the creation and running of nationalised industries to the design and adjustment of company law, the term is one that has special force in relation to the multifarious forms of government tinkering with specific industries substantially or wholly in the private sector.

It is at this point that useful connections can be made between regulatory politics at the various junctions between the national and international levels. Regulations made by governments on health, safety or pollution standards, for example, are rarely made in isolation from events in other countries. This is not to say that such moves are concerted, or that governments, when they use different tempi, are nonetheless following the same score. Diversity, rather, is the norm. Regulations in such areas are idiomorphous: they reflect the distinctive character of the national political setting, and the particular blends of interests and values brought into play by different

15

players in the national regulatory game. Some of the assumptions, though, may be transmitted to international arenas and, in turn, some of the policy implications of debates at the international level may be translated into national regulatory contexts.

The extent to which this happens – or, when it does, how significant it is – is not clear. On the first point, studies of the external sources of national regulatory standards have been inhibited in practice by two sets of constraints. Students of international relations have tended to look more at interactions between states, or among the variety of actors that make up the contemporary international system; at issues of a manifestly 'high' political character; or at technical bureaucracies within states more as potential sources of foreign policy and, hence, of international outcomes than as arenas in which the forces of such consequences work themselves out. Similarly, students of regulatory processes have tended to focus either on one particular country, or else on a group of countries investigated in comparative fashion. Again, some important parts of the complex web of causes and effects may be overlooked.

On the second point – whether all this matters – the literature of international relations gives a number of conflicting leads. Some writings of functionalist theorists, and of observers of trends in the relations between societies and between governments, suggest a wider peace-building significance to changes in the aerial mosaics of such links in the last three or four decades. When criteria at such grand levels of synthesis are manoeuvred into position, however, subtle differences of coloration or marking may also disappear from sight. Many forms of cooperative endeavour between states may be irrelevant to questions of war and peace. In Sir Charles Webster's phrase of the 1930s, such interlocking links between nations may turn out to prove 'no stronger than the cobwebs across the mouth of a cannon'.[1] These bigger questions are not our concern in the present study. The focus is on one particular area of policy – the regulation of pesticide chemicals – and on the various connections between national and international forms of regulatory politics. Both sets of connotations of the malleable word 'regulation' are needed. We will be looking at the ways in which states approach and move around within international institutions, and also at the multiple layers of relations between government and industry in the international system. Before turning to the investigation itself it is useful to take some soundings in the intellectual and policy depths through which we will be steering.

REGULATION AS AN ISSUE

Greater attention to issues of government regulation of industry has emerged as a result of changing public and political moods in several western countries. Critics of the changing relations between the state and the economy pointed to what they saw as a qualitatively different magnitude of government intervention from that which characterised regulatory forays in the 1930s and 1940s. This context of debate is revealing because of the ways in which some of the issues, assumptions and frustrations have been transmitted to the international level.

Critics of regulatory burdens on industry in the United States have highlighted implicit threats to democratic processes, the allegedly illusory character of the pursuit of safety, the high cost to industry, the indirect costs in terms of innovation and international competitiveness, conflicts between productive and regulatory norms, and the inflexibility of application of regulatory standards. The first was derived by leading Republican politicians and others from the supposed lessons of the previous decade. As Governor Reagan formulated it in 1976:

Both in the field of health and in the economic field, government has grown to such an extent that I'm afraid it is showing a lack of respect for the average citizen. With government fostering the idea that the citizen can't even buy a box of Post Toasties for himself without being cheated, one wonders how voters are supposed to be able to pick people for government who are wise enough to make all these decisions.[2]

Regulatory standards in the fields of health and safety or environmental protection were perhaps more vulnerable because they could more readily be portrayed as irrelevant or gratuitous marks of government interference. Debate on the marketing of carcinogenic products was central also because of changing technologies. Regulatory bodies were developing technical capabilities for detecting contamination or the causes of hazards to health at much more sophisticated levels than previously. These in turn brought into question the validity of extrapolations from test animals to humans traditionally used in toxicological studies shaping regulatory determinations in these areas. An ability to detect in a product designed for human consumption the presence of a toxic contaminant of the order of a few parts per billion (thousand million) naturally raises the issue of the limits to which governments should go in the matter of protecting consumers' interests. A simple principle, that governments should not allow carcinogenic products to be consumed, involved more difficult judgements of degree with the growth of knowledge and the refinement of techniques. More generally, society's safety and health problem, one writer argued, was:

> not how to guarantee everyone the maximum level of safety technologically possible. If that were the case, we would have a national speed limit of five miles per hour, no military establishment, no large dams or bridges (which are dangerous to build), and no airplanes. Rather, our national safety and health problem is choosing the desirable level of risk – level of risk that takes into account the sad fact that safety and health are costly.[3]

It was also in the United States that industry tended to be most vigorous in protesting the direct costs of regulation. One General Motors estimate was that between 1974 and 1978 the cost to the company 'to comply or to prepare to comply with the regulations imposed by all levels of government' averaged $1.2 billion (thousand million) a year. Dow Chemical put its costs during 1976 of complying with federal government regulations at $186 million. Of this, around 55 per cent was estimated to have arisen from regulations governing the safety of workers or consumers; much of the rest was criticised by the company on the grounds that it represented a duplication of regulatory effort by different agencies, or else regulatory burdens which went beyond the ensuring of good practices in science-based industries.[4] A link could be made, moreover, with innovation in industry and from there with the competitiveness of industries in international markets. In the United States most research and development appears to take place in the largest firms and the most concentrated industries. This has been particularly the case in five sectors: chemicals, electrical equipment and communication, motor vehicles and transportation, machinery, and aircraft and missiles. During the 1960s and 1970s the 400-500 largest companies accounted for nearly 90 per cent of private research and development expenditures.[5] In specific cases like agricultural chemicals and pharmaceutical products the research and development costs per marketed product in the 1970s and 1980s have been variously estimated at between $20-70 million.[6] Declining rates of product and technical innovation might be expected to occur for other reasons in 'maturing' industries; industry's argument was that government should not needlessly reinforce any such tendencies by increasing the regulatory load at all phases of the product cycle, from the initial stages of research through to the sale of goods.

Regulatory assumptions and styles collided at several points with those of companies, critics argued:

> Perhaps the most salient characteristic of the regulatory process is that regulators (and the legislators who created the regulation) are looking for simple decisions, for certainty, for a dichotomous world in which yes–no answers can be given to problems that in reality are very complex and uncertain. They are uncomfortable with uncertainty, with probability distributions, with a world that is continuous rather than dichotomous.[7]

There is nothing startlingly new in the observation that civil servants and businessmen think differently. Sustained efforts have been made in a number of countries with the aim of narrowing the gap, and of thereby making governments more effective in the pursuit of broader economic policy objectives. Indeed there is also a long tradition in the United States of criticism of different kinds of regulatory bodies or administrative agencies for being too close and responsive to the industrial or agricultural sectors they were designed to regulate; the charge was repeated in relation to various activities of the Environmental Protection Agency, for example on the issue of toxic waste disposal, in the late 1970s and early 1980s. Some collisions are to be expected, then, and their absence treated as indications of regulatory failure. According to some assumptions, regulatory agencies, in aiming to maximise social welfare, will inevitably be drawn into such conflicts; this is entailed, by implication, in the belief that 'industry interests and prerogatives, such as profitability, should be given no weight per se, and should be protected only insofar as they are instrumental to the service of consumer or other general interests.'[8] The complaint of many companies, then, was that these and other assumptions were becoming more pervasive and more firmly embedded in regulatory practices affecting industry. The objection was at times as much to the apparently mindless and inflexible application of regulatory standards to a variety of specific situations as to the substance of the original provisions.[9]

Within the obvious limits set by prevailing and shared assumptions about state ownership, as distinct from regulation, of industry, such debates in the United States were often more sharply polarised than their functional equivalents in Europe. The Industrial Revolution in Britain, and the more protracted transformations in France, took place against a backcloth of criticism of older and accepted practices of state intervention. These frequently involved extension of notions of privilege and ascribed rights into the marketplace. The tradition was attacked by Adam Smith: it was 'the highest impertinence and presumption . . . of kings and ministers to pretend to watch over the economy of private people.'[10] While the tenet fitted comfortably with the American critiques just noted, later practices of state involvement in the economy in Britain took the countries on divergent paths. The practices may have had their origins not so much in ideological constructions or the rise and fall of political parties, as in the more pragmatic responses of governments to emergency conditions. Regulation of industry during World War I, one historian later suggested, had far-reaching effects: 'The economic breakwaters which, if seen as a whole, would have caused cries of alarm, grew like coral islands through the unseen activities of the industrious, but silent, insects of the civil service.'[11] But whatever were the factors at work, the greater presence of the state, whether as reformer of working conditions in industry in the nineteenth century or entrepreneur in its own right in the twentieth, meant that appeals to a golden age of non-regulation had far less uncontestable validity.

Relatively ignored in these various debates, international regulatory efforts involving the participation of many governments have affected a number of policy areas since the mid-1940s. The issues in only a handful of international negotiating arenas have played much of a part in arguments inside countries on the impact of or requirements for regulations in specific sectors. These have included environmental policy areas to some extent, partly because of the internationalist orientations of pressure groups typically to be found there, but have more often centred on general issues of international trade. More specific regulatory exercises, for example those dealing with various aspects of the chemicals industry in the Organisation for Economic Cooperation and Development (OECD) framework, or with health standards through that of the World Health Organisation, have been chiefly of concern to the more restricted range of participants immediately involved. Where the issue of a state's participation in international institutional arrangements has arisen and found its way into domestic debates – as with criticism in western nations of policy, budgetary and decision-making trends in UNESCO and FAO in the mid-1980s – public attention has tended to be short-lived, sporadic, and questionable in terms of its impact on governments. Many of the issues that have structured the debates on regulation – the costs to industry, the potentially detrimental effects on innovativeness, the impact of changing technologies on the design of appropriate regulatory procedures — have nevertheless also emerged at the international level.

THE POLITICS OF REGIME CONSTRUCTION

Criticism of international organisations is part of the background noise of their environment, a kind of universal constant like the radiation from the Big Bang. For the most part the more technical bodies of the 1920s and 1930s were able to escape the full force of the criticism directed towards the League of Nations as a whole. Even so, while items of technical cooperation between states assumed an expanding proportion of League expenditures (25 per cent in 1921 to 50 per cent in 1930), only the more clearly non-controversial activities could successfully withstand budgetary attacks.[12] Since the early 1950s the areas of political controversy in the universe of discourse on international technical questions have grown proportionately. Sales by western companies in developing countries of cigarettes, pharmaceutical products, infant foods, or pesticides, became during the 1970s and 1980s significant issues on the agendas of a variety of international bodies and domestic groups in western countries. This broadening of the scope of the items which tumble on to international agendas – from wars to the sale of television sets, from the uses of outer space to the migration routes of wild birds – has important implications for the workings of late twentieth-century international institutions.

Firstly, the spread of issues has exacerbated the problems of duplication of effort and lack of coordination and contact between such bodies. For any given international question, a number of organisations are ready, waiting in the wings to enter with a recital of their credentials for assuming lead roles. Any new coordinating body or programme may thus fall into place eventually as just one additional component part of a sprawling and disorganised whole. The United Nations system has achieved an often deserved notoriety in this regard. One commentator has noted the stubborn persistence of various aspects of the problem since the 1950s. There have been 'unresolved differences of view regarding the respective competences of different agencies in particular fields; and of the UN regional economic commissions and the specialised agencies in regard to action at the regional level; and there continue to be cases of duplication and overlapping, of lack of cooperation among organisations and their staffs, of failures to consult, and divergencies of objectives.'[13] Such difficulties are partly a reflection of the overall extended structure of the UN; many of the technical bodies – WHO, FAO or other Specialised Agencies – exist as autonomous entities, with their own memberships, funding, programmes and secretariats. But while the fragmentation is a reflection of underlying structural and constitutional realities, these are not the sole causes of failures to rectify the attendant problems. During the 1970s western governments in a number of international forums pressed for greater attention to the virtues of more effective coordination on the part of technical agencies.

Secondly, the wide range of issues that have a significant international aspect, combined with a background of general disenchantment with existing inter-governmental organisations, has led to an institutional proliferation. This is particularly, though not exclusively, the case at the non-governmental level. One assessment, by Judge and Skjelsbaek, suggests that the rate of change in the world of international non-governmental organisations is itself increasing: 'Increasingly rapid organisational creation, evolution, adaptation, and dissolution is to be expected with rapid membership turnover and constantly changing patterns of inter-organisational interaction, including splits and mergers.'[14] It is not easy to bring neat classificatory schemes to bear in the resulting profusion. In the case of some organisations, for example, different categories of membership – states, government agencies, private groups, even individuals – may coexist, and qualify the utility of distinctions between inter-governmental and non-governmental organisations. Further, the regulatory character of many of the issues being handled in various international forums, as in discussion of codes of conduct for multinational enterprises, means that companies or industry associations may take on more active political roles.

Thirdly, the resulting complexity and financial cost to governments of even elementary levels of participation in international organisations is likely to continue to compel reappraisals and tighter monitoring. Foreign policy reviews in several western countries have already encountered this problem. That by the Central Policy Review Staff in Britain in 1977 drew attention to the large number of international bodies to which the United Kingdom belonged. Reviews were particularly needed in relation to minor forums, the authors of the report wrote, because of an impression they had had 'that, while new organisations are not joined thoughtlessly, there are instances (for example in the scientific area) of confusion over the interests to be served by joining [and] that having joined, the level of participation develops a momentum of its own and can become unnecessarily active.' Continued monitoring was thus needed 'both to guard against creeping inflation in the number of fora to which the United Kingdom belongs and in the resources put into them, and to take account of any change in the degree of UK interest in different areas.'[15]

If we look at the changing attitudes of governments and publics in western countries with regard to peace and security issues, or at the statistics on the rate of creation of certain types of international organisations, it seems to be undeniably true that, as one analyst has put it, 'the heyday of the international organisation appears to have passed'.[16] Paradoxically, this did not check a wave of rising expectations during the 1970s. Attention increasingly turned to the capacity of reformed, and more effectively coordinated, international institutions to promote and manage change: but for the most part in economic or functional, rather than security areas. Discussion of requirements at global levels – in relation to food, population, the environment, human settlements, energy, telecommunications, desertification, or the exploitation of the resources of the sea-bed – pointed consistently to a presumed need for international organisations with significantly enhanced powers. Debates about international institutions and world problems were returning, it seemed to some observers, to an older, idealist tradition in which the realities of power in the international system could be lightly glossed over and the requirement of world government taken for granted.[17]

We have so far been talking of international organisations. From some perspectives it is more useful to refer to international regimes. The term can be defined in various ways. It can denote the cumulative outputs of international agencies in particular policy areas. In his study of health, meteorological, and food standards regimes, David Leive tends to restrict use of the term in practice to the sets of recommended rules or regulatory standards produced by international organisations, and more particularly by the Specialised Agencies of the UN system. Thus regimes:

variously include legislative processes, formal and informal procedures and techniques for administering and interpreting the regulatory instruments, and means for promoting compliance therewith. The term 'international regulatory regime' thus refers to the complex of regulatory instruments and the attendant legislative, administrative, and quasi-judicial procedures and organs, as they work in practice.[18]

In more comprehensive formulations the activities of international institutions are seen as part of, rather than as identical with, international regimes. A definition which draws attention to the full range of principles, norms, rules and procedures accepted in varying degrees by states in a given policy area points towards a much broader spectrum of activities and of actors. The international trade regime embraces the external trade policies of individual states as well as the broad frameworks of GATT procedures and rules; in relation to the peaceful uses of nuclear energy, one central international body, the International Atomic Energy Agency (IAEA) occupies a pivotal role within a context of state policies and bilateral and multilateral agreements on nuclear cooperation, and safeguards against misuse of materials for weapons purposes.[19] Whether or not the language of regime studies is used, however, it is clear that study of the various forms of collaboration between governments in a particular policy area has to take account not only of the workings of international institutions of various types, but also of those policies of states which have effects beyond their territorial borders.

Yet in practice it may not be so easy to define sets of issues in such a way that a significant measure of analytical coherence is not lost. There are no simple dividing lines here, like Jordan curves in topology, for neatly demarcating a plane into separate and distinct policy areas. Issues are interconnected. Questions of nuclear cooperation overlap on one side with broader questions of energy resources and uses, and on the other spill over into problems of disarmament and arms control. Environmental issues have proved rich sources of specific sets of questions each with relatively discrete policy actors. Those actors engaged in the area of oil pollution of seas or beaches, for example, may have little connection with those in the area of national parks and protected areas, or of the management of toxic chemicals. Specific sets of cooperative arrangements between states have emerged in some, for example in relation to the international trade in endangered species, and these display many of the characteristic features associated with more formal definitions of international regimes.[20] Some actors, such as many environmental pressure groups, engage in activities across a wide spectrum of such issues and moreover employ definitions of their own roles that serve to integrate a number of otherwise relatively separate areas.

Study of these kinds of activities and arrangements often takes the observer of international relations into areas either uncharted or only sketchily mapped because of a presumption of their comparative insignificance. There are several reasons for paying greater attention to such regions. First, on a kind of *ex pede Herculem* assumption, we may be able to make use of information and interpretations from such areas as a means of making tentative extrapolations to areas of a higher order of policy importance. The extent to which this might be possible is obviously limited by a number of factors, including the structural dissimilarities that may distinguish one issue area from another, or the degree to which actors base their engagement on subjective rankings of the importance of different areas. Secondly, distinctions between relatively high and relatively low politics are not set in stone. Issues rise and fall in visibility and significance.[21] Fisheries have emerged as areas of major negotiations between governments. In 1884 the heads of government of the major European powers would probably have been surprised to be told that their counterparts a century later were deeply immersed in issues such as the amount of milk that cows in Ireland should be allowed to produce. Thirdly, students of politics generally can often contribute usefully to debates in areas where policy discussion tends in practice to be contained within the ranks of technical specialists, or to move out among interested publics only sporadically. Much writing on environmental questions, for example, has in the past employed many of the devices of a wisdom literature; a tendency to use excessively simplified models of political processes, and a desire to compensate for apparent gaps in attention scans by governments, has also produced programmes for institutional and policy change more at the ethereally grand than at the working level. And finally, the bulk of the activities carried on by governments in the international system do in practice involve low-politics interactions.

But whatever the issues, accounts of the emergence or desirable future course of regimes in economic and in technical areas have increasingly focused attention on the activities of multinational companies. Perceptions of these actors vary of course, as do evaluations of their power in a world of states. The larger international companies can be viewed in some areas as transmitters of processes of development and of the promotion of economic welfare, or else as threats to the control of resources by states and constraints on the capacities of governments to manage and nurture economies. Increasingly from the 1950s on, export markets formed a significant part of the production and sales planning of the major western companies, a process of which local production overseas was an important integral component.[22] Economic activities thus gave rise to and structured a growing number of policy issues for governments and international organisations.

Many of these can be viewed as broadly regulatory in character, in both senses of the term with which we began this discussion. First, the search for internationally agreed codes of conduct tended to rest on the assumption that governments individually, particularly those in developing countries, in practice would have a limited capacity to create an effectively operating legal and political environment for company activity.[23] Overlapping this strategy were, secondly, moves in some western countries to secure tighter regulation of the external operations of domestic firms by unilateral government measures. Several specific export issues emerged in the United States and other countries during the 1960s and 1970s and highlighted this approach to regulation: the sales of pharmaceutical products in developing countries, for example, or pesticides and other toxic chemicals, or certain kinds of specially treated children's clothing. From another direction the politics of codes of conduct through the United Nations and other forums also overlapped with a third level of regulatory activity in the form of the considerable variety of relationships between developing countries, or, more properly, the economic and political elites in these countries, and the multinational enterprises. These three broad categories were linked in various ways. More particularly, each tended in practice to be grounded in an appreciation of the more disorderly and unmanaged aspects of international relations, and to use such observations as a rationale for greater regulatory authority for various kinds of global institutions. While thus raising by implication the more general question of the nature of the international system, these debates also reactivated older problems concerning the separability, or the respective dominance, of economic and political spheres. These were central themes in controversies surrounding domestic regulatory issues.[24]

The questions dealt with in this study are rather more narrowly defined. The primary focus is on the regulatory frameworks in states which govern the markets in, and use of, pesticides, and on the ways in which regulation at the national level interacts with the politics of international regulatory efforts. The more distant perimeters of these areas will for the most part be left undisturbed. Thus questions of broad economic policy affecting pesticides sectors in Third World countries will not be tackled in depth; and neither, more specifically, will negotiations between the governments of developing countries and multinational chemical companies on such matters as access, local production facilities, joint ventures, or ownership, though these will be touched on where appropriate as forming part of the policy and economic environment of pesticides regulation. Many of the regulatory issues posed by these toxic chemicals arise regardless of who has ultimate control over production and other processes within these sectors. Central to the study, however, are questions of the impact of international regulatory politics on governments, and of the ways in which states cooperate, compete and coalesce in international regulatory forums. The actors at this level are not only states, but comprise also inter-governmental and non-governmental organisations as well as chemical companies and industrial associations. Before reviewing the cast, we must look more closely at the science and economics of pesticide chemicals. This brings us to the theme of the next chapter.

3 The Political Economy of Pesticides

The structure of the chemical industry is a function both of the nature of the science and technology involved in the design and manufacture of its products, and of the kinds of regulatory activities affecting these processes that governments engage in. Production of a pesticide is a science-based enterprise. Crucial to the fulfilment of regulatory objectives, as we saw in Chapter 1, is the acquisition and effective handling of scientific data. At the heart of the regulatory task lies bargaining between government and industry about the treatment of data that could be used to advantage by competing companies. An account of the main kinds of scientific enquiry involved in pesticides research and development is outside the scope of the present study. A short summary is useful, however, as a means of coming to grips with some important features of industrial structure that have a bearing on regulatory processes.

FROM CHEMISTRY TO ECONOMICS

At the risk of some over-simplification, the history of pest control strategies in agriculture can be divided into several distinct but overlapping phases. Each has been associated with a characteristic form of industrial organisation. Firstly, and traditionally, controlling organisms that destroyed crops was one of the essential tasks of the farmer or the community. Some pests could be attacked directly, for example by manually removing insects or larvæ or by burning diseased foliage. Checks could also be imposed by more indirect methods, even if the processes at work were not fully understood: the rotation of crops, for example, or the parallel cultivation of interacting species. Secondly, the use of products manufactured and sold for the specific purpose of combating pests marked a stage in which the enterprise of agriculture diverged from the related enterprise of plant

28

protection. In regulatory terms, this kind of phase has tended to be characterised by government interest in regulating the market to the degree necessary to guard against the circulation of fraudulent products. It merged with a third, in which large-scale scientific work, involving the mass screening of thousands of chemicals for possible pesticidal activity, became the organisational basis of the pesticides industry. The study of the variation, or the attempted manipulation, of molecular structures now put pesticides firmly within the larger chemicals industry. Pesticide companies were typically component parts of larger industrial enterprises producing pharmaceuticals, paints, fertilisers, or any of the large numbers of compounds required by a modern industrial society. Regulatory attention shifted to the protection of consumers, pesticides users or non-target wildlife species from the hazardous effects of these products; and regulatory arenas were marked by greater variety, complexity and public interest. This most recent phase may be changing into a fourth, as pesticide manufacturers confront ominous signs of maturity in the industry: a slow-down in the appearance of fundamentally new compounds, lack of growth in many traditional markets and a heavy burden of perceived over-regulation.

Pests of one kind or another have inflicted tumultuous havoc on communities throughout the history of agriculture. Indeed there is some irony in the fact that pesticides are now viewed as a problem. The communal ritual accompanying pest control in many traditional societies suggests that more was at stake than the instrumental purposes of protecting crops. The last sheaf to be cut might be kept until the following year, perhaps nailed to a cowshed in medieval England or Germany, in order for it to impart its concentrated virtue to the fresh crop. Appreciation of the dangers is shown in the ancient Chinese *Book of Songs*:

Avaunt, all earwigs and pests,
Do not harm our young crops.[1]

In the harsher climates of Biblical tradition, detection of the handiwork of an angered God is not surprising:

He turned their waters into blood, and slew their fish. Their land brought forth frogs in abundance . . . there came divers sorts of flies, and lice in all their coasts. . . . He smote their vines also and their fig trees; and brake the trees of their coasts. He spake, and the locusts came, and caterpillars, and that without number, and did eat up all the herbs in their land, and devoured the fruit of their ground.[2]

Regular and numbing encounters with ecological disaster did not, however, deter experimentation with a variety of practical devices to control pests. In these we can find the historical origins of the modern pesticides industry. In both ancient Egypt and China successful efforts were made to protect crops by using various sulphur, mercury and arsenic compounds. The use of bitumen boiling to rid grape leaves of pests by fumes was known to farmers of the Roman empire. Pyrethrum was used in seventeenth-century Persia against human pests, and the introduction of tobacco from the New World stimulated a variety of uses of nicotine products, for example against diseases of soft fruits.[3]

In nineteenth-century Europe and the United States such tools began to be investigated and used more systematically. The American market in mid-century was still relatively small, but gathered pace later with the spread of small manufacturing businesses. These circumstances, and the temptations to easy fraud occasioned by the growth of mail-order sales, led to the emergence of federal regulations on the subject and the beginnings of a regulatory framework for the pesticides economy. The second half of the century saw the introduction of several new compounds. Following research on various arsenic compounds, paris green was introduced in 1867 for use against the Colorado potato beetle; Bordeaux mixture was used from 1885 to counter downy mildew of the vine. Such events were important turning-points. While inorganic compounds continued to be used, as did others drawn from plants, the emphasis was put increasingly on synthetic organic compounds. This gave a significant advantage to larger firms which could employ research staffs and exploit economies of scale in production. German chemical companies had produced several synthetic organic insecticides by the turn of the century, and the first organo-mercury seed dressings by the start of World War I. The early 1900s also saw the synthesis of various analogues of pyrethrins, nicotine compounds and others which had already demonstrated pesticidal properties in agriculture.

This phase of development of pesticide science included several dramatic demonstrations of the destructive power of agricultural pests, as well as the potential of the new generation of synthetic chemicals. In the 1860s and 1870s the indigenous European species of grape-vine proved incapable of withstanding attack by the *Phylloxera* louse. In this case use of existing chemicals was ineffectual. The solution eventually reached was the drastic one of grafting the original vines on to immune American stock. A once more viable industry resulted, marred only by the occasional grumble from the more fastidious port wine drinker. Another event took the pesticides industry into a new era.

This was the revolutionary impact of the compound DDT. Though first synthesised as early as 1874, it did not reveal its full powers until the 1940s. Its discovery has been described as 'one of the most significant events in the history of insect control, even, perhaps, in the history of civilisation.'[4] The significance of DDT as far as industrial structures were concerned lay not least in the screening and testing procedures that led to its discovery. Patented in 1940 following research in the Geigy laboratories in Switzerland aimed largely at producing moth-proofing compounds, it first indicated its potential in agriculture by checking an outbreak of the Colorado potato beetle there in 1941. This was as nothing, however, compared with its spectacular success in controlling a typhus epidemic in Naples in 1944. When eventually revealed publicly after secret wartime production and research in the United States and Britain, it seemed a panacea: DDT was highly effective, relatively cheap to produce, and apparently safe to use. Though some problems were known in the 1940s, such as the toxicity of the compound to mammals and early evidence of insect resistance, DDT did not begin its controversial course through the pathways of the American political system until the 1960s.

While research continued on other kinds of organochlorine compounds, development of another class – the organophosphorus compounds – was a more direct product of wartime. Shortages of insecticides led to a search for alternatives by German chemists working in this area, and to the discovery of several organophosphorus compounds with insecticidal properties. Others emerged as indirect consequences of military research into the design of toxic nerve gases. Two other large groups of pesticides made their appearance at around the same time. The basis was established in Britain in the early 1940s for the later development of herbicides, and the early carbamate compounds were developed there and in Switzerland in the mid-1940s.

These kinds of discoveries entailed further changes in the pesticides industry. In the nineteenth and early twentieth centuries the industry was characterised by relatively small-scale production of a limited number of products. The four decades since the end of World War II have, by contrast, been identified with large-scale research based primarily on the mass screening and testing of large numbers of chemicals, and by high – though eventually declining – rates of increase in production and consumption of pesticides. During this period the costs of research and development became a significant factor in the economics of the industry. Some of these costs were attributable to the requirements of regulatory authorities in the leading producer countries. A further trend during the latter part of this period was divergence in the world pesticides market and the appearance of new markets in the developing countries of the Third World. These threads will be taken up in later chapters. We turn now to some of the leading trends in pesticide science and technology in recent decades.

For some purposes it is useful to classify compounds according to the interests of the user and the type of pest being targeted. The range of compounds we are dealing with thus covers the main types of insecticides, fungicides, and herbicides, together with an array of more specialised groupings such as rodenticides, avicides, molluscicides, acaricides, nematicides, bactericides, and anti-virals.[5] Such classifications are rarely free of ideological or political problems. In some settings it is hazardous to identify wild birds as pests and to identify avicide requirements. And, as we saw in an earlier chapter, user-centric definitions are somewhat arbitrary. 'If evolution had taken a different turn', one writer has observed, 'an intelligent insect could certainly have devised selective mammalicides.'[6] Distinctions also have to be made between the various component parts of pesticides. The active ingredients of pesticides exist in western countries in a variety of formulations and under a large number of trade names. In practical agricultural or forestry terms, the formulation is at least as important as the active ingredient as regards the biological efficacy of the product. Further, mixtures of different compounds tend to be more common, particularly for insecticides, than production of individual compounds under various trade names.

Let us take insecticides as an example. It is customary to divide these into at least four main groupings: botanicals, or insecticides derived from plants or plant products; and three broad classes of synthetic organic insecticides – the organochlorine, organophosphorus, and carbamate insecticides.[7]

The first of these groupings includes products derived from nicotine, rotenone or pyrethrum, and synthetic compounds such as alle-thrin. Of these, pyrethrum provides a good case study of research and development processes. Use of the crushed flowers of this plant has a long history. Its cultivation in Kenya, Tanzania, and more recently Rwanda, forms a key sector in their national economies. Research was initiated in England, at the Rothamsted Experimental Station, from the late 1940s. The aim was to identify compounds for future use which, unlike DDT and others in the organochlorine group, had low mammalian toxicity. Synthetic compounds related to pyrethrum formed the crucial part of this research. Products derived from the plant had admirable qualities, such as low toxicity to mammals and a rapid knock-down effect on flying insects, but suf-fered from a number of defects. Notable among these was lack of stability in sunlight. Even after the discovery of allethrin in the United States in 1949, results came slowly. Resmethrin was discov-ered in 1967. Though more active than the natural pyrethrins and less toxic to mammals, it had the same major drawback. It was not until 1973 that the group of researchers announced the discovery of permethrin, a compound which finally combined the desired attributes of being highly active, stable in sunlight, and having low mammalian toxicity.[8] This developmental picture is more the exception than the rule. Nicotine, for example, happens also to be one of the most rapidly acting and toxic substances for humans, a factor which con-strains the likelihood of substantial further development of synthetic compounds. Similarly, while rotenone and related compounds gener-ally have low toxicity to mammals, no related compounds more active than the parent molecules have been synthesised.[9]

DDT has been the most publicly visible of the organochlorine compounds. Others include methoxychlor, toxaphene, lindane, al-drin, dieldrin, chlordane, heptachlor, endrin and endosulfan. It is this group as a whole that has been most frequently and most systematically targeted for attack by regulatory agencies, particularly in the United States, and environmental pressure groups. DDT itself could not stand up for long against intense regulatory scrutiny of its high mammalian toxicity, high stability and persistence in the envi-ronment, and its decreasing effectiveness in the long term against resistant insect species. The controversy it generated, however, often obscured the benefits. Since the 1940s, Kenneth Hassall has written, 'several billions of people have been exposed to DDT, yet outside the range of industrial accidents or attempted suicides, one has to search assiduously for even disputed evidence of serious medical side effects from this compound. Conversely, probably no chemical made by man – not even penicillin, streptomycin and the sulphonamides – has saved so many lives as has DDT.[10] Organophosphorus alternatives have nonetheless tended to be more prominent in research programmes in industry. The compounds here include parathion, malathion and tepp. It was German research in the 1930s into new military instruments that led to discovery of the insecticidal, or more properly the aphicidal, properties of tepp, and to the synthesis of parathion. Introduction of malathion in the United States in 1950 marked the culmination of research into compounds of the group less toxic to mammals. Around 100 000 organophosphorus compounds have been screened for possible insecticidal action, and over a hundred marketed.[11] Some of these chemicals have particularly useful properties. Fenitrothion, for example, is a derivative of parathion, but with lower toxicity; leptophos is useful against some pests in warmer climates. In other words a considerable variety of uses can be accommodated by different members of the organophosphorus family. The carbamates have also demonstrated a capacity for wide structural variation and an extensive range of properties.

Before leaving this short review mention should also be made of herbicides. These compounds will be discussed more fully in later chapters. They are significant for two reasons. First, their value in agriculture, forestry and a number of industrial settings has resulted in a large expansion of sales in recent years, and an increased percentage share of the overall pesticides market (to around 40 per cent of the world market in the 1970s). Secondly, the real and the alleged hazards associated with the use of herbicides have made these compounds the focal point of intense regulatory and group pressures in nearly all western countries. Discovery in the 1960s of a contaminant entering the manufacturing process of one group of herbicides, particularly 2,4,5-T, and identified as an especially toxic dioxin, has turned these compounds into the most controversial of pesticide chemicals in the early and middle 1980s. This attention is comparatively new. Generally speaking the herbicides have not been subjected to the same kinds of research and development efforts as those classes of compounds just described; nor have regulatory agencies had a long history of difficulties in dealing with them, as has occurred with some of the organochlorine compounds. This is partly a result of the uses to which they are put. If used along railway lines, for example, persistence in the environment is a virtue for weedkilling purposes rather than a drawback. Similarly, because the link with residues on food crops has tended to be more tangential than direct, herbicides as a group have in the past been relatively neglected by national and international regulatory bodies. But it is also partly a result of the sharp contrast between the balance of available scientific evidence, which tends to support the proposition that they are safe to use, and the persisting margins of doubt pointed to by their critics.

RESEARCH PROCESSES AND INDUSTRY STRUCTURES

Much of the scientific research on related questions is submerged from view inside the chemical industry. Companies are not motivated by altruism. High research costs represent a production factor to be covered at the marketing and pricing end of the development cycle. This research-intensive character of the pesticides industry, then, is a product of the wide variety of the requirements of users; the potential for structural manipulation of and variation in chemicals which might have pesticidal activity; the constraints imposed by regulatory demands in the major producing nations for stringent toxicological and other testing as a pre-registration hurdle; the development of resistance in some pest species and the consequent need for new compounds; and, finally, the competitive state of relations between the world's leading chemical companies. This last factor is qualified, as we shall see, by the fact that a relatively small number of such firms dominate many markets. The costs of entry to the industry are high.

The research and development and production costs of a pesticide are not, of course, the only determinants of price. As with any other product a major factor is what the market will bear. The initial expenditures involved, however, are substantial. Not counting investment at the stage of manufacturing, estimates in the 1970s of the research and development costs varied between $10–20 million or more for each pesticide. A comparable estimate for the pharmaceuticals sector was of an average of $24 million.[12] More recently it has been calculated that a pesticide product introduction would be likely to have nearly $70 million of research and development money riding on it, together with in excess of $30 million allocated to manufacturing facilities for the product.[13] These figures represent significant increases over those of the early 1950s. The cost of meeting regulatory requirements at the pre-marketing stage is only one of the cost factors involved, but one that companies are fond of seizing on. One 1979 estimate was that the cost of toxicological testing was increasing at about 30 per cent a year.[14] In one recurrent nightmare scenario, patents then expire and a free-for-all ensues before a break-even point is reached.

From the perspective of the corporate planner, uncertainty in the economic and political environment is more a problem than research and development costs. There is no guaranteed route to marketable products. The state of different markets, and of competitors' positions, several years down the road are not amenable to easy predictions. In what often appears as a volatile political setting, moreover, the regulatory hurdles facing a product at the registration stage may change in number, type and stringency over the several-year period of product development in ways that cannot be foreseen at the start of this process. For all these reasons there are incentives to minimise the role of the largely hit-and-miss methods of traditional approaches to pesticide discovery. Otherwise a company that is seriously in the business of developing new products may have to count on the screening of 10 000 or more chemicals annually.[15] Synthesis of analogues of known active molecules can cut corners; but as the synthetic pyrethroid case shows the basic research period may still span decades. Insights can be derived from closely related chemical sectors, such as pharmaceuticals. Some discoveries owe debts to knowledge of natural processes. Those of 2,4-D and MCPA, for example, drew in part on knowledge of the behaviour of natural plant hormones.

The pesticide company or division, however, has a unique character. In fertilisers, for example, the closest family relative as far as many users are concerned, little research investment takes place. Demand for the limited numbers of ways in which nitrogen, phosphate and potash can be combined is unlikely to have high elasticity. Lack of the toxicity factor also minimises regulatory intrusions. At the research and develement end there is more scope for collaboration or integration with pharmaceuticals or other kinds of chemicals sectors. The same compound may prove to have widely different uses. Warfarin, best known as a rat poison, is also used in the treatment of thrombosis in humans; the herbicide aminotriazole was earlier used as an intermediate in colour-photographic dye production; the dithiocarbamate fungicides were first produced as ancillary compounds in rubber processing.[16]

But whatever opportunities present themselves for this kind of cross-fertilisation of ideas and findings, the link between research costs and regulation remains a close one for pesticides manufacturers. The more demanding the regulatory setting, the higher the costs of the testing phases of research and development; the higher the costs of research and development, the more reluctant are chemical companies to take the risk of handing over information to regulatory agencies. Few companies operate, moreover, with an eye to particular markets in individual countries. Given the wide variation in national approaches to pesticide regulation, industry associations representing pesticide manufacturers have taken initiatives to press for greater harmonisation and uniformity. Even where such broad objectives find sympathetic echoes in government institutions, as in those of the European Community (EC), the forces for retention of regulatory variation remain strong. Some companies, for example, can benefit from the existence of distinctive non-tariff barriers at their own national borders; and rigorous pursuit of harmonisation may logically lead to costly demands for an upgrading of the stringency of regulations in some countries. The harmonisation issue is examined at greater length in Chapter 5.

THE INTERNATIONAL PESTICIDES ECONOMY

While pesticide manufacturers have been quick to protest threatened new additions to the regulatory burden, this has nonetheless proved itself a resilient industry. Profits continue to be made and, more important, to be expected. World market growth has remained steady in the 1970s and 1980s at around 5 per cent a year. Even the ending of patent protection for a compound does not necessarily, or even usually, signal the beginning of a collapse of profit margins.

Observers of the industry have pointed, however, to signs of maturity. The term usually connotes low growth and innovation rates. Certainly there are some indications that discovery of new compounds has passed the plateau reached in the 1950s and begun a downward trend. One significant new compound was introduced during the 1930s, 9 in the 1940s, 18 in the 1950s and 19 in the 1960s. The 1970s opened with markedly lower rates of discovery; only 3 appeared in the first half of the decade.[17] The statistics on significant new products also shows evidence of a diminishing flow. The frequency of invention in the late 1970s was about 16 products a year; by contrast the figure for the late 1960s was 25.[18] These trends do not reflect a drop in interest on the part of chemical companies in research and development efforts, but rather the increased difficulty over time of bringing new pesticides on to the market. The number of compounds screened per marketed product has been estimated at 1800 in 1956, approximately 10 000 in 1972, and perhaps 12 000 towards the end of the 1970s.[19] Plotting these kinds of statistics against time and arriving at some form of flattening S-curve is not a source of great encouragement for manufacturers looking ahead a decade or two.

Such concerns may prompt momentary qualms on the way to the bank, but only a few shops actually bring down the shutters. The pesticides industry is increasingly a concentrated one, with less room now than in the 1950s for the small or medium-sized manufacturer. The phenomena of a maturing industry are countered by several considerations. First, new introductions, when they occur, can take off rapidly. This was the case with the synthetic pyrethroids. Following discovery of permethrin in 1973, a protracted commercial stage of development by ICI followed complex negotiations with other companies which led to it, or more precisely ICI Americas, acquiring rights to develop, manufacture and market the compound. The large potential US market against cotton pests was the major incentive. Partly as a result of emergency registrations granted by the EPA in situations where existing pesticides were proving ineffective, permethrin and other compounds then managed in the later 1970s to achieve high rates of penetration of between 60–75 per cent in key markets such as that against the cotton boll-worm in the United States and horticulture in the Netherlands.[20] Secondly, the large number of products on the market attests to the continued vitality of the industry. Whereas in the mid-1940s about 50 basic farm chemicals were in use in the United States, the figure had risen to several hundred by the mid-1970s, with perhaps 50 000–70 000 commercial formulations available.[21] Thirdly, overall production figures for pesticides worldwide since the 1940s indicate largely unchecked and occasionally rapid growth (though production figures in some sectors, such as some of the more politically delicate organochlorine compounds, have tended increasingly to be put into the category of sensitive information by some companies). In 1974 US manufacturers produced 643 000 tonnes of synthetic organic pesticides with a total value of $1732 million; total British sales in 1975 were £159 million, almost equally divided between home and export sales.[22] In 1980 it was estimated that US production of pesticides could reach $6 billion by 1990.[23] Much of this production, moreover, is accounted for by products relatively cheap to manufacture, and which have passed the break-even point of returns to cover research and development costs. Exports are one way of coping with a maturing industry and government regulation. Since the 1960s this aspect has been crucial to the pesticides industries of most western countries. Chemicals generally have constituted Britain's third largest export.[24] Between them the United States, West Germany, Britain, France, Italy and Japan accounted in the 1960s and 1970s for around 75 per cent of world chemicals production; and the international trade in chemicals was one conducted in the main between these countries.

Growing attention has been paid, however, to markets in Third World countries. Companies have emphasised that no dramatic sales figures can be expected from this quarter. The early 1980s estimates of continuing world market growth of about 5 per cent per annum during the decade still focused in the main on the major 20–25 country markets as being those that would be the leading ones in the early 1990s.[25] Pessimism about developing country markets generally is grounded in several factors: lack of government investment in agricultural sectors, or of foreign exchange reserves, finance problems facing small farmers, illiteracy or lack of attentiveness to the potential of technical innovation, and generally impoverished national economies. One projection in 1983 of future world markets put the overall Third World share in 1990 at the same level as that in 1982, at 22.5 per cent; sales by the later date were anticipated at around $8 billion.[26] Built into some of the more optimistic industry projections have been expectations that urgent food production needs in poorer countries will lead to pressures for greater international agency and bilateral aid and technical assistance. In Africa, for example, significant expansions of sales have usually been thought of as being a decade or more away for these reasons. For the short- and medium-term future, pesticide companies have tended to put more faith in those regions of the Third World where agricultural modernisation programmes indicated prospects of increasing dependence on pesticide supplies; these considerations have pointed more to Latin America and certain parts of South-east Asia.

Expansion of the trade in agrochemical products from North to South, as opposed to the traditional concentration of trade patterns within the advanced industrialised nations, has brought with it a renewal of the vigour of pesticide debates in western countries. These debates had a more international flavour in the 1970s and 1980s. Some evidence has indicated that chemical companies have viewed developing countries, particularly those with the weakest regulatory barriers, not only as means of circumventing saturated and over-regulated markets in the industrialised world, but more especially as opportunities for selling compounds subject to major restrictions on safety grounds at home. Some developing countries may be loosely categorised by companies as 'short' markets, where the likelihood of rapid penetration, assisted by energetic advertising campaigns, in-creases the chances of getting back investment money quickly. By the late 1970s the toxic chemicals trade with developing countries had emerged as a major issue in a number of international forums, as well as in countries, particularly the United States, where the charge of toxic chemical dumping in the Third World could be exploited in the context of domestic issues surrounding the chemical industry. We will come back to these debates in later chapters.

If only by virtue of sales patterns, then, the pesticide industry is international. It is also located in the wider setting of the world chemical industry. The heavy emphasis on research and development has already been noted as one contrast with the neighbouring ferti-liser industry, and as one structural similarity shared by pesticide and pharmaceutical manufacturers. Pesticides, largely unlike fertilisers, are also subject to some short-term fluctuations in demand. Britain experienced a wet summer in 1958, and supplies of copper fungicides for use against potato blight could not keep up with the demand; there was then little demand for these products in the following dry summer.[27] There are a number of other similarities between the pesticides and pharmaceuticals sectors. Both deal essentially with the biological effects of chemicals; they are both highly diverse industries which have experienced similar patterns of overall market growth; and both have to confront significant regulatory constraints as well as criticism of their operations in developing countries. By contrast, important parts of pesticide production processes tend to be local-ised. Formulation can most economically be carried out in local plants near predictable markets. This means that developing coun-tries intent on bringing more of the pesticides sector under state control, or in expanding the role of local entrepreneurs, can do this with least difficulty at the formulation stage of the production cycle. These kinds of differences with even closely related chemicals sectors are also reflected in political organisation, in that the pesticides sector – partly in response to more direct regulatory attack – has tended to display more interest in organising in ways that would allow compa-nies to lobby governments and international regulatory bodies. Pesti-

:ides decisions, then, including responses to regulatory trends, are :ypically made interdependently with decisions affecting other chemi- :als divisions of the same company.

ICI and Ciba-Geigy are two cases in point. In ICI, major decisions affecting future agrochemicals investment began to be made as early as the 1920s. At that time the major issues centred on such matters as the expansion of fungicide production. Leading figures in the com- pany also tended to be ignorant about the general state of the market for agricultural supplies.[28] During the following decade there was growing awareness of the fact that embarking on agrochemicals production did not mean just the introduction of new product lines. It was apparent that chemical research at basic levels would have far-reaching implications for the chemical industry generally, and in areas such as pesticides particularly. Yet major decisions on pesticides emerged slowly out of inter-divisional competition. Several existing divisions or groups within ICI had an interest in the newly emerging pesticides area in the 1930s and 1940s. Indeed this fact has been put forward as one which in practice hindered pesticide development; shared control of the agrochemicals area by competing divisions as diverse as those dealing with dyestuffs or general chemicals had an inhibiting effect on investment of resources in pesticides research and development and manufacturing. The company's position was also affected by the presence of others on the outside who arguably had a stronger competitive edge in the pesticides area. One result was an early agreement, in 1937, with the firm of Cooper, McDougall and Robertson which amongst other things had the effect of restraining ICI growth in this sector. Under its terms, for example, ICI was kept out of the trade in protective dips for farm animals and the agreement also restricted profit levels. Other ICI divisions, moreover, showed resentment of the company (Plant Protection Ltd.) through which ICI moved itself into the pesticides area in a major way.

A similar pattern of internal and external competition emerged out of the history of Ciba-Geigy in the agrochemicals area. Here, however, the two constituent companies had already by the 1950s carved out for themselves distinctive niches in the European and world markets for pesticide products. Geigy's success was based practically on one product class as far as agrochemicals were con- cerned: the triazine herbicides; it also concentrated heavily on the two markets of the United States and France. Ciba, on the other hand, with about one-quarter the agrochemicals sales, had developed a wide variety of diversified products, and was also more active in marketing in many more countries. The agrochemicals area supplied several reasons for integration into a unified company. There were expectations of a long-term decline in demand for the triazines, based on experience of an increasingly saturated US market. Ciba was experimenting with a number of new areas, such as the launching of insecticide products in Third World markets using package approaches that took more account of local conditions. Diversity on the Ciba side was such that it provoked criticism as an organisational weakness; regional organisation, it was argued, had been neglected, and the company tended to lack a broad set of overall objectives or a working philosophy that could weld together the many diverse areas – synthetic resins, photochemistry, rare metals and others, as well as pesticides – in which it was engaged.[29]

The pesticides industry is thus characterised by vertical integration, a high degree of export orientation, product diversity, and a variety of important connections with national economies generally. It is also a capital- and research-intensive industry, involving dominant market positions by relatively few large companies and by a leading role on the part of relatively few countries. The effect of chemical production by some Third World countries in the 1970s and 1980s has been significant in some national markets, for example in India, but in general has been minimal. Here as in the wider chemicals industry the more important trends have been the rise of Japan as a major producer and exporter and increased competition from east European countries.

COMPANIES AS POLITICAL ACTORS

Economic and political processes are linked. More specifically, the regulatory environment in which pesticide manufacturers operate has become an increasingly important factor in the making of decisions on the research, development or production of pesticides by companies; and in turn industry structures have both set limits to and provided opportunities for regulatory innovations by governments. In some ways, for example, the task of regulation is facilitated by the relatively confined states of some markets. Highly specific ones, such as those for corn herbicides or tobacco plant growth regulators in the United States, tend to be restricted in practice to very few firms, either because the high costs of entry have a deterrent effect on other companies or simply because users have set buying habits. Similarly, synthetic pyrethroid insecticides is an area which means, in practice, ICI Americas together with Shell and FMC.[30]

A combination of shifting public perceptions of toxic chemicals and heightened attention to pesticides by a variety of national and international bodies has brought about changes in industry approaches to regulatory issues. Before the 1960s, the assumptions made by companies that pest problems could be handled effectively by the development of new compounds tended to be shared by users, publics and governments. Occasional questioning of the assumptions, for example as a result of the evidence from the late 1940s of the development of insect resistance to orgonochlorines, had few political implications. During and since the 1960s, by contrast, pesticides and other toxic chemicals have become subjects of intense political debates in the United States and many other western countries. More widespread anxieties about the extensive use of chemical compounds in modern industrial societies were reinforced by incidents such as the Seveso explosion in 1976, and the debates that have surrounded issues such as toxic chemical waste disposal, the hazards and benefits of additives and preservatives in foods, as well as particular controversies such as those over asbestos or thalidomide.

Pesticides have been fairly consistently in the firing line of such attacks. Some shifting of political gears on the part of pesticide manufacturers has been detectable. Political environments affect consumption patterns, and not only through the direct consequences of regulatory changes. Industry's proposition was essentially that stringent regulation in the interests of consumer and environmental safety carried with it a potentially high cost in terms of the discouragement of innovation, with consequent effects for employment, the general state of the economy and a country's competitiveness in world markets. During the 1970s the point was felt to have been inadequately grasped by politicians, publics and the media who tended, it was argued, to be susceptible to alarmist calls from environmental pressure groups. In a sense manufacturers were constrained from acting more publicly by a conviction that the basic proposition was so self-evidently true as not to require an elaborate defence. This slowly changed:

There has been a lot of arm-waving by companies in the past saying that the regulations 'cannot be so' or 'what do politicians know about all this?' In fact the companies in the early stages did not know how to react appropriately and they contented themselves

with maintaining a low profile while gaining experience. Now they
accept that they have to live with these regulations and also do
something to reverse them where they are intolerable. The low
profile attitude cannot be maintained and the industry has recognised that it must speak out.[31]

Up to a point, of course, companies have always been political
actors. It makes good business sense to have good political sense.
The moods of publics have to be catered to where they cannot be
directly led. A large chemical company is likely to be influenced in
some manner by vaguely defined, if expedient, notions of responsibility. Its biographer has suggested that there has been in ICI 'sufficient political skill and sense of public responsibility to respond to
movements of power and opinion in the world at large and to adjust
policy continually to the mood of the times.'[32] In some respects this
kind of company is self-regulating. Instances can be cited, for example, of pesticides being withdrawn from the research and development processes of large companies because of discoveries of obscure
toxicological effects, including some that might have evaded the
notice of regulatory authorities. Such companies tend to be critical of
the 'cowboys' whose operations, for example in Third World countries, can bring their own products under closer regulatory or media
scrutiny and, through the workings of a kind of Gresham's law, affect
the profitability of their own operations.

INDUSTRY AND INTERNATIONAL REGULATORY
POLITICS

Pesticide companies have also undertaken activities in relation to the
international institutions that will be discussed in the next three
chapters. There are several points of access to this machinery. Some
manufacturers have representation in advisory roles on member-state
delegations to international conferences. This happens in the case of the
Codex Alimentarius Commission activities concerned with the formulation of international standards on levels of pesticide residues in
foods. Industry associations are somewhat better placed to gain
participation rights as observers, or acquire various forms of consultative status. Within such broader transnational associations individual companies remain autonomous, but their employees may in

practice participate in various ways in the international regulatory work involved.

The pesticides sector has tended to be the most effectively organised of the various parts of the chemical industry, with the possible exception of pharmaceuticals. Because of the structure of the international pesticides economy, however, the main international bodies have at times been more European in character, US companies often being content to confine their interest in regulatory questions to the national context. The close connections between many European markets, and the harmonising objectives of European Community institutions, have accented this tendency. During the 1970s some US pesticide companies questioned whether their own national association, the National Agricultural Chemicals Association (NACA), should maintain such an active international role. Funds spent on participation in the main international body, the Groupement International des Associations Nationales de Fabricants de Produits Agrochimiques (GIFAP), met with some criticism. Earlier, US financial support of this organisation had peaked at around 50 per cent of its budget, a figure eventually brought down to a less controversial 23 per cent of GIFAP funding. As one NACA official put it in 1976, 'We have felt for a long time . . . that it was not quite right for the NACA to support an organisation in Europe to the tune of half their budget.'[33] Thus a more equitable sharing of the costs of international operations has characterised the period since the mid-1970s, even though the requirement for national pesticide manufacturers' associations other than that of the US to increase their share encountered a few veiled threats of withdrawal.

By the end of 1983 GIFAP membership comprised the national agrochemical industry associations of 21 countries. These included the leading pesticide producing and exporting nations of the United States, Japan, the Federal Republic of Germany, Britain and Switzerland. Only two of these members were from developing countries (Brazil and India), but a class of 'associate' membership extended the range to Argentina, the Philippines and Mexico.[34]

In terms of its own organisation the grouping has aimed to demonstrate, firstly, a continuity of representative membership that merits its participation in international pesticides regulatory discussion, and, secondly, the reliability and authority of the scientific and technical judgements which it contributes to such meetings. Thus apart from an annual General Assembly of member associations, the regular running of the organisation is in the hands of a Board and an Executive Committee; the secretariat staffs the headquarters offices in Brussels. However, much of the continuing work of GIFAP of a technical and evaluative nature then flows through its working group and technical committee structure. These bodies are important because they constitute the main locations of the expertise which the organisation brings to international regulatory bodies, and assure its effective participation there. One group acts as a kind of general review body for all international regulatory matters; a second handles more general concerns having to do with manufacturers' liability, confidentiality of data, good advertising practice and related issues; a third deals with educational and informational matters; and a fourth with pesticide transportation questions. Reinforcing this work, and also comprising individuals from companies whose national associations are members, are a series of technical committees on such matters as usages in agriculture and test methods, pesticide residues, the specifications of pesticides and toxicology.[35]

The general objective of protecting the interests of the world pesticides industry breaks down in practice into a number of more specific goals and concerns. During the 1970s and early 1980s these focused particularly on the problems and politics of harmonisation of pesticide regulations. Industry involvement in international negotiations on approaches to pesticide registration is examined in Chapter 5, and the particular area of pesticide residues standards in Chapter 4. In addition GIFAP has also aimed to encourage moves which would have the effect of taking unreasonable and heavy regulatory burdens off the shoulders of the pesticides industry; to ensure that adequate recognition is given to principles involving industrial property rights, including the confidentiality of proprietary data; and, in general, to publicise the requirements of growing populations for agrochemically-safeguarded food supplies.

Some national groupings of agrochemical industries have also projected an active international presence in their own right. This is particularly true of the United States. The approach of the NACA to international regulatory questions has varied according to the inclinations of its member companies. Some have periodically been critical of too many overseas diversions. The questions have largely been resolved by a measure of functional separation between the association's domestic and international regulatory policies and activities. The working rule evolved that member companies with a significant involvement in international trade, or a particular interest for other reasons in following international regulatory issues, should pay a special assessment to the association. This contribution funds the international side of its operations, which primarily means participation in GIFAP. About 7 per cent of the overall NACA budget was devoted to the international side during the 1970s.[36] This division has been reflected organisationally, for example in the creation of a new international affairs committee in 1978. The NACA has also taken initiatives to promote wider industry interest in international regulatory questions, and particularly in the significance of the work of the Codex Alimentarius Commission for US pesticide manufacturers. Early in the 1980s the association became more active in relation to international issues being handled by Congressional committees; it pressed at one point, for example, for withdrawal of most-favoured-nation status from Hungary because of an alleged lack of respect for chemical patents by that country.[37]

REGULATORY *DRAMATIS PERSONÆ*

Whether directly themselves, or more indirectly through broad industry groupings, chemical companies have thus approached international regulatory forums with clear definitions of the issues at stake. Unfortunately for those sectors with a special interest in promoting harmonisation of pesticides regulations across countries the number of such forums is large; none can be specially targeted as that most likely to bring about results in terms of changes in government policy at the national level. The qualities of pesticides that give them their staying power in political arenas also stimulate the formation of organisations of different types, both inter-governmental and non-governmental. Officials of a national regulatory agency face a similarly confusing proliferation of would-be regulators in the international system.[38] Depending on definitions and criteria of evaluation employed by the observer, around three dozen international bodies can readily be identified as having a particular interest in taking part in the international regulation of pesticides. There is some risk, then, that developing countries will find the regulatory task that confronts them magnified, rather than made more manageable, by this daunting profusion.

In practice many of the international actors occupy relatively distinct niches in the overall system, either by design or as a result of negotiated demarcations of functions with other organisations. In practice, too, the more important bodies are not difficult to identify. First, among inter-governmental organisations of a global character, both FAO and WHO have taken central roles in the international pesticides area since the 1950s. Their respective approaches have reflected differences of general organisational goals and interests. These, in turn, have had implications for relations with other actors. FAO, for example, operating on the basis of definitions of pesticide supply requirements in agriculture and forestry, has tended to approach the question of relations with industry with a more openly collaborative outlook; WHO has usually been more concerned to preserve some distance between itself and companies. The two were joint founders of the Codex Alimentarius Commission, designed in the early 1960s as a body to oversee and promote improvements in food standards in their various member states. Many of their own programmes continued to overlap with the pesticides components of this machinery, which have rested primarily on the work of a pesticides residues committee (the Codex Committee on Pesticide Residues, or CCPR); in turn, the work of this committee, which consists of delegates from member states, has been dependent for scientific and technical advice in relation to particular compounds on the Joint Meeting on Pesticide Residues (JMPR), comprising individual experts nominated by FAO and WHO.

A full listing of the organs within the UN system which have moved into the pesticides area would be very much more extensive. The UN's Environment Programme (UNEP), a creation of the early 1970s, has not monopolised the environment area; environmental health aspects of pesticide use are a continuing and traditional part of WHO's activities, as are the environmental criteria for pesticide registrations for FAO. Since toxic chemicals issues were a prominent feature of the environmental debates of the late 1960s and early 1970s, however, UNEP has retained an organisational interest in pesticides matters. This has centred on support for programmes encouraging integrated pest management strategies, and on data collection regarding pesticides and other compounds through its International Register of Potentially Toxic Chemicals (IRPTC). Towards the end of the 1970s, WHO also took an initiative to build on pesticides safety questions in which its activities overlapped with those of the International Labour Organisation (ILO) to create an International Programme on Chemical Safety (IPCS). Similarly FAO for several years in the 1970s was cooperating with the International Atomic Energy Agency (IAEA) in a project designed to use nuclear techniques in the detection of pesticide residues in developing countries. Of the main economic development parts of the UN system, the Development Programme (UNDP) and Industrial Development Organisation (UNIDO) have promoted the growth of pesticides industry sectors in Third World countries, though primarily at the formulation rather than the active ingredient manufacturing stage. A number of the UN's regional bodies have been active in some pesticides areas; the Economic Commission for Europe (ECE), for example, has produced major studies of the international trade in pesticide chemicals, and engaged in some cooperative work with parts of the Codex machinery. Other world bodies, within and outside the UN system, have had connections with these activities in specific instances, as in GATT's role in the mid-1980s in the construction of notification procedures to aid regulation of the international trade in agrochemicals.

Secondly, regional inter-governmental organisations, particularly in the industrialised world, have been attracted to pesticides regulatory issues. The Council of Europe, while generally lacking power and political visibility, has nonetheless been one of the more noted pesticides actors by virtue of its widely circulated sets of recommendations to guide registration procedures. Harmonisation has also been a goal pursued by the Commission of the European Communities (EC); several directives relating to different aspects of pesticides regulation in member states have resulted. Attention has been given to similar questions as part of the growing interest during the 1970s of the Organisation for Economic Cooperation and Development (OECD) in chemicals policy generally. The OECD also emerged as the main institutional framework within which the conflicting approaches to chemicals regulation on the part of the United States and Europe were examined, particularly with a view to the minimising of their non-tariff barrier implications. Technical cooperation on related matters of pesticides residues, plant protection products, and the environmental consequences of pesticide use, have also been a feature of the work of the Council for Mutual Economic Assistance (CMEA).[39]

Thirdly, there is a considerable variety of organisations predominantly, though not always exclusively, non-governmental in character. Questions of analytical methods can be highly controversial ones in this area because of the registration and marketing implications of some, particularly since changing technologies have increased the number of regulatory demands that it is technically feasible to place on a manufacturer. Various recommendations of bodies such as the Collaborative International Pesticides Analytical Council (CIPAC) have been criticised on the grounds of the elaboration and sophistication of tests and the high degree of technical expertise required to carry them out.[40] Expert technical bodies in the area also include the International Union of Pure and Applied Chemistry (IUPAC), which has augmented its activities in the 1980s with the CHEMRAWN series of conferences on a wide variety of pesticide use and regulatory issues; the International Union of Biological Sciences (IUBS), particularly through its long-running International Congress of Plant Protection meetings; and related bodies such as the internationally-oriented British Society for Plant Pathology (BSPP).

Multi-purpose environmental non-governmental organisations have often adopted pesticides issues with enthusiasm. The classification here is frequently difficult, however, since concerns and memberships may overlap more development-oriented groups, which typically have been relatively more responsive to supply problems. Generally critical lines on pesticides have been characteristic of leading organisations, such as the International Union for Conservation of Nature and Natural Resources (IUCN), as well as more specific or regionally organised transnational groupings such as the European Environment Bureau (EEB), or the Pesticides Action Network (PAN) of the International Organisation of Consumers Unions (IOCU).

Fourthly, we must for the sake of completeness also make note of the companies and industry associations discussed earlier in this chapter. As we have seen, these have been increasingly active players in the international regulatory game. Whereas formally their role in some forums, such as the Codex organs, may be that of non-participating observers, it is more useful to regard the more active representative bodies as participants in the politics of regulation; viewing them as groups aiming to exert pressure on regulatory organs is a limited perspective at the international level, given the absence of authoritative rule-making bodies.

This brings us, finally, to states. On the criterion of rule-making capability, these remain the crucial actors. They also give shape and structure to a diffuse and unorganised system. The priorities and rankings of governments thus give useful indications of the parts of this system that can in practice be regarded as the more important. This process of elimination is not wholly trustworthy, since the working relations between a part of a state agency and a relatively obscure transnational group may have significance for some issues, and may go largely unnoticed at higher bureaucratic levels. Using this criterion, though, we can reduce the spread of actors to more manageable numbers, and essentially to the major inter-governmental and government–industry forums of FAO and WHO, the Codex system, the OECD and the European Community, and possibly a few others. Governments not only take part in the framing of potentially important international recommendations, they may also institute domestic measures which have broader international repercussions. The general approaches and specific determinations of some government agencies, particularly the Environmental Protection Agency (EPA) in the United States, create sizeable ripples throughout the international pesticides regulatory system; by a kind of protective mimicry, some may be adopted and applied in other countries. Similarly, the degree to which the export procedures of states call for data on chemicals to be transmitted to importing countries clearly has major implications for the broader international regime. The ways that governments have approached pesticides regulation through international bodies will be examined in three contexts in the following chapters: pesticides residues in foods, procedures governing the registration of pesticides by governments, and issues surrounding the environmental costs of pesticide use.

Part II

4 Residues of Pesticides: the Codex System

Chemicals used to guard crops from attack by insects and other pests may leave traces of themselves behind. Even ostensibly safer pesticide chemicals can pose hazards for the consumer if applied carelessly: if, for example, due regard is not paid by farmers to the appropriate interval between application and harvesting. Consumers for their part may neglect to take elementary precautions when preparing food. Upon these facts have been built imposing and complex edifices of international regulatory politics. This is partly because the readily observable fact, that residues of pesticides exist in foods, does not so easily lend itself to neat regulatory solutions. How much consumption of a pesticide in this fashion should be permitted? What are the criteria on which the decision should rest? What if little in the way of a technical or administrative infrastructure exists – as in most developing countries – so that no sustained monitoring of residue levels in different foods is feasible?

These kinds of questions provide one basis for the interest of some international organisations in pesticide issues. The general area of consumer protection, additives, food standards and related questions of environmental health, however, has on its own lacked the driving force which has propelled much international attention to pesticides in the last quarter-century. The other factor is the international character of the residues issue. Agricultural products are traded across national frontiers. So are the chemicals used in agriculture. For a government to attempt to set pesticide residue levels in isolation from the rest of the international community, or at least from the countries which constitute its major trading partners, is potentially self-defeating. Different standards might apply in other states. Imported agricultural products might then have unacceptably high levels of toxic residues. Exporters, similarly, if they are to be successful in penetrating foreign markets, will have to take into account the residues standards applying there.[1] At the same time, such regulatory frameworks provide temptations to protectionism. Rules on pesticide residues may in practice serve as significant non-tariff barriers behind which can hide local agricultural or agrochemical sectors.

THE CODEX SYSTEM AND PESTICIDE RESIDUES

The Codex Alimentarius Commission, a joint creation of FAO and WHO aimed at establishing internationally accepted food standards, is the main international body dealing with these kinds of issues. The machinery is in principle relatively simple. On residues questions the Commission operates primarily through a Committee on Pesticide Residues (CCPR). This makes judgements on acceptable levels of pesticide residues in selected food commodities with a view to these recommendations being eventually incorporated into the Codex and implemented in the form of national regulations. Its members – delegations representing member states of the two parent agencies – perform this task on the basis of scientific evaluations submitted by a group of experts. This body, the Joint Meeting on Pesticide Residues (JMPR), comprises specialists drawn primarily from the relevant pesticides groups of FAO and WHO. This basic picture remained intact until the early 1980s, when some institutional alterations took place which will be discussed later.

Since its origins in the early 1960s the system has gradually evolved into a complex and ambitious scheme which can be regarded as the core component of the emerging international pesticides regime – 'the centrepiece of the international regulatory work concerned with pesticide residues in food', as one official closely associated with its operations has described it.[2] Its slow-moving pace, however – apparently an unavoidable product of its twin goals of scientific credibility and political influence – has attracted criticism over the years. So has the lack of universal, or even widespread, adherence by governments to agreed and recommended standards. Some of these complaints have sprung from differing expectations of its roles and objectives. It can variously be viewed as a bulwark of the industrialised nations against the spread of non-tariff barriers and protectionist impulses, as part of the international network of actors combating threats to the environment, as an instrument for the promotion of effective strategies of agricultural development in Third World countries, as a means of protecting consumers from adulterated foods, or simply as a forum of debate and deliberation rather than as an inter-agency collaborative effort aimed at influencing government policies.

The mechanism originated in FAO discussions of pesticides issues in the late 1950s, and overlapping WHO interest in health aspects of pesticide use. Two lines of institutional development followed: that of meetings of experts of the two agencies, and that of the overarching Codex framework. The latter started life in 1963 with the establishment by the two organisations of a joint programme on food standards. The principal organ of this programme was to be the Codex Alimentarius Commission. The CCPR, the specialised subgrouping dealing with pesticides, was set up shortly afterwards. Regular exchanges between experts in the early 1960s were then formalised in 1966 with the initiation of the parallel Joint Meetings series.

From the outset the two broad objectives of eliminating hazards to consumers and of combating the spread of non-tariff barriers shaped the approaches of these bodies. The purpose of the Food Standards Programme as a whole was defined as being:

> to protect the health of consumers and to ensure fair practices in the food trade; to promote coordination of all food standards work undertaken by international governmental and non-governmental organisations; to determine priorities and initiate and guide the preparation of draft standards through and with the aid of appropriate organisations; and to finalise standards and after acceptance of governments publish them in a Codex Alimentarius either as regional or worldwide standards.[3]

The workings of the programme also have to be seen in the context of growing fears on the part of countries with high stakes in the international trade in agricultural products – the United States, Canada, Australia – that divergent food standards regulations could increasingly pose a serious threat to this trade. As one participating official later put it: 'The suspicion was that as tariffs were being reduced on agricultural products as a result of GATT negotiations, selective enforcement of national food standards legislation could develop into a significant non-tariff barrier to shelter domestic agricultural interests.'[4] In one sense the roots of the Codex system lie in the creation of the EEC. Though still a fledgling enterprise in the early 1960s, the leading world agricultural exporting nations saw in its future growth the possibility of their progressive exclusion from European markets.

Other actors had an interest in these goals. The 'enormous repercussions' on the trade in agricultural products of the setting by governments of different pesticides residue levels were still a major concern of manufacturers in the 1980s.[5] Representatives of Group of 77 states participating in the Codex framework also increasingly turned to this forum as a means of pressing for more resources from international agencies to assist with agricultural development generally and the use and management of agricultural chemicals in particular.

We can see in some of the complexities of Codex processes reflections not only of the intrinsic technical difficulty of making sound judgements on pesticide residues, but also of the variety of actors that have an interest in shaping these outcomes. The broad institutional setting consisted in the 1980s of the Codex Alimentarius Commission itself and its Executive Committee, together with fourteen commodity and six other committees. The subjects covered range widely over food standards issues. Apart from pesticide residues, others include special problems of cereals, pulses and legumes, and cocoa products and chocolate, as well as more generally applicable questions such as food additives, labelling, methods of analysis and sampling, and food hygiene. In addition four regional coordinating committees (for Africa, Asia, Europe and Latin America), formed at intervals during the 1960s and 1970s, attempt to inject greater cohesion and consistency into the various component parts of this functionally fragmented system. Two other expert groups have been formed jointly with the UN's Economic Commission for Europe (ECE). Representation on the major Codex bodies is of states and by one of the common UN geographical distribution formulæ. The Executive Committee, for example, consists, in addition to its chairman and three vice-chairmen, of six members elected from among FAO and WHO member states from Africa, Asia, Europe, Latin America, North America, and the South-west Pacific. Each member has one representative at Commission sessions and one vote.[6]

More specifically, the role of the committee on pesticide residues is:

(a) to establish maximum limits for pesticide residues in specific food items or in groups of foods;

(b) to establish maximum limits for pesticide residues in certain animal feeding stuffs moving in international trade where this is justified for reasons of protection of human health;

(c) to prepare priority lists of pesticides for evaluation by the [JMPR];

(d) to consider methods of sampling and analysis for the determination of pesticide residues in food and feed;

(e) to consider other matters in relation to the safety of food and feed containing pesticide residues; and

(f) to establish maximum limits for environmental and industrial contaminants showing chemical or other similarity to pesticides, in specific food items or groups of foods.[7]

This list, from the 1981 definition, reveals the impact of change and debate in the period since 1963. The question of animal feeding stuffs (b) posed at times controversial issues. The final objective (f) was the product of prolonged discussion on whether or not the terms of reference could legitimately be extended to encompass pollutants. The catch-all provision relating to 'other matters' (e) has also at times sparked heated disputes on such questions as the authority of the committee to act as a source of advice to governments on general items of agricultural policy and practice.

For the Joint Meetings, on the other hand, the organising principle is individual scientific expertise. Both FAO and WHO, as the main UN sources of this expertise, have a long-standing institutional interest in residues questions.[8] The role of the joint body is basically to respond to questions put to it by the Codex pesticides residues committee. In practice, somewhat distinct sets of tasks have tended to be allocated to the respective agency sub-groupings.[9]

The spark which sets the engine in motion might be an approach by a government requesting that an internationally agreed maximum residue limit be set for a particular pesticide in relation to a specific food commodity. Assuming that the CCPR agrees that a case has been made for the establishment of such a limit, on the basis of the data accompanying the proposal and of its own deliberations, the Joint Meeting of experts is then asked to carry out an initial scientific assessment. At its own annual meetings the JMPR reviews these various questions put to it and examines known residues data as well as existing judgements about acceptable daily intakes of each pesticide investigated. If sufficient data are available, the Joint Meeting may at this point recommend limits and return the matter to the residues committee; if not, the item is likely to reappear on subsequent JMPR agendas. An important filter in this process is a sub-grouping of the CCPR which decides on priorities (in line with objective (c) above). This has proved a crucial innovation for helping to ensure that the machinery is neither random nor passive in its intermediary role between member governments and its own experts. As for other Codex organs the pesticides committee follows a step-by-step procedure of decision-making, which will be reviewed shortly.

Here, then, is an international regulatory system in microcosm. Behind the striving for objective scientific determinations on pesticides residues issues lie the interests of states in protecting and promoting important sectors of their respective economies, whether the production of grapefruit or apples or the marketing of fungicides and insecticides. The Codex structure is a tacit acknowledgement that such interests exist, and have to be accommodated if scientific recommendations on residues are to avoid an ivory-tower abstractness. Representatives of the pesticides industry also have direct access to this machinery. On the sidelines, though rarely neutral as regards the interplay of scientific and political forces, are a variety of non-governmental organisations and other international agencies. The workings of the system, and the respective impact of different factors, can most conveniently be approached by examining first the character of the scientific decision-making process.

SCIENTIFIC DECISION-MAKING

Several considerations have rendered the making of scientific judgements on these matters either painfully slow and tortuous, or else simply impossible. First, the state of the art of residue analysis continues to change and develop.[10] In the early and middle 1960s international pesticides meetings could not just refer to a tested and widely accepted set of findings and methods. The Codex meetings have themselves played a significant role in the evolution of this field. Underpinning this scientific work at various times, however, have been a number of assumptions or relatively arbitrary judgements which, taken together, have meant that specific questions can seldom escape prolonged discussion.

Some of the basic terminology is such as to allow a variety of judgements to be applied in particular cases. The notion of a maximum residue limit, or MRL, has been defined as 'the maximum concentration of a pesticide residue that is allowed in or on a food commodity at a specific stage in the harvesting, storage, transport, marketing, or processing of the food, up to the final point of consumption'.[11] This is related to judgements of acceptable daily intakes (ADIs) of particular pesticides, defined as 'the amount of a chemical that could be ingested daily without appreciable risk to the consumer, in the light of all the information available at the time of the evaluation'.[12] The phrase 'without appreciable risk' can be defined more, or less, rigorously. The leading WHO official on the subject has taken it to mean 'the practical certainty that injury will not result after a lifetime of exposure'.[13] In practice, the amount of reliable toxicological data on a given pesticide can vary; and, in principle, any resulting figure 'remains an expression of opinion which carries no guarantee of "absolute" safety. Such a guarantee would be impossible.'[14] This kind of approach conflicts with more extreme formulations, for example some put forward in the United States on the basis of the so-called Delaney clause on the marketing of possibly carcinogenic compounds. The Codex approach represents a compromise. Pesticides are there to be used; some risk has to be accepted.

Other kinds of assumptions are more widely applicable. For obvious ethical reasons, much toxicological work has to rest on extrapolations to humans of investigations of test animals. But as the toxicologist Bernard Oser entitled a 1981 paper, 'Man is not a big rat'.[15] Some extrapolations may have limited validity. Dietary intakes of pesticide residues also vary as a result of individual preferences, custom, agricultural practices, cultural or religious rules, income levels, or health. There may be more complicated synergistic effects of residue reactions with food additives, pharmaceuticals, environmental contaminants, or other pesticide residues inside the human body. The fact that assumptions are made in the course of a scientific investigation does not, of course, in itself invalidate any results. They do mean, however, that regulatory evaluations, no matter how well grounded in an inter-subjective consensus of expert opinion, cannot avoid having a contingent quality.

A second set of constraints emerged from debate on the terms of reference. Early in the game participants discovered that it was impossible to agree quickly on the meaning of the term 'pesticide residue'.[16] But more importantly, the basic reference point was food. Cotton is not a food; so discussion of problems associated with pesticide use against cotton pests, for example in Latin America, has been out of order. The Codex Commission ruled in 1979 that tobacco could not be considered, for the same, if less valid, reason. On a different tack, Finland in 1981 raised the question of whether the residues committee should be able to deal with residues from drugs used in veterinary practice, and cited as an example thiabendazole, which leads to residues in meat or milk products.[17] An earlier decision, in 1967, maintained that the committee was empowered to discuss pesticide residues irrespective of their origin, and so could investigate residues left by animal feeding stuffs.[18] The environmentalist atmosphere of the 1970s produced a fresh batch of such issues. The consensus at first was that contaminants other than pesticides should not be considered. Poland took a strong line in arguing that PCBs and dioxins were legitimate parts of CCPR work. The case against moving in this direction was put in pragmatic terms. In practice it would be difficult to generate information on the basis of which maximum limits for industrial and environmental pollutants in food could be established; and even if it were possible, it would mean a vastly increased work load for the committee. The compromise eventually reached was that contaminants which showed 'chemical or other similarity to pesticides' could be brought to the attention of the CCPR, and this phrase was duly added to the roster of objectives (as (f) in the list in the last section).[19]

Thirdly, there have existed a number of competing methodologies and test routines. Should recommendations on maximum limits be made for pesticides only, or for their metabolites as well? The answer that provides the largest margin of safety is clearly yes. This, though, would be costly in terms of time, organisational effort and data-gathering. Similarly, analytical methods vary in their sophistication and elaboration, as well as in the cost and level of technical expertise involved. Industry representatives have occasionally been critical of test methods advocated by some scientific bodies on these grounds. There are also practical implications for developing countries. Making excessively elaborate procedures the norm could bar many from effective participation in such debates. Codex work was set back for months, or years in some cases, as a result of the discovery in the late 1970s that findings from one of the leading US toxicological testing laboratories, Industrial Bio-Test Laboratories (IBT), were of poor quality.[20] Choices of test methods, then, have more than an academic significance.

Fourthly, the operations of the Codex residues system have been hostage to the politics of data. The Joint Meetings had to confront major gaps in the toxicological data available. Very few governments tended to submit information directly, the experts complained. Submissions by industry were largely deficient in the residues data required for the evaluation of compounds. When information was passed on, it was usually meagre. As a result Joint Meetings were often put in the difficult position of trying to reach sound scientific judgements on the basis of grossly inadequate data. Some of the information available was several years old by the time the JMPR was reviewing a compound, and did not therefore comply with increasingly exacting standards of testing applied in the period since.[21]

An over-zealous protection by firms of proprietary data was frequently at the root of this frustration. Pesticides vary in composition. This is particularly the case with some compounds, such as toxaphene or other chlorinated terpenes and technical grades of BHC(HCH), and presents acute regulatory problems in situations where several manufacturers are engaged in production. Companies tend to be reticent, however, about releasing this kind of information. And governments, when they are in possession of relevant information of this kind, are not necessarily responsive to overtures from international bodies such as the various Codex organs. Guarding and nourishing their own delicate relations with companies in their own countries may be a more pressing concern. Participants in the Joint Meetings, indeed, have often found themselves in the situation of knowing that crucial data existed, but of being unable to put their hands on it.[22]

The pesticides industry has shown some flexibility over the term 'trade secret'. How much depends in part on the international organisation concerned. The Codex forums have probably fared better than most. This is partly because of industry access to the machinery, and partly because the government participants in it have tended to be attuned to the sensitivities of industry on this point. When the question of modifying these procedures arose in 1980, the head of the Australian delegation spoke vigorously of the need to protect the confidentiality of and proprietary rights to data on pesticides.[23] The Joint Meetings have attempted to go some way towards meeting industry concerns. It was essential for the JMPR to have access to detailed information on such matters as impurities in technical grade pesticides, it pointed out in 1977, but it was 'not usually necessary' for such information to be published afterwards.[24] Usually, however, these organs have been able to do little more in practice than draw attention to their plight, urge governments and international agencies to cooperate with them, and try to reassure pesticide manufacturers and industrial associations of their respect for property rights while persuading them that it is in their interest too to collaborate with international regulatory bodies.

A final set of problems affecting scientific decision-making has arisen from the close link between toxicological studies of residue hazards on the one hand, and actual patterns of use and consumption on the other. Different countries have differing pest control requirements. How agrochemicals are used in practice does not necessarily follow efficacy or safety guidelines. Consumers' dietary patterns and their intake of pesticide residues are also subject to wide variation. So conscious had some CCPR participants become of these kinds of constraints by the early 1970s that they questioned seriously whether the elaboration of pesticide residue tolerances was feasible. There was some support for the idea that the work of the CCPR, then almost a decade old, should be discontinued.[25] Instead, the committee reinforced its efforts to gather use and consumption data. Studies carried out during the 1970s in Canada, Britain, the United States and Australia suggested that pesticide residue intake was safely below ADI figures. But given the inadequate resources at the disposal of the committee, and the limited spread of such surveys, the utility of the results could be open to question. Some monitoring programmes were under way in developing countries in the 1980s, for example in Brazil, but in general Third World regions represented huge gaps in knowledge.

The CCPR has also given thought to the issue of greater standardisation of agricultural practices. Meetings in Canada and Denmark in the late 1960s and early 1970s first brought the question into prominence. Requirements varied greatly from country to country, an important Australian paper argued during the course of this work. There were inevitably differing levels of residues and differing requirements for tolerances. Fungicides, for example, had to be applied frequently in regions where temperature and humidity were high.[26] Making recommendations on agricultural policy, though, raised some sensitive questions. Governments had the right to work out their own policies; it was not clear that the CCPR or the Codex system generally should try to insinuate itself into such deliberations. It was evident, too, and acknowledged in CCPR discussions in the 1960s, that that body could run into considerable political difficulties if it appeared to be trying to standardise pesticide usage on a global basis. A less controversial approach was to expand the amount of reliable information on the subject. This was done primarily through a Canadian initiative from the early 1970s, which led to the collection of statistics on patterns of use of different pesticides in various countries.[27] But a feeling that more was required than fact-gathering persisted. Dutch officials had argued in the late 1960s that the CCPR should endeavour to define guidelines for good agricultural practice in the use of pesticides. A set was later produced, but the committee tended to conclude that it was not its purpose to provide more than general principles which should be considered by governments and users; specific recommendations were not its function. This conclusion also applied to the idea that certain compounds should be designated by it as restricted or discontinued, where it was felt that their use was not in accordance with accepted definitions of good agricultural practice. Such attempts to move the CCPR in more environmentally activist directions failed. Judgements of this sort, it was concluded, were best left to national authorities.[28]

THE REGULATORY PROCESS

Codex work has thus been slow and laborious. But there have been results. A general assessment of their impact is reserved for later in this chapter. First we must look at the process itself. The bulk of the work of a typical CCPR meeting is taken up with discussion of proposals for maximum residue limits in a variety of draft stages. The one in 1982 examined a total of 47 compounds, each in relation to various foods. Some matters can move quickly. A proposal for a residue limit of 0.5 mg/kg for diazinon on kiwi fruit, based on data generated in New Zealand in supervised trials, had met with no objections from governments in the preceding months, and a couple of the steps in the committee's procedures could be skipped.[29]

These carefully designed 'steps' are the central structure in the regulatory process. Based on general Codex procedures, the underlying aim is to ensure maximum opportunity for governments to express opinions and reservations at each point along the line from the initial scientific appraisals of a pesticide to the final formulation of a standard. Each pesticide thus becomes the subject of a set of multilateral negotiations, the character of which is different for each one. The initial strategy, when the CCPR began its work, was to tackle residues on a commodity by commodity basis, but this was soon dropped in favour of the approach of investigating individual compounds. The process begins with recommendations on maximum limits made by the technical experts of the Joint Meetings. These are distributed by the Codex secretariat to governments and interested international organisations for comment following preliminary drafting by the CCPR (steps 1-3). In the following two steps member governments taking part in CCPR work examine any comments submitted and formulate recommendations for proposed draft standards. The drafts are also distributed to governments and other international bodies (step 6), and the subsequent responses evaluated by the committee (steps 7 and 8). In the final steps in this sequence (9 and 10) recommended standards are circulated to governments for possible acceptance, and published as approved Codex maximum residue limits.[30]

The exercise, duplicated simultaneously for each of the several dozen compounds that might be at any of the steps at a given time, can be wearisome for the impatient. From the start there have been proposals for accelerating the process. Israeli delegates in 1969, critical of the length of time it took to establish a Codex tolerance, argued that the time schedule involved could have a deterrent effect on the development of new pesticides by industry. The Federal Republic of Germany took up the theme in 1977. Codex procedures were too lengthy and needed to be streamlined and made more flexible. German limits, it was pointed out, were normally reviewed every two years, something that would be impossible if a procedure such as that of the Codex Commission had been adopted.[31] In practice, some flexibility is possible, as the example of kiwi fruit residues indicates. Changes have been implemented in the procedures over time. Further, the CCPR has benefited from a Dutch chairmanship which has taken full advantage of opportunities for changing into higher gears by setting and reminding delegates of deadlines, and taken initiatives to expedite deliberations by such means as asking delegates for early clarifications of their positions. But there are limitations to this. Governments need their opportunities to comment on proposals going through the system. Gaps in the data may have to be plugged. Too zealous a commitment to results, then, can be counter-productive in terms of both the scientific and the political goals of the exercise.

The increasing number of pesticides examined by the residues committee and the Joint Meetings has provided fuel for these kinds of complaints. From 1970, for example, the Joint Meetings have tackled various herbicides and the politically sensitive nature of some of these compounds for some delegations has caused problems. In general, though, the system has been able to cope with large numbers of issues. This has depended on the ability of delegates to order their priorities. At its first session in 1966 the CCPR agreed on two lists of priority compounds which were subsequently examined by the Joint Meetings. Production of three later lists, however, prompted the expert group to seek some guidance on priorities. The formation of a priorities group within the CCPR was thus an important development which went a long way towards removing earlier and relatively more unsystematic approaches to tolerances. The criteria for priority were in practice wide use of a pesticide and/or the existence of residues that were of concern to public health authorities; given the workload of the committee, in other words, a very much lower priority was given to potential problems of this kind that might arise in the future. Judgements about priority compounds also rested in part on the empirical use data collected as a result of the Canadian survey work during the 1970s.

Despite this innovation, the Joint Meetings have still at times been restless partners in the venture. The reverse has also been true. Member state representatives on the CCPR have complained both of information overload and at the same time of information inadequacies. The United States delegate, in a major 1974 statement, noted the sheer amount of work demanded of the residues committee. In one meeting alone the members of the committee had been called upon to examine several hundred proposed pesticide residue limits. It had had on several occasions to recommend that matters be returned to the JMPR.[32] Other critics maintained that experts from developing countries were rarely included by FAO among its expert group sent to the Joint Meetings; that insufficient attention generally was being paid to the needs of growers in developing countries; and that pest control expertise on which standards of good agricultural practice might be judged was only lightly represented at these meetings. As a result, it was argued, the Joint Meetings were increasingly unable to provide recommendations and advice on compounds, or to prepare such opinions in good time for CCPR meetings.[33] The technical experts of the Joint Meetings have thus had at times to bear the brunt of member state alarm at the magnitude of the information gap confronting the international regulatory network. A strengthening of their support facilities has been proposed from time to time, but it has been clear that this in itself would not solve the problem.

Some data in the hands of industry are just not there for the asking, no matter how persistent the asker.

NATIONAL AND CORPORATE INTERESTS

The nature of the international regulatory process affecting pesticide residues, then, is such as to encourage the expression of views from governments and a variety of international organisations at each step along the way to the formulation of a regulatory standard. Pesticide companies have several points of access to this machinery. Member state delegations to the CCPR are one. Governments vary considerably, however, in the composition of their delegations. Two of the countries which can be regarded as among the leading participants – the United States and Britain – regularly include industry representatives on their teams. At the 1982 CCPR meetings, for example, the United States was represented by eleven individuals. They included three representatives of the California and Arizona citrus industries and two from leading agrochemical companies. The British delegation (of nine members) included a representative of both the Food and Drink Industries Council and the British Agrochemicals Association. Some western countries simply send officials from the appropriate ministries. Of those at the 1982 meetings, eight other countries included agrochemical industry or agricultural sector representatives: the Federal Republic of Germany (five), the Netherlands (four), Switzerland (three), and Australia, France, Italy, Spain and Sweden (one each).

Since 1977 companies or industry associations have also taken part in consultations held by FAO and WHO prior to the Joint Meetings. This is a procedure separate from the meetings themselves. It has been described officially by WHO as an extension of the process by which industry collaborates with the Joint Meetings framework by submitting toxicological data on compounds. The consultations are open to JMPR participants, but they are not obliged to attend. For WHO, the ground-rules for the sessions have been defined in such a way as to emphasise their non-official status. Industry representatives 'may at their own initiative introduce a subject they consider of potential interest to the meeting', but 'will not be allowed to elaborate on these subjects unless requested to do so by the committee through the chairman.'[34] A similar procedure exists for meetings between industry representatives and FAO officials, though these sessions have in practice tended to be more open and less formally structured.

The main pesticides industry grouping, GIFAP, has observer status at meetings of the Codex pesticide residues committee. Indeed it has frequently sent along what amounts in practice to the largest single grouping present of more than thirty members. While the meetings are held on the principle of member state representation, this industry presence can have an appreciable impact on the atmospherics of the discussions. Apart from this more intangible factor, GIFAP also participates in several more direct ways. Its representatives may request permission to make statements to the meeting; these are then published in the official report of the sessions. Members also take part in the activities of the various working groups created from time to time by the CCPR, for example those on priorities, regulatory principles, and methods of analysis. More informally, the organisation of the sessions creates opportunities for contact with national delegations, especially where these also comprise industry advisors from pesticide firms. All this means that on occasion retention of the state representation principle requires a subtle chairmanship, especially since some national delegations tend to be more sympathetic to the view that companies are best seen and not heard. Others, particularly though not exclusively the United States in recent years, are more ready to see industry representatives as partners in a broader collaborative exercise.

Industry representatives thus make use of these various opportunities to defend certain positions. Many concern the treatment of data. Toxicological and other data acquired by pesticide companies at considerable cost have to be protected. A GIFAP representative argued in 1982 meetings that basic producers of pesticides were concerned at the failure of many governments to treat data developed for a specific product as proprietary to the manufacturer who had developed the product. Data submitted by a company to the Joint Meetings could, following publication of the proceedings of these sessions, be used as the basis for commercial registration of a pesticide in some countries, resulting in a loss of the proprietary value of the data concerned.[35] Discussion of the issue revolves around the adequacy of possible protective measures that might be taken by regulatory bodies to guard against release of sensitive information. For industry the reservation about the various Codex-related bodies in this regard tends to centre not so much on its traditional character, which is that of a predominantly western and technical organisation, as on the potential for it to evolve into a more universally representative institution like other UN organs. Among other things this might mean the intrusion of what tend to be perceived as 'political' issues and stances, leading possibly to various blacklisting attempts levelled at certain compounds or companies. Of the socialist states only Czechoslovakia, Poland and Romania are members, with the German Democratic Republic attending as an observer. But even this limited range of participation still raised the question of proprietary data reaching governments who might not then accord it due protection.

The interests of member-state delegations also reflect those of domestic agricultural sectors. Spanish citrus fruits have provided an interesting case of the blend of science and politics that permeates Codex pesticide residues deliberations. In 1982 Spain pursued energetically one ostensibly minor methodological issue. The delegation raised an objection to the expression of maximum residue limits on the whole fruit, on the grounds that these were fruits with an inedible peel. Citrus fruits have pesticide residues concentrated in the peel, so that a limit set high does not necessarily mean that the consumer is more at risk; however, a perception of citrus fruits as agricultural produce drenched with toxic chemical residues would not help sales, and the limits could raise problems in some importing countries. So Spain argued that most pesticides used on citrus fruits did not penetrate into the edible part, and in cases where the skin was indeed consumed this was normally after cooking, which would destroy most of the residues. Maximum residue limits, that is, should be set only for the edible portion. There followed lengthy debate. Israeli delegates pointed out that many citrus varieties might in fact be eaten, or processed into edible commodities, with the peel included. Alternatively, limits might be set in principle both for the whole fruit and, separately, for the edible portion (as West Germany, Thailand and Canada observed); but such a compromise procedure would still not have resolved Spain's reservations since the product traded would have to comply with both sets of limits. After prolonged discussion the Spanish argument was rejected.[36]

Many of the national delegations, at least those from the western countries, consist of government and industry participants. They vary in the extent to which consultations prior to meetings lead to the formulation of negotiating positions and strategies. Of participating member-states the United States has the most complex and regularised system of intra-governmental and government–industry concertation. The nature of the subject-matter is such that no single agency in Washington has sole right to speak on residues questions. The lead, however, is clearly that of the Department of Agriculture, with representation also from the EPA and the Food and Drug Administration. The more critically anti-pesticides positions adopted by the EPA in the 1970s at home have not surfaced in CCPR sessions; indeed the spirit of the exercise tends to mean that EPA participants are socialised into more 'realistic' ways of thinking by the approaches of Agriculture people. In between CCPR meetings a consultative infrastructure ensures good preparation of the US case in relation to various compounds being evaluated internationally. Apart from regular monthly meetings of CCPR delegation members (and the wider institutional context of Codex consultations) contact is also maintained with industry. Even before the more sympathetic de-regulation atmosphere created by the Reagan Administration in the 1980s, companies could expect a reasonably good chance of overtures in relation to specific compounds succeeding. As with the citrus interests, companies have also taken initiatives to secure direct participation as industry advisors on delegations.

The United States has also had more extensive public and industry discussion of Codex issues generally. The Department of Agriculture organised a national conference on US participation in the Codex system in 1976, which was designed to review activities and future goals and in general to alert companies to the importance of Codex work, including its pesticide residues components. This followed a broad-ranging government–industry conference on the pesticides aspects of the machinery organised by the National Agricultural Chemicals Association earlier the same year. Indeed the existence of a 13-member Codex Alimentarius Committee at this time is itself a measure of the importance attached by NACA to Codex activities. A subsequent meeting on US participation in the Codex system was organised by the Department of Agriculture in 1981.[37]

Such consultations also extend internationally. Officials from the United States, Canada and Britain have adopted the practice of engaging in informal tripartite exchanges, held in rotation in each country, as a prelude to Codex pesticide residues sessions. As leading countries in the enterprise, all three have stakes in different ways in the international trade in agricultural or agrochemical products. Washington is also the chief national arena within which many key pesticides regulatory issues are fought out. In addition Britain has a long history of participation in international pesticides discussions, particularly through FAO programmes. Other countries bring different kinds of influence to bear, and in varying degrees, in Codex sessions. The heads of some delegations, for example that of Australia for many years, have been important participants in their own right by virtue of expertise or the vigour of their promotion of the underlying principles of operation of Codex pesticides work. The Netherlands has provided the chairmanship of these sessions and, though the national delegation is distinct from the chair, this fact and the geographical location of meetings in The Hague have given Dutch officials marginally more weight, for example in the unravelling of compromise positions. The small size of many delegations restricts their contributions. Some developing countries have simply designated as their representative a non-specialised embassy official from Brussels or The Hague. At the 1982 meetings, for example, twelve of the forty-four delegations to the CCPR consisted of only one official, and a further thirteen of two officials. During the 1970s, however, increasing numbers of developing countries began participating in Codex activities. The impact of this trend is noted in Chapter 7.

CODEX OUTCOMES AND NATIONAL STANDARDS

How is all this work translated into action at the national level? Participants are not engaged in an abstract scientific endeavour. Most would probably also repudiate the notion that their role is to talk, investigate, and clarify issues, with consequences percolating through to governments by a kind of osmosis. Several delegations to CCPR meetings, as we have seen, have from time to time expressed criticisms of slow rates of progress towards results. Other critics have questioned the value of the effort on the grounds that it remained to be demonstrated whether governments would in practice accept a significant number of recommended pesticide residue limits.[38]

The rate of progress has been assisted by two factors. Firstly, Codex deliberations have tended to be little known to the general public. Discussions take place in ways that are relatively insulated from the heat of pesticide politics in many western countries. Some basic differences of approach occasionally are revealed, as in the debates on good agricultural practice or on the accommodation of Third World concerns. In general, however, the spectrum of debate in Codex forums tends to be more restricted than that outside, in part because of the underlying terms of reference and in part because of the nature of the official and industrial expertise present. Further, dietary intake studies carried out in the United States and other countries have tended to conclude that consumption of pesticide residues from foods is well below the acceptable levels recommended by FAO and WHO.[39] Monitoring occasionally reveals more cause for concern. A 1983 survey in Britain, carried out by the Association of Public Analysts for the government, found that one-third of the fresh fruit and vegetables in samples contained pesticide residues and that the level was significant in one-seventh.[40] For the most part, however, delegates do not approach CCPR sessions with a sense of burgeoning crisis.

Secondly, the goal of standardisation has been helped by the general Codex approach of devising procedures which serve to minimise gaps between national and internationally recommended standards. Central to this scheme has been flexibility in the definition of the circumstances in which a government can be said to have 'accepted' a given Codex standard.

Thus three broad categories apply to pesticide residues limits. These are 'full' acceptance, where a government ensures that all foods in the country comply with the limit; 'limited' acceptance, where a country undertakes not to hinder the importation of a food which complies with the limit; and 'target' acceptance, where a country can indicate its intention of giving either full or limited acceptance to a standard after a stated number of years. These categories, adopted by the Codex Alimentarius Commission in 1974, also specify a number of definitions of 'non-acceptance', which depend on the degree to which a government is prepared to allow distribution within its territory of products which comply with recommended Codex standards.[41] Instead of a simple yes/no choice, governments thus have six options, from full acceptance to the category of non-acceptance/no distribution, in relation to any recommended standard on pesticide residues. Taken together with the step-by-step procedure described earlier, these serve to blur the distinction between international recommendations on the one hand, and national decisions on the other.

The Codex machinery has, however, gone through relatively passive and active phases in its approach to government compliance. The early preoccupations were largely with methodological, procedural, data-gathering and organisational questions. But as the volume of maximum residue limits in various stages of drafting grew, more attention was turned to the national decisions at the end-point of the procedures. Already in the 1960s some countries were getting impatient with an apparent lack of commitment by some states to harmonisation goals. Australia and New Zealand, both of which had an interest in securing greater regulatory uniformity in the markets for their agricultural products, pointed in 1969 to the great number of reservations being brought forward by governments regarding proposed tolerances. This attitude could only lead to 'serious retardation of the international agreement in this field'.[42] Lack of public visibility here was a double-edged weapon. While it could be said to aid the scientific sobriety of the discussions, it also meant that recommended standards were deprived of a potentially nourishing atmosphere of political debate when the time came for making an impact on national regulations. A campaign, led chiefly by the United States, attempted in the mid-1970s to overcome these obstacles. The resulting 'drive' for acceptances highlighted the importance of achieving this kind of impact. It had also a practical outcome in the form of production of coded lists of government acceptances of various proposed standards for the first time. The first compilation was circulated to governments in 1977, and provision made for regular updating.[43]

By the early 1980s a total of six lists of recommended standards on pesticide residues had been submitted to governments. In all a total of 102 pesticides was involved. The Codex system was then dealing with 122 pesticides at various stages of formulation of standards, and some 1689 tolerance proposals when these were combined with various food commodity groups. The percentage of acceptances by governments, in one or other of the various categories noted earlier, was close to 70 per cent, with full acceptance of recommended tolerances at just under 50 per cent.[44] In addition the Codex Alimentarius Commission generally had developed by that date 148 product standards as a result of the work of Codex committees in other areas, with a further 19 in various stages of development, together with 21 codes of hygienic and/or technological practice, and 54 methods of analysis and sampling. By mid-1981, 64 countries had responded to give a total of 511 full acceptances, 149 target acceptances, and 148 acceptances with specified deviations.[45]

This record indicates some gathering of speed from the mid-1970s. However, the pesticides residues committee and the Codex machinery generally face a number of constraints. Firstly, governments differ in the amount of investment put into these negotiations. The

United States, for example, has engaged in a series of reviews aimed at bringing earlier national standards into line with emerging Codex recommendations. Secondly, pesticides residues regulations are approached in a variety of ways. Britain's traditionally voluntary regulatory system cannot readily incorporate formal tolerances. It was suggested in 1979 that the difficulties experienced by some countries in accepting maximum residue limits were due more to legal problems than to any lack of willingness on the part of governments to react favourably to the Commission's recommendations.[46] Thirdly, rules on residues have to be seen in the context of agricultural practices. Lack of information on the agricultural practices involved in the establishment of maximum residue limits as recommended by the Joint Meetings was put forward by the United States in 1974 as one of the major contributing factors to the difficulty some countries had in accepting proposed limits.[47] Fourthly, the broader Codex consultative network is unevenly developed. Codex contact points have been identified in most countries; but in some this has amounted to little more than the in-tray of an official of a general standards agency. Relatively few countries have developed the network by investing significant pesticides residues expertise at this point. Finally, even after formal acceptance, the actual practice of compliance might be more limited. Many countries have inadequate monitoring capabilities for checking on the observance of residues limits.

THE POLITICS OF RESIDUES

The Codex negotiations, then, have not been devoid of results. The comparatively slow rate at which these have been achieved, however, has provided ammunition for the system's critics. In the longer term, the struggles to reach agreement on issues of procedure and approach are perhaps more important. The Codex pesticides residues scheme represents the outcome of prolonged attempts to construct an international regulatory system that would be recognised by states as authoritative because of the key points of access (in the 'steps' and elsewhere) they had to it. The substantive issues, moreover, have been both highly technical and often politically delicate. Since its beginnings in the mid-1960s Codex pesticides meetings have provided many instances of the inseparability of many technical questions from tangible economic interests. The limited, though expanding, participation of developing countries has increasingly been recognised as a constraint; this has forced the western governments who have traditionally formed the bulk of the membership to draw wider attention to the paucity of resources which in effect acts as a barrier to wider and more effective Third World engagement.

5 Registration of Pesticides: Intersection of the National and International Levels

Regulatory standards in the pesticides chemicals area are subject to wide variation among even western nations, let alone among all states in the international system. Not only do standards differ; there is tremendous variety in the styles and philosophies that govern approaches to chemicals regulations. In consequence there are many views about the best, or least unsatisfactory, methods of approaching greater uniformity. International regulatory politics on these matters are marked by a proliferation of actors, a multitude of possible regulatory solutions, clashes of ideological approaches to regulation, and a large backlog of unresolved questions of substance and approach.

In this chapter we are concerned primarily with the registration of pesticides. Since this step determines whether or not compounds can legally be sold, it represents the main set of regulatory issues. Here, too, as in relation to the various questions discussed in the last chapter, manufacturers and industry associations have been active promoters of the goal, or slogan, of harmonisation. We begin by looking briefly at the prevailing approaches to registration policies in some of the leading manufacturing countries. These have a broader international significance. Some, such as the contrasting regulatory approaches to be found respectively in Britain and the United States, have at various times been proposed as models which contain more widely applicable lessons for the harmonising of national registration systems, or as bases for greater administrative rationality in the approaches of international agencies. The capacity of registration questions to generate non-tariff barriers to trade is also significant, or at least has been perceived in this way by a number of international

77

actors. Companies themselves have the most obvious interest in some kinds of change. Greater harmonisation, if it came about, would largely free them of the requirement to go through the variety of different obstacles erected by regulatory bureaucracies in different countries. We shall also in this chapter examine the regulatory impact of a number of regional organisations, notably the European Community and the OECD, as well as those within the UN system.

DIVERSITY IN NATIONAL REGULATORY SYSTEMS

The way an issue is defined affects the kinds of administrative bodies to which it might be referred, the structure of regulatory instruments, and the range of actors which may have some impact on regulatory processes. Changing technologies are a productive source of altering regulatory rationales. Pesticides have been viewed in a variety of ways historically. Legislative approaches in many countries have been derived from nineteenth- or early twentieth-century concerns about adulteration, counterfeiting, and false advertising. In the United States, for example, large numbers of small producers or dealers, and the lack of knowledge of many farmers, led in the late nineteenth century to fears about adulterated products and their impact. The Insecticide Act of 1910 resulted from pressures by farmers' organisations and the activities of sympathetic Congressmen and Department of Agriculture officials; it specified the percentages of certain ingredients for paris green and lead arsenate, and initiated a new regulatory era for pesticide chemicals.[1]

Early approaches to pesticide regulation in western countries emerged, then, out of a context of broader regulatory efforts by national authorities. This is not surprising when we recall that contamination of sugar, flour and other basic staples was the norm. Indeed the variety of compounds deliberately or inadvertently added by manufacturers, retailers or middlemen to foods and other products often constituted hazards far outweighing in significance those chemicals which have become the focal point of more recent debates. Such issues have not disappeared. In some developing countries the importance of pesticide residues in foods is much less a source of public and regulatory concern than adulterated products. Similarly, an illicit trade in fraudulently-labelled compounds in some European countries periodically surfaces as a major concern of pesticide manufacturers.

Of all western countries, the United States has the most complex regulatory system for pesticides, as well as that with the most important international implications. The modern regulatory period begins in 1945. The trigger for change was the emergence of a modern chemical pesticides industry following the developments of the 1930s and World War II. Compounds were now more complex structurally, more toxic and more widely available to consumers and farmers. They were also more potentially damaging in their effects on wildlife and other non-target species. The Federal Insecticide, Fungicide, and Rodenticide Act (FIFRA) of 1947 required for the first time that all pesticides be registered before they could be marketed. Labels had to specify contents. However, the law has been described as more a continuation of past regulatory assumptions than a major change of emphasis. It was 'an extension of classic consumer protection objectives. A rational user is assumed and the problem is defined as the disclosure of sufficient information for the user to make an informed choice.'[2] The efficacy of the compounds concerned was still the primary regulatory concern; and the major basis for denial of registration was that the label contained claims that differed from those made to the Department of Agriculture.

Different regulatory assumptions came into play in the altered atmosphere of public and Congressional debate on pesticides in the 1960s. Criticism now focused on the inadequacies of the safety provisions of the 1947 act, including lack of any effective review procedure. Objections were also raised to the provisions which in practice allowed companies to market compounds even where these were being challenged on safety grounds by regulatory bodies. The authority of these was strengthened as a result of tougher approaches taken by both the courts and Congress. The courts began to adopt an interpretive strategy which in practice gave the appropriate regulatory agencies discretion to ban pesticides on the basis of comparisons of costs and benefits. Further, the area of acceptable risk in the use of such compounds was restricted. Congress, similarly, began to move towards the different regulatory principle which emphasised degrees of probability of hazard, rather than absolute proof that damage would be done by a chemical. Other criteria entered the domain: injury to wildlife species, as well as to economically valuable plants and animals.

These changes laid the basis for the Federal Environmental Pesticide Control Act (FEPCA) of 1972. This represented a new high point of environmentalist attack on pesticides. It required the EPA to refuse to register a pesticide unless it were determined that 'when used in accordance with widespread and commonly accepted practice it will not cause unreasonable adverse effects on the environment'. The criterion was defined as 'any unreasonable risk to man or the environment, taking into account the economic, social, and environmental costs and benefits of the use of any pesticide'.[3] These kinds of phrases were clearly open to differing interpretation. But a significant shift was the emphasis now put on conditions of use of pesticide chemicals, rather than on more abstract analysis of their toxicological properties. As a result some environmentalist critics of pesticides took the view that a substantial showing of benefit was required if any finding of risk was made in relation to a compound. Shortly afterwards, however, the opposite criticism mounted of failure by regulatory authorities to take adequate account of the needs of agriculture. This was reflected in amendments to the 1972 act. The hand of the Department of Agriculture was strengthened in decision-making; and a scientific advisory body was created with the aim of countering some EPA assumptions that tended to maintain that lack of knowledge of the effects of a pesticide constituted a valid basis for banning it.

Later in the 1970s, in other words, the regulatory dilemmas were accentuated. While their fate was affected by changes of administration in Washington, the trend was for greater stress on the need to accept that risk was an intrinsic feature of pesticide use, and that neither the risk nor the use could be outlawed. While the legislative framework in the United States has become more complicated in the period since, its detailed evolution need not concern us here. We will take up later in this chapter the discussion of the international ramifications of the later Toxic Substances Control Act (ToSCA).

The EPA, the main regulatory body for pesticides since the early 1970s, has been a controversial institution from the start. Its procedures for evaluating the risks and benefits of particular compounds have sparked wide debate not only in the United States but also in the broader international regulatory contexts which in practice have to pay close attention to developments in that country. The agency's Rebuttable Presumption Against Registration (RPAR) system, adopted in 1975, has been at the centre of these debates.[4] The regulations were aimed at identifying and evaluating those pesticides that appeared to cause 'unreasonable' adverse effects on human health and the environment. Each pesticide, together with its metabolites or degradation products, was measured against a set of risk criteria, such as acute or chronic toxicity in humans, domestic animals or non-target wildlife species. If one or more of these was reached, the agency's procedure was to issue an RPAR. The onus of responsibility thus fell on those – manufacturers, users and others – who wished to rebut the charge that the compound was too dangerous to be in circulation.

Pesticides have formed only part of the basis of criticism of the EPA. During the 1970s it was regularly targeted for Congressional enquiries. In 1975–76 a Senate subcommittee chaired by Senator Edward Kennedy concluded that the pesticide safety and health data available to the EPA were in a state of disarray, and that many of the long-term chronic toxicity data were inadequately reported or of poor quality.[5] The agency was also criticised for placing too much emphasis on carcinogenicity as a criterion. Officials tended to respond by arguing that there was no such thing as an acceptable level of risk associated with a known carcinogen, and that other effects were indeed part of the RPAR and other procedures.[6] Criticised on the one hand for over-regulating the chemical industry in the 1970s, it was then attacked in the 1980s for its allegedly over-lax dealings with agricultural interests. Thus among de-regulation goals affecting the EPA under the Reagan Administration from 1981 were reductions in the average time needed to process applications for registration of a pesticide. A further consequence in practice was growing use of some pesticides under non-federal registrations authorised under the emergency exemptions procedures of FIFRA. The number of these 'Section 18' emergency exemptions rose from 180 in 1978 to 750 in 1982.[7] Environmental critics argued that state bodies were often too inadequately staffed to deal with such applications, that the local environmental costs could be serious, and that the state level was significantly less rigorous than the federal.[8]

Central to regulatory debates in the United States on these matters has been the interpretation and handling of the provision of the Food, Drug and Cosmetic Act known as the Delaney clause. This expressed the general principle that any substance found to induce cancer when given to an animal species under test conditions must be excluded from human foods. Critics took the principle to task on the grounds that its full application would make questionable the legality of many products that for all practical purposes could be regarded as safe. This was particularly the case as a result of changing technologies. Some techniques have since been developed which would permit detection of compounds at the level of a few parts per billion.

This is one of the several points at which regulatory approaches in Britain and the United States can be contrasted. The prevailing

assumption in British practice has tended to be that a goal of removing all risk from pesticide use is illusory. In addition it has been
assumed that such matters as risk to consumers from pesticide applications on food crops werè best handled by the provision and wide
circulation of advice on good agricultural practice. Legally binding
regulatory schemes have also traditionally been rejected in favour of
largely voluntary collaborative exercises between government and
industry designed to ensure that hazardous compounds were not
marketed. Finally, though this characteristic is in process of being
changed in the 1980s, the regulatory arena has tended to be more
restricted than that in the United States. Some of its main features
have more recently been undergoing alteration as a result of the
impact of EEC provisions, but it is useful to look first at the British
traditional system.

This rested on the Pesticide Safety Precautions Scheme (PSPS),
which was designed to deal with clearance of the safety aspects of
pesticides.[9] The frame of reference covered a wide range of criteria
from toxicological testing, investigation of residues, and environmental impact, to day-by-day management of relations with industry. The
Agricultural Chemicals Approval Scheme (ACAS) was set up to deal
with questions of biological efficacy, but has tended to remain largely
secondary to the main stream of pesticides regulatory activity
channelled through the PSPS. Thus the British Government, unlike
the US Administration, has traditionally had no formal scheme for
the statutory regulation of maximum pesticide residues limits in foods
(with the exception, for reasons of legislative history, of arsenic and
lead). If a product is cleared under this scheme, official recommendation sheets are issued. Control of residue levels is thus accomplished
by the tendering of advice on good agricultural practice in the use of
compounds. In addition, monitoring by the Government Chemist is
carried out in practice; residue levels when detected have usually
been well below the figures proposed as acceptable by international
regulatory schemes such as the Codex system.

Whereas in the United States regulatory processes have often been
characterised by protracted battles between the EPA and chemical
companies – or alternatively, in the eyes of some critics, by too great
a readiness to work to company bidding – the approach in Britain has
had good working relations between government and industry as a
sine qua non. The voluntary scheme came into existence in 1957
following such consultations. The regulatory goal is defined very

broadly: 'to safeguard human beings (whether they be users, consumers of treated produce, or other members of the public), livestock, domestic animals and wild life, against risk from pesticides.'[10] Companies proposing to introduce a new pesticide, or new uses for an existing one, notify the agriculture ministry, provide specified information, and then refrain from introduction of the product until agreement has been reached on the appropriate precautionary measures. Under the terms of ACAS, a product containing a new active ingredient cannot be approved until its safety has been considered by the authorities under the PSPS, and the necessary precautions recommended.

Since in the last resort it has lacked statutory enforcement powers, the system has thus relied on extensive and close working contacts between government officials and the agrochemicals industry. Indeed it is emphasised in accounts of the scheme that manufacturers, importers, formulators or others are 'urged to consult informally, at an early stage' with officials involved with the notification procedure 'so that, when the notification is made, the information accompanying it may be as complete as can be reasonably expected'.[11] The same cooperative principle has then been the foundation of BASIS, the British Agrochemical Supply Industry Scheme, an understanding between industry and government that producers would ensure that only PSPS-approved pesticides are marketed.

Two sources of change emerged during the late 1970s. The first arose as a consequence of British membership of the European Community. The PSPS was called into question because of the clash of principle it entailed between a traditionally informal set of arrangements on the one hand, and the more statutorily-inclined thinking of the Community institutions on the other. In 1981 products intended for users in other EC member-states were imported into Britain. These entered without clearance under the PSPS, and indeed did not even have labelling in English. The question thus arose of whether or not the government did indeed have any statutory authority under back-up legislation to control such imports. Industry, through the British Agrochemicals Association (BAA), took the view that the government would not be breaking Common Market law by insisting that products identical in origin to ones already on the UK market should be cleared by the PSPS prior to sale. However, because of the various notification provisions of the Treaty of Rome (primarily under Article 85) it was thought that schemes such as BASIS, as they stood, might well infringe Community law.[12] The broader context of EC pesticides policy is discussed later in this chapter.

A second source of change came from the altering climate of the pesticides debate in Britain. From the late 1970s these encompassed a far broader range of political actors than ever before. Many of the traditional working assumptions of regulatory approaches were challenged. Greater protection was needed, it was argued, for consumers, agricultural workers and the natural environment. While much of this broader public debate took place on an emotionally anti-pesticides plane only minimally affected by scientific norms, it nonetheless served to focus attention more specifically on regulatory procedures for pesticides registration and use. Some critics, for example, drew attention to alternative approaches contained in mechanisms such as the Health and Safety Executive (HSE). This had been set up under legislation in 1974 as the enforcement arm of a commission tasked to protect conditions in the workplace. There was representation in the scheme not only of government and industry, but also of trade unions. When pesticides – and more specifically herbicides such as 2,4,5-T – emerged later in the 1970s as a major source of dispute between the agricultural workers' unions and employers, the HSE structure appeared an attractive alternative. At its annual conference in 1980, for example, the Trades Union Congress (TUC) passed a motion calling for the transfer of responsibility for the control of pesticides to the HSC.[13] In practice, however, the room for manoeuvre of newer bodies was constrained by the continuing importance of the traditional regulatory bodies, and by the government–industry relationship built up over many years through PSPS consultations.

Two other examples of regulatory systems in OECD countries can be cited briefly before we summarise the international implications of these approaches. Legislation in the Federal Republic of Germany calls for registration of pesticides following their notification to the Federal Institute of Biology for Agriculture and Forestry (BBA). Biological and residue data have to include the results from official trials carried out inside West Germany in accordance with guidelines laid down by the government. The BBA checks the biological reports, the composition of the product being considered, and its physical and chemical properties. Toxicology and residue data are reviewed by the Federal Health Office (BGA), which considers the toxicity classification and where applicable the official maximum residue limits.[14] As in other approaches to these subjects at national and international levels, this pesticides procedure has tended to remain somewhat apart from other legislative instruments dealing broadly with chemicals, for example the government's general statement of environmental goals of 1971, and the Chemicals Act of 1980. This last included provision for a new statutory authority and chemicals notification scheme and for control of toxic chemicals in places of employment.

While the United States, Britain and West Germany have been closely involved with international harmonisation discussions through the OECD, FAO and other bodies, this has been much less the case with Japan. A regulatory insistence there on data obtained in Japan is similar to provisions in many other countries. In the Japanese case, however, it has given rise to rather more scepticism about the link between regulatory stringency and the protection of the domestic chemicals market. Criticism by foreign companies is in part a product of the rapid rise of Japan as a major world producing and exporting nation. Production of pesticides in that country doubled between 1965–70, and doubled again between 1972–74; production of pesticides was valued at 12 773 million yen in 1955 and at 202 627 million yen in 1974.[15] The legislative framework followed the US pattern in some respects. Thus an early act, of 1948, was designed to prevent the movement of inferior or illegal chemicals. A number of animal poisoning cases, and the spread of environmental debates, led to change in the 1970s. The Japanese Environment Agency (JEA) was created, and this body shared responsibilities in relation to pesticide registration and related questions with the Ministry of Agriculture and Forestry; the change signalled that environmental protection and the safeguarding of human health were to be the primary regulatory criteria in the future.

These kinds of variations in regulatory approaches among OECD countries are significant in terms of international regulatory politics for several reasons. Where markedly divergent, they define the condition of minimal order that characterises the pesticides regime. There is no guarantee that the regulatory authorities in any country will reach the same conclusions, or base their decisions on the same sets of detailed criteria and data, as those in other countries. Though autonomous, however, the regulatory system of any country is in practice set in a broader international context of multiple influences. The policies and conclusions of at least the leading countries are regularly taken into account by regulatory authorities in others. This affects patterns of transnational politics. A ban or restriction of use of a pesticide in one country is likely to be communicated quickly to groups in other states, and then becomes part of the weaponry of the argument for imitative adaptation. Further, depending on the rules which may govern export practices – as in the export notification scheme for toxic chemicals in the United States – national regulations can have direct impact on other countries. Similarly, domestic regulations setting residues limits which in practice have the effect of barring imports of some agricultural products, for example from developing countries, cannot be regarded as solely of national interest. And finally, some national regulatory schemes have international significance because of their model-making potential as possible guides for the design of regulatory systems elsewhere. Considerable variety, nonetheless, is the rule. Herbicide politics provides a good example.

THE CASE OF 2,4,5-T

Chemicals have pathways through political systems. In the case of some pesticides, research and development follows a well-defined and for the most part uncontroversial path of testing and registration. Herbicides, however, like the organochlorine compounds before them, raised issues in the 1970s and 1980s that could not so easily be resolved.

The compound, 2,4,5-T is used primarily for weedkilling purposes in agriculture. There are a variety of uses in forestry management. Mixtures of related compounds were also used in military operations in Malaya in the 1950s and Vietnam in the 1960s as a means of destroying the protective habitats of guerrilla armies. The compound derived its controversial character from the discovery after many years of use of a potentially dangerous contaminant introduced during the manufacturing process. This was one of the dioxins, that is, one of the chemicals in the family of polychlorinated dibenzo-*p*-dioxins (PCDDs). Of these, one – 2,3,7,8-tetrachlorodibenzo-*p*-dioxin (2,3,7,8-TCDD) – is by far the most toxic of the possible 75 or so isomers in the group. PCDDs generally are by-products of manufacturing processes, notably of the chlorinated phenols used directly or indirectly as herbicides, fungicides and other agents. Thus in the course of producing 2,4,5-T this particular contaminant happens to be formed. The degree of contamination varies according to a number of factors. Normally it would be at a level which most regulatory authorities would regard as safe. In cases where certain chemical reactions take place in the manufacturing process, however – particularly, it appears, where increasing temperatures are involved – higher levels of PCDDs can be produced. Other contaminants are produced at different stages of the process, for example the polychlorinated dibenzofurans (PCDFs), which as a group are also highly toxic.[16]

In its path through the political systems of the western world, including the main international regulatory bodies, 2,4,5-T has had mixed reactions. Several kinds of intractable issues have arisen: whether such contaminants were unavoidable features of herbicide manufacturing; how specific they were to these industrial processes, as opposed to others such as those in fossil-fuelled power plants; what the carcinogenic or teratogenic effects, if any, were; what level of contamination of the compound was acceptable; the manner in which effects were produced, for example in agricultural or industrial workers or forest sprayers, inhabitants of neighbouring areas, consumers of sprayed commodities, or other users; what kinds of controls by regulatory authorities would be acceptable and workable; and, finally, the ways in which governments should approach issues of risk management in such relatively uncharted areas. The last of these has made the 2,4,5-T case a particularly important one. Major literature reviews and other investigations by regulatory authorities have tended to conclude that the level of risk associated with 2,4,5-T use was negligible or minimal. Contradictory evidence was based on a number of disputed studies. The political issue hidden on agendas was thus just as much the appropriate mechanism by which regulatory decisions should be made.

The question emerged in the United States in the late 1960s. A report of 1969 linked 2,4,5-T with teratogenic effects in rodents. It led to restriction on the use of the compound in spraying programmes. The suggestion that these properties might be due to contamination with 2,3,7,8-TCDD came in 1970. Knowledge of the presence of a highly toxic impurity in 2,4,5-T had been available as early as 1950, however, and this had been identified as a dioxin in 1965. At the beginning of the 1970s, US regulatory officials juggled with definitions of acceptable levels of contamination. By the end of the decade the EPA was confident that even its earlier recommendation of limits of dioxin contamination to no more than 0.1 ppm, posed an unacceptable risk to health.[17] The regulatory contest in the United States involved conflicts of interpretations and judgements by EPA on the one hand and the chemical companies, notably in this case Dow Chemical, on the other. The incidental factor of use of herbicides in warfare expanded the range of political actors and their engagement, and by encouraging polarisation increased the stakes. The 1976 Seveso incident, in which a cloud of various chemicals including 2,3,7,8-TCDD was released, had political repercussions in both the United States and European countries and added fuel to the dioxin debate.

In some countries regulatory action was taken without much accompanying public debate. France, for example, limited dioxin content in 2,4,5-T in various measures in the mid-1970s, and also banned ærial spray programmes. In the United States, Britain and the Federal Republic of Germany, however, politicisation of the central issues led to more protracted regulatory struggles.

A temporary lull followed a ban on the use of 2,4,5-T on all food crops except rice in the United States in 1970. Scientific evidence linking human exposure to harmful consequences tended to be lacking. In 1979, however, the EPA suspended the registration of the herbicide for use on forests and rights of way following studies that claimed to find a significant correlation between 2,4,5-T spraying and local miscarriage rates in Oregon.[18] This emerging regulatory trend contrasted sharply with that in the United Kingdom. There the government's Advisory Committee on Pesticides concluded among other things that the Oregon study was not valid 'either in scientific or statistical terms'. Its general conclusion, therefore, also in 1979, was 'that the allegations made recently about the adverse effects of 2,4,5-T spraying are either not sufficiently documented or, where they have been thoroughly investigated, cannot be substantiated'.[19] Developments in the United States then had the effect of narrowing this difference. The EPA's scientific advisory body, for example, concluded that the available data gave no evidence of an immediate or substantial threat to human health or the environment and recommended that no cancellation proceedings be taken against the compound as far as its use on rice and rangelands was concerned.

While in the United States the main participants in the debate tended to be the EPA, Congressional committees, industry, and environmental groups, the pattern in Britain was of an active role also by trade unions and political parties. The three main trade unions whose workers were most immediately affected pressed for bans on the use of 2,4,5-T, and for union representation on the regulatory bodies dealing generally with pesticides. Technical decisions made by experts were portrayed as lacking realism.[20] The case was also developed by the Labour Party. Appeals to anti-chemicals prejudice and fear, however, were also prominent features of the campaign. A further review by the government's advisory body in 1980 came to essentially the same conclusions. The risk was negligible, it argued, given levels of exposure to the herbicide likely to be encountered in established use patterns. Evidence was published during 1982 in support of the view that there were links between exposure to the phenoxy acid herbicides or their contaminants and a certain type of cancer. The government again concluded at the end of 1982 that formulations of these herbicides as cleared under the PSPS scheme could continue to be used.[21]

Similar kinds of conflicts have marked herbicide debates in West Germany. The regulatory bodies withdrew registration for all preparations containing 2,4,5-T in 1981; a court dispute ensued when the objections of chemical companies were overruled. Further reviews, however, by the federal government's biological and health institutes produced the conclusion that the available scientific evidence did not in fact justify refusal to grant an extension to the period of registration of 2,4,5-T and products containing it. The arguments as to the compound's carcinogenic properties could not be substantiated. Registration for the period 1982–85 was accordingly granted.[22]

Treatment of the issues in these three countries gives some measure of the variation possible between national regulatory approaches, and also of the mix of scientific and political factors that shape regulatory outcomes. The particular question of 2,4,5-T appeared to be resolved in practice late in 1983 when Dow Chemical said that it was no longer economical for it to participate in a clash with the EPA over restrictions on its sale in the United States; the EPA announced shortly afterwards that sale of the herbicide would be illegal once existing supplies were depleted.

HARMONISATION IN THE EUROPEAN COMMUNITY

As indicated earlier, these national efforts to formulate rules governing the registration of pesticides do not take place in isolation. Apart from regularised contacts in forums such as the Codex Alimentarius Commission meetings on pesticide residues, several major inter-governmental efforts have been made to bring about greater uniformity in approaches to registration. That in the European Community in the 1970s and 1980s has constituted a sustained and continuing programme of progressive harmonisation in this area.

The earliest approaches to harmonisation among European countries, however, took place in one of the forerunner institutions of the European idea, the Council of Europe. These exercises merit discussion, firstly, because they established a precedent for the handling of pesticides matters at the inter-governmental level in western Europe, and, secondly, because some of the outcomes continue to play a role in global deliberations. The common institutions of the Council of Europe, though, are more exhortative than policy-making in character. On the other hand, they are not restricted in the scope of subjects they may discuss, with the exception of security issues. The Council of Europe's authority in the pesticides area derives from a Partial Agreement (that is, one which did not immediately encompass all member-states) of 1959. This covered many aspects of public health policy. In the implementing machinery set up by this agreement the Social Committee has included one body which has the specific task of investigating dangerous chemical substances, and the Public Health Committee has overseen the work of a specialised sub-committee on pesticides.[23]

Several outcomes of these activities have had an impact on international pesticides regulatory discussions either in the EEC context or more widely in the international community. The best known product has undoubtedly been a set of guidelines on pesticides registration, several editions of which have been published since the first in 1962. Because of the nature of the Council of Europe the guidelines lack authority; they do, however, enjoy very wide circulation internationally as concise statements of hypothetical but workable ideals. A number of more specific instruments have highlighted the policy importance of pesticides registration questions. For example, following guidelines drawn up by the Public Health Committee in 1978, the Committee of Ministers adopted a resolution on those 'which national authorities should consider including in their publications on the use of pesticides' in 1979. They included general principles on topics such as safe handling, accidents and storage of pesticides.[24] Similar wide-ranging resolutions have dealt with such questions as the minimising of risk from the domestic use of pesticides; disposal of surplus pesticides and pesticide containers; the use of pesticides in premises where food is produced, processed or stored; and the contamination of animal products for human consumption which might result from pesticide residues in feeding stuffs intended for livestock.[25]

The involvement of the European Community in pesticides issues is more politically significant. Since the EC does not consist of a set of institutions with full decision-making authority across such policy sectors, and since the policy process in the Community is a complex one, evidence of the growth of harmonisation in the area of pesticides registration has been slow to emerge. Community competence in the area is derived from various provisions of the founding Treaty of Rome, particularly Articles 43 and 100. Two lines of policy are relevant. The first deals specifically with pesticide registration and closely related matters; the second concerns the implications of the more controversial and ambitious objectives with regard to toxic chemicals generally contained in the so-called 'Sixth Amendment' provisions of 1979.

In the first of these the Community's institutions have tended to favour a bits-and-pieces approach rather than a comprehensive package of measures related to registration of pesticides in member-states. Thus the Council of Ministers passed a Directive in November 1976 on maximum residue levels of pesticides in fruit and vegetables. The lengthy policy process leading to this outcome had been set in motion in the late 1960s. The Directive took as a starting-point the observation that member-states had different methods for avoiding risks posed by pesticide residues, and different regulations on maximum permissible levels. These therefore 'can help to create barriers to trade and thus hinder the free movement of goods within the Community'.[26] This constituted the main rationale for Community involvement. The main aim of this Directive was defined in Article 3(1): 'Member States may not prohibit or impede the putting on the market within their territories of [the agricultural products concerned] on the ground that they contain pesticide residues if the quantity of these residues does not exceed the maximum levels laid down in Annex II.' Several qualifications were injected. An agreed maximum limit might legitimately be considered by a government to pose a risk, in which case it could temporarily reduce that level (Article 4 (1)); and the preamble stressed the point that member-states could permit circulation of products with residues higher than the agreed maxima under certain conditions. Further, it was 'not necessary' to apply the provisions of the Directive to fruit and vegetables intended for export to third countries. In addition, detailed technical implementation was to be through a Standing Committee on Plant Health, consisting of member-state representatives voting according to one of the Community's weighted voting formulæ (Article 7). Moves were later initiated inside the Commission to extend the provisions to cereals intended for human consumption and foodstuffs of animal origin.[27]

More direct attempts to focus on central registration issues faced considerable difficulties. Some environmental groups in the middle and late 1970s were calling for the banning of certain pesticides in the territories of member-states and for provisions which would apply also to products exported to developing countries. A Council of Ministers' Directive of 1978, which also drew on the principle that obstacles to trade could arise from differing member-state regulations, was designed to ensure that products containing one or more of a number of listed active ingredients could not be placed on European markets or used (Article 3).[28] But the general principle was also subject to various qualifications which had been inserted during the course of member-state negotiations preceding adoption of the Directive. Like the residues Directive of 1976 it did not apply to exports to third countries (Article 5). An emergency use procedure was defined which could allow a member-state to use a listed compound for a period of up to 120 days (Article 7 (1)), and Article 4 also allowed use of these compounds in certain specified cases. The list in the Annex, though short, and consisting of mercury compounds and a group of highly persistent organochlorine compounds, nonetheless set a precedent for the Community's entering directly into member-state pesticide registration processes.

These processes have also been affected, though more indirectly, by spin-offs from the second line of evolving Community policies. The origin of this was the important Council Directive of June 1967 on 'the approximation of the laws, regulations and administrative provisions relating to the classification, packaging and labelling of dangerous substances'.[29] The Sixth Amendment of this Directive, by the Council in September 1979, constituted a comprehensive and far-reaching statement of toxic chemicals policy. The general aim was to ensure that substances could not be placed on the market, on their own or in preparations, unless they were notified to 'the competent authority of one of the Member States', and packaged and labelled in accordance with certain specified definitions, criteria and tests (Article 5 (1)).[30]

The integrationist aim was thus to create a Community-wide notification system for chemicals. In negotiations the issues centred on the degree to which notification in any one state thereby bound the authorities in others. The outcome was a complex procedural formula. The competent authority of one state could consult that in the state receiving the original notification or the European Commission itself on specific details of the data submitted; however, it 'may also suggest that further tests or information be requested' (Article 10 (2)). A state could then refuse to divulge information to another state. A procedure was set down (in Article 21) by which the Commission could take a decision in cases where there was disagreement between two or more governments on whether additional information or amendments in study programme were needed with respect to any particular compound. A further attempt to protect the principle of confidentiality came in Article 11. A company could under this provision indicate that information given to a regulatory authority was 'commercially sensitive', that is, its disclosure might harm the company industrially or commercially, 'and which [it] therefore wishes to be kept secret from all persons other than the competent authorities and the Commission'. In such cases 'full justification' had to be given. The secrecy principle could not apply to such matters as the trade name of the substance, possible ways of rendering it harmless, or interpretation of toxicological and ecotoxicological tests and the name of the body responsible for these. In general, however, 'confidential information brought to the attention either of the Commission or of a Member State shall be kept secret' (Article 11 (4)).

Though it had implications for approaches to pesticides, the aim of this instrument was to tackle questions of toxic chemicals other than pesticides. A Council Directive of 1978, which also followed on from the 1967 scheme, did deal specifically with pesticide chemicals, but with a much less ambitious end in view. It aimed to set up a classification scheme for pesticides by degree of toxicity – similar in principle to the WHO and other international agency systems – with labelling and packaging provisions to ensure that the classification formed the basis for sales of pesticides in member-states. As in other Community instruments exports to third countries were specifically excluded (Article 1 (2)(c)).[31]

Even for the pesticides sector, however, it was the Sixth Amendment that provoked more controversy. This was partly due to the fact that its provisions represented a series of carefully structured compromises. Some Community actors persisted with their aim of eventually enhancing their stringency. The Commission had originally proposed in 1974 a far greater tightening of the market in hazardous chemicals, and incorporated a version of these ideas into its formal 1976 proposals for a further amendment of the dangerous substances Directive of 1967. The Community's Economic and Social Committee called for tough controls in 1977. Member-states, however, were divided. For Britain, flexibility of testing requirements was essential. This objective met with wide industry and scientific support during the consultations and exchanges of 1977–78. Exemptions were also urged for new chemicals manufactured or imported in quantities less than one ton.[32] The Federal Republic of Germany, on the other hand, tended to be more sympathetic to the concerns of chemical companies who confronted not only a variety of regulatory hurdles in member-states, but also unpredictability in the building or adjustment of these. Accordingly a basic set of tests was advocated for all new products. Further tests could be added as production increased beyond initial minimal levels. In the event it was agreed that the notification package was to contain a base set of tests for all substances produced in excess of one ton per annum, but British concerns on the question of flexibility were also accommodated. The issue of data and its confidentiality also held up the pace of negotiations. Environmental groups in some countries, including the Netherlands and West Germany, were demanding greater public access to information submitted by companies, together with a lengthier period of government review in order to ensure more careful scrutiny of the data. An extension of the processing time from 30 to 45 days was eventually agreed, but the principle of restricted access remained intact.

It was during the course of early explorations of the subject that it became clear that the provisions could not apply to all toxic chemicals. Pesticides, one of the sectors already most heavily regulated in member-states, were excluded. Articles 5–7 (on such matters as notification, labelling and packaging, and the submission of data) were explicitly stated not to apply 'to pesticides and fertilizers, in as far as they are subject to approval procedures which are at least equivalent to Community notification procedures or procedures which are not yet harmonised' (Article 1 (4) (b)). Even so, the regulatory style of the Sixth Amendment laid down a number of principles which had an impact on the pesticides sector. Because of the structure of chemical industries, moreover, what happened in one area had repercussions for others. Further, at the implementing stage some governments appeared to be confused over the scope of the Amendment or else to be using it as a means of extending its approach to pesticide chemicals.

This was a point of concern for pesticide manufacturers. In Britain the HSE was criticised for attempting to incorporate agrochemicals within the range of application of the Sixth Amendment.[33] France's legislation in 1979 on control of chemical products did exclude pesticide active ingredients, and this position was maintained after Sixth Amendment implementation in 1981. West Germany's 1980 chemicals law also in practice followed the general lines of the 1979 Directive. One interpretation, given to pesticide companies by the European Commission in 1979–80, was that active ingredients were chemical substances like any other, and that therefore all new active substances regardless of their use should indeed be notified according to the terms of the Amendment. Later, however, the Commission's expert group on Sixth Amendment questions reported that it was not necessary to notify if the substances were sold to a company exclusively for use in a pesticide or medicine.[34] Specific decisions, that is, would have to be made on a case-by-case basis.

Respect for proprietary rights, particularly of the first applicant to an EC member-state, was also an issue on which companies and industry associations were active. There were bound, it was felt, to be slips, some of them intentional, no matter how well policed was the confidentiality principle.

The pesticides Directives and the Sixth Amendment thus proved to be important turning-points in relations between government and industry on a Europe-wide basis. They emerged at a time, in the late 1970s and early 1980s, when industry attitudes were in a state of flux and transition. The Director-General of Britain's chemical industries association raised the more general question in 1979:

I suppose the most frequent comment, or question, I get from industrialists about the EEC, is 'does it matter?' Many business-men, scientists and technologists, feel that Brussels is very far away from their daily problems, and faced with the great costs and frustrations of work at the Brussels interface, they seem to hope that it will go away if they shut their eyes . . ... Mind you, I never get that comment from the larger transnational companies! They know that what is happening at the level of the EEC is vitally important to them, and not only to them, but to all of our industry.[35]

From the middle and late 1970s the shift of outlook became more pronounced. European Community institutions were clearly and irreversibly dealing with core principles of concern to the chemical industry, such as the confidentiality of data and the protection of basic industrial property rights more generally. With activities such as that of the IRPTC – the toxic chemicals registry work of UNEP discussed in the next chapter – the approach tended to be more pre-emptive in character; it was shaped by the possibility that with growing environmental activism in western countries, and an antipathetic attitude towards multinational enterprises by many developing countries, such exercises might one day take on more practical significance, perhaps as the cornerstone of new and far-reaching licensing strategies. In the case of the European Community, however, the issues were much more immediate.

The pesticides industry thus paid close attention to Sixth Amendment developments while raising specific concerns in relation to the Community's pesticide policies. There was no objection to the principle of harmonisation itself. On this the industry and the European Commission were agreed. Reservations centred on the manner in which the goal of harmonisation was pursued and defined. Companies were also restless with Community decision-making procedures. Europe appeared to be a bureaucratic jungle. Companies complained that it was often difficult to know on what bases decisions were being taken, since information on such matters was frequently not released. Different parts of the European Commission, the Directorates-General dealing respectively with environmental and agricultural policy matters for example, often seemed not to know what the others were doing. The EC was also criticised for departing from internationally established norms. The point was developed by pesticide companies and members of the European Parliament sympathetic to the interests of agriculture in connection with the Directive on pesticides residues levels in foodstuffs of animal origin. The Commission's experts, it was argued, were deviating from Codex standards. The EC was in effect creating fresh trade barriers.[36] Community institutions and member-states, moreover, took an inordinate amount of time to agree on anything.

This amalgam of hunches, perceptions and concrete interests on the part of the pesticides industry was revealed in the case of one further measure. This was the Directive for common registration of agrochemicals, and for which the 1978 harmonising Directive on classification, labelling and packaging of pesticides could be regarded as a prelude. Preparations for the registration directive were under way in the late 1970s and early 1980s. The issues were divisive for member-states. The principle that registration decisions should be retained by national authorities was defended by Britain and Denmark. Other states, particularly the Federal Republic of Germany, were under strong domestic pressure both from industry and from environmental groups urging tough regulatory steps against pesticides. Some of the positions taken in Bonn, indeed, were criticised by others on the grounds that no chemical tests existed for some of the regulatory questions being posed. The idea of establishing an EEC-wide registration system for agrochemicals, first proposed by the Commission in 1976, confronted several obstacles. It clashed more directly than had previous developments in this area with the principle of member-state sovereignty. It raised again the delicate question of data handling: the rules that were to govern an application for registration for the same product from a second applicant, for example. The Commission also tended towards the view that a registration applicant needed only an office somewhere in the territory of any member-state; several governments took the position that an applicant had to be based in the state where the application was made, so that producers or distributors operating in a given area could be more easily identified by national authorities. Finally, agreed provisions were needed in relation to imports of pesticide compounds from third countries; if their free circulation was to be allowed, pesticide companies tended to argue, then various kinds of reciprocal deals should be negotiated. Harmonisation was a desirable goal, that is, but not if it was defined in such a way as to lead to an influx of American or Japanese products.

REGULATING THE INTERNATIONAL TRADE IN PESTICIDES

Because of the character of the international pesticides economy, almost any national regulatory system can have effects on the international trade in agrochemicals. The various frameworks discussed in this chapter have three levels of consequences: for trade between the member-states of the European Community; between western countries more generally, and particularly between the United States and Europe; and, finally, between the advanced industrialised countries and the Third World. The first of these has already been touched on.

Here we will concentrate on the regulatory issues arising in connection with the other two sets of trade relations.

The emerging European Community regulatory systems on pesticides and on toxic chemicals more generally coincided in time with a series of parallel developments in the United States. These centred more especially on the Toxic Substances Control Act (ToSCA). The Act included various pre-marketing notification provisions for toxic chemicals. Thus the later 1970s and early 1980s saw developments on both sides of the Atlantic that generated mirror-image fears on the part of pesticide manufacturers and exporters; at the same time there was some common ground of criticism of world regulatory trends. US companies protested that the pre-marketing notification provisions of ToSCA in effect meant pre-manufacturing notification. Decisions would thus have to be made about development of a compound at a much earlier stage than previously. Because of EPA powers, firms might also be faced with an almost limitless series of tests at different stages of development and production. Companies also were critical of the requirement that claims for confidentiality had to be made at the time of the initial notification. US manufacturers were uneasy too with the potential obstacles to their products contained in the EC's Sixth Amendment, as were European companies about the implications of ToSCA.

These emerging US and European frameworks contained divergent elements. The political systems on either side were different: the Sixth Amendment was not a piece of national legislation, but required implementing measures by member-states. Differences of interpretation could emerge on such points as the flexibility of testing requirements (on which the British authorities continued to insist), the handling in practice of sensitive data, or the treatment of 'old' or already existing compounds. The two were similar, however, in that both ToSCA and the Sixth Amendment formally excluded pesticides from their scope. Other differences included the far greater interest of ToSCA in earlier stages of the pesticide production process; its wide scope to include the hazards of both old and new compounds; and the approach to the question of confidentiality. Confidential status for data could be requested under ToSCA by a notifier, but it was limited to data meeting the legal standard for trade secrets; no information relating to health and safety studies could be included within the definition.[37]

The OECD emerged as the main forum within which the trading implications of these differential standards were explored. This choice was partly due to US strategies. Washington was more interested in working through a mechanism which would include western countries other than the member-states of the EC. Any resulting agreement could then cover the major trading countries. The OECD also allowed greater scope for the United States to make use of negotiating alliances with other governments. In addition, the common EC negotiating approach was more likely to be diluted in a framework in which the member-states had individual rather than a collective representation. The EPA, for its part, was attracted to the prospect that chemicals agreements within the OECD framework could strengthen its hand in relation to chemical companies in the United States.

Considerable progress was made, within certain limits, towards the objective of greater harmonisation by way of OECD channels. In the organisation's Chemicals Group, for example, several technical problems were dealt with successfully. Specific expert groups, in which individual countries assumed a lead role, examined questions of ecotoxicity, biodegradation, and physical and chemical methods. More general questions, such as good laboratory practice (GLP), information exchange and the confidentiality of data were approached in the context of the OECD's Special Programme on the Control of Chemicals of 1979–82 (later renewed until 1985).

This groundwork led to agreements in a number of important areas. Two decisions were made at OECD Council meetings in 1981. The first outlined the set of minimum pre-marketing data (MPD) that would be appropriate for inclusion in the notification package for chemical compounds. The second required that each OECD member accept toxicological data packages from other member-states, provided these were prepared according to the prescribed test guidelines and the standards on good laboratory practice.[38] These were significant steps towards international harmonisation of chemicals registration procedures. The OECD's Second High Level Meeting on Chemicals, in 1982, then endorsed a set of principles to guide the exchange of confidential data on chemicals between governments which would ensure protection of any proprietary rights attaching to the data concerned.[39] A Council decision later the same year called for sufficient information to be made available to ensure that the potential health and environmental effects of chemicals could be adequately assessed before they were placed on the market. Thus agreement on basic data to be required before marketing of toxic chemicals went a considerable way towards reconciliation of diverging US and European viewpoints. The flexible application of the MPD rules was also provided for. Due regard could be given, 'on a case-by-case basis, to the scientific and economic factors that may influence the need for and scope of testing'. Member-countries, moreover, could 'omit or substitute certain tests or ask for them in a later stage of initial assessment, as long as they can justify their course of action'.[40]

The second level of negotiations and exchanges on the regulation of the international trade in chemicals has been that of North–South transactions. Here, however, pesticide chemicals were much more directly at the heart of the debate. No negotiating framework such as the OECD, though, has existed. Instead the issues have been aired in a variety of international forums such as Governing Council meetings of the United Nations Environment Programme, which will be examined in the chapter following. More important, in many ways, were debates inside western countries, and within regional groupings such as the European Community, on the unilateral regulation of the export trade in toxic chemicals.

Debate on these regulatory questions emerged in several western countries during the 1970s. The most far-reaching effects were felt in the United States. There was mounting criticism during the decade of the hazards presented to developing countries by western exports of pesticides. Critics took as scapegoats companies allegedly exporting pesticide chemicals banned or restricted in their own country. Much use was made of the various WHO statistics on deaths and injury in Third World nations resulting from pesticides. Risks to western consumers were cited. In 1976, for example, the US Department of Agriculture refused entry to about half a million pounds of DDT-contaminated beef from El Salvador.[41] Environmental groups put forward evidence of various cases of poisoning and fatalities in Brazil, Colombia, Pakistan and Egypt involving use of pesticides sold by US companies for which restrictions were in force at home.

The issue was one that readily provided links with many others. Indeed the catalyst for more intensive Congressional action was not so much pesticides, though these were assuming increasing importance in the middle and late 1970s, as the export of treated children's sleepwear alleged to be hazardous; this question stimulated much interest on the part of Congressional committees in 1978. The regulatory trend in the later years of the Carter Administration was to move towards greater export restrictions where feasible, for example by requiring stricter attention to labelling and a tightening of several export procedures. This trend was checked, however, early in the life of the succeeding Reagan Administration from 1981.[42] The general principle of export notification, however, remained, and the issue continued to rumble through Congressional bodies during the 1980s. As one Congressman posed the regulatory dilemma in 1982: 'Will the workings of the marketplace ferret out hazardous products and reward safety? Does the US have either a moral or ethical obligation to share with other countries the knowledge about hazardous products this Nation has developed through either bad experience or regulatory caution?'[43]

Similarly, environmental groups in West Germany pointed to the high percentage of pesticides produced in the country that entered the export trade, especially to Third World countries, and demanded tighter restrictions of the kind that were being discussed in the United States. The response of federal regulatory bodies was that in practice pesticides that were either banned or restricted in West Germany formed only a small part of this trade; and it was reasonable to expect differences in regulatory standards between different countries. Lack of registration for a compound, that is, did not necessarily imply hazard in all possible circumstances. The more controversial banned products that were exported to developing countries covered a restricted range, chiefly mercury and HCB. For the most part, the regulatory authorities maintained, the non-registered pesticides that were exported consisted of products applied either to crops that did not grow in West Germany (rice, cotton or exotic fruits) or, where the same crops were involved, in the context of control programmes aimed at pests which did not occur or did not have the same economic significance domestically.[44] While pesticide manufacturing interests in European countries took the same anti-regulatory approach as their counterparts in the United States, some interesting differences emerged. American companies at times during these debates found themselves in the difficult position of arguing both *against* toxic chemical export regulation and *for* the spread of whatever regulations did exist to all western countries so that companies would be equally disadvantaged in their attacks on Third World markets.

Developments in United Nations forums in the early 1980s were significant influences on the handling of these issues. The background of international agency activities which contributed to these developments are discussed in the next chapter. In its 34th and 35th sessions the UN General Assembly passed resolutions calling for more effective information exchange systems in relation to the trade in hazardous chemicals generally. The particular object in view was

more effective control over pesticides and pharmaceutical products
that were banned, restricted or unregistered in exporting nations.
The UN's Commission on Transnational Corporations was asked to
study ways of improving the exchange of information. The immediate
culmination of this activity was the passing of resolutions by the
Economic and Social Council (ECOSOC) on the question in 1981
and 1982. These drew particularly on a report on toxic chemical
information exchange requirements prepared by the Secretary-
General, which built in turn on the work of UNEP's data-gathering
team in Geneva.[45]

Such resolutions do not, of course, have binding effect, nor necessarily much impact. In this case, however, the UN lead was adapted
by the European Commission to its own toxic chemicals strategies in
the Community. Following the 1982 ECOSOC resolution in particular, the Commission turned more energetically to the exports issue.
Because of member-state objections and reservations regarding
Community competence, exports, as we have seen, had been excluded from the scope of the EC's pesticides Directives of the 1970s.
But this was a potentially sensitive area in which the Commission had
a restricted area of manoeuvre. The instinct of officials was to let
other international efforts develop more momentum first, particularly those in the OECD. Internal Community pressures, however,
were pushing the Commission towards early action. Contacts between European environmental groups and Third World countries
had expanded by the 1980s. A considerable amount of evidence had
been gathered on the pesticides problems confronting a number of
countries.[46] Consumer protection groups had been actively forging
transnational links through such bodies as the International Organisation of Consumer Unions (IOCU). This established a Pesticide
Action Network (PAN) in 1982. Support for the creation of strong
and effective export regulations was a major theme of a conference of
European non-governmental organisations arranged by the European Environment Bureau (EEB) in 1983 in Schneverdingen. But in
the interplay of Community forces there was also pressure for a more
cautious approach. The more development-oriented groups attuned
to the pesticides issue, such as Oxfam, were constrained in the vigour
of their pursuit of toxic chemicals export controls by appreciation of
the requirements of Third World countries for pesticides in agriculture and public health programmes. And as debates in the European
Parliament showed, no easy consensus could accommodate the calls,
for example by some members of the socialist group, for some form

of export notification scheme for agrochemicals on the one hand, and for greater attention to the concerns of industry and the export needs of European chemical companies on the other.

THE PESTICIDES CONSULTATIONS OF 1977 AND 1982

Global efforts to secure greater uniformity in pesticide registration schemes have been for the most part less politically visible. As was seen in relation to the Codex work on residues levels, they have also tended to be restricted in practice to a narrower range of actors. Environmental groups, for example, have not usually placed great emphasis on this activity. The main harmonising goals within the UN system have been pursued by FAO. Though some attempts to institutionalise broader patterns of cooperation during the 1970s were less successful, FAO has, on balance, usually been the international agency within the UN grouping least distrusted by industry. At the same time its espousal of integrated pest management strategies has allowed it to escape attack by those environmental groups that have been aware of its activities. In two major international conferences on pesticides, in 1977 and 1982, FAO set out to consolidate its credentials as the main international forum on pesticides regulation.

The precursors of these events lay both in the agricultural development programmes of FAO in the 1960s and in major international conferences of the 1970s. The World Food Conference of 1974 set this particular pesticides sequence in motion. Included among its resolutions, largely as a result of FAO efforts behind the scenes in Rome during the conference, was one calling on the leading international agencies concerned to convene on an urgent basis an *ad hoc* inter-governmental consultation on pesticides matters.[47] However, the World Food Conference was also important more generally for setting the intellectual framework for the ensuing debates. Pesticides, that is, were regarded unequivocally as an urgently needed tool of economic development. Uncertainties of supply, together with the high costs of some compounds to developing countries with limited foreign exchange funds, were central to the agenda. One preparatory assessment of developing country requirements for agrochemicals drew attention to low rates of usage: 'the full potentialities of the soils, the irrigation water and the high-yielding varieties will not be realised until it becomes normal to use much larger quantities.'[48] The overall picture painted by the conference was pessimistic. An estimated 35 per cent of potential agricultural yields in developing countries was being regularly lost because of pests; there were forecasts of impending global deficits for pesticide requirements of the order of 20–30 per cent. The goal, then, was to assist developing countries:

(a) in obtaining the pesticides required for meeting urgent needs and for implementation of their plant protection programmes;
(b) in proceeding to develop their own pesticide industries where feasible;
(c) in strengthening their plant protection capabilities through training, consultant missions and supporting research activities; and
(d) to launch breeding programmes for horizontal resistance to disease and to promote the development of integrated control programmes of insect pests.[49]

It followed that moves towards greater harmonisation of the registration schemes for pesticides were to rest on assumptions of their value and benefits rather than of their hazards.

This orientation towards pesticides in developing countries underpinned the resulting pesticides conference of 1975. The meeting was largely technical in character, and explored problems connected with pesticide supply and demand, training, the registration procedures for compounds, integrated strategies, the roles of various international agencies, collaboration with industry, emergency situations of pesticide need in developing countries, and specific problems such as weed control and the methodologies for estimating crop losses due to pests. A strengthening of efforts to secure greater harmonisation was urged. The 'highest possible degree of uniformity in such laws and in the outlook of those that administer them' was essential, one paper argued. The active ingredients of pesticides were international commodities. If highly specific and environmentally acceptable pesticides were to be developed, then the high costs of research and development had to be kept as low as possible and commensurate with the relatively small potential demand to be found in many developing countries.[50]

The 1975 consultations thus set the scene for the major harmonisation exercise that followed in 1977. Its aim, as defined in one of the resolutions of the earlier meeting, was 'to analyse and discuss the basis for harmonising the requirements of registration of pesticides in different countries'. Anticipation of the event centred on its identification of registration and harmonisation as the crux of the pesticides issue. Thus pesticide companies, while not approaching the lead-up to the conference with high hopes of success, at the same time used the occasion to publicise their own defence of harmonisation objectives. Differences in national regulations, it was argued, represented significant trade barriers. Pesticides, moreover, were particularly vulnerable since they were in any case always subject to government regulation. 'Differences in regulation may not pose an absolute barrier to the manufacture, transport or use of a product', one company official said, 'but they create uncertainties, both real and potential. As a result, those who make, sell, and transport these products must invest considerable sums in order to meet the varying requirements.' Harmonisation, or at least partial harmonisation, of laws and regulations was 'a prerequisite for solving the world's food problem. Harmonisation is in everybody's interest.'[51]

A leading US industry journal identified seven main sets of objectives for the 1977 consultation. The suitability of a pesticide, it argued, should be judged on the basis of laboratory tests 'that are uniformly conducted throughout the world'. The protocols for these tests should be standardised in meetings comprising 'internationally-oriented scientists' and representatives of industry. The basic criteria for registration of pesticides should be chemistry, physical properties, toxicology, residues, the effect on environment and wildlife, and efficacy. Registration, moreover, should ideally be conducted in phases. The confidentiality of research information should be respected by regulatory bodies. Negotiations should be continued to establish internationally accepted tolerances for pesticide residues – a reference to the work of the Codex Alimentarius Commission – and an 'independent board' should be established to stimulate implementation of uniform registration requirements.[52]

The consultation convened in October 1977. Represented were 41 countries, and 7 international organisations, including FAO itself, WHO, and the Commission of the European Communities. In line with the aims of the exercise GIFAP had a delegation, whose members played an active role in the committee sessions of the conference. The six committees established dealt respectively with chemical and physical properties; the assessment of biological activity, efficacy and crop safety; toxicology; the determination of pesticide residues in food and feed; environmental impact potential of pesticides; and problems of labelling. Delegates were presented with working and background papers on specifications, toxicology, registration, residues and other topics, prepared by FAO and WHO staff and other experts. GIFAP itself submitted documents outlining its view of the pesticide industry's assessments of the need for greater harmonisation.[53]

While this was not a gathering likely to be marked by any sharp dissensions over pesticides policy, differences did arise over pursuit of the most appropriate path towards a greater degree of harmony in registration practices. Industry representatives, for example, developed the case for far more flexible initial procedures such as phased registrations for compounds. Suggestions for adoption of various kinds of step-wise introduction methods were criticised by a number of delegates who pointed out that existing legislation in many European countries could not accommodate this approach. The overall aim, though, fitted in well with industry objectives. Even limited use of expensively developed compounds during trial or limited registration periods prior to full registration would allow earnings to be made earlier, and over a longer span of the period of patent protection. Disagreement also emerged over the data requirements of registration. More particularly, the central issue of harmonisation was the extent to which data submitted for registration in one country could be used in connection with regulatory procedures in another. But some countries, as was seen earlier in relation to the politics of European Community harmonisation, were, in practice, firm in their conviction that basic decisions on the registration and marketing of toxic chemicals should remain with governments: if this added to the costs of pesticide manufacturers, then it was simply a price they would have to pay each national market. The resolutions of the conference left some room for manoeuvre. One recommended that procedures should be constructed so as to allow limited marketing of pesticides during a control period for field trials; that FAO investigate further the possibility that existing step-wise introduction procedures be extended; and finally 'that registration authorities should use to the fullest extent possible, data and evaluations from other countries and international agencies, where these can be extrapolated'.[54]

There was, similarly, a consensus on the criterion of 'reasonable requirements' in registration procedures, but a considerable area of dispute as to what this meant. No calls were issued for significant reversals of regulatory trends in some countries that had earlier been denounced by industry as excessively stringent. The conference recognised, however, that 'in the evaluation of safety of pesticides some degree of risk must be considered acceptable to society, bearing in mind that the alternative would be needless prohibition of important benefits'.[55] This represented a discreet assault on zero-risk assumptions prevailing in some regulatory quarters in the United States. More criticism was also levelled in this context at some regulatory practices in the Third World. Developing countries, that is, were ill-advised to adopt as the core of their regulatory schemes principles and approaches derived from the richer nations. Yet in this they faced a dilemma. Since many regulatory procedures required highly sophisticated tests, some countries argued, many developing countries had delayed taking action on registration 'with the result that they experience a high incidence of accidental poisoning due to the general availability of highly toxic compounds, mostly without proper labelling and warning notices'. Others did adopt rules, but lacked the expertise to implement or monitor them; a practice that was especially self-defeating where the rules themselves simply called in practice for a duplication of tests carried out elsewhere.[56]

The 1977 consultation did not add anything fundamentally new to the stock of international knowledge and assumptions about pesticide use and regulation. Many of the main conclusions echoed debates in FAO and other settings earlier. The meetings were important, rather, for focusing sustained attention on these questions, and for initiating a sequence of distinctive implementing steps. Indeed FAO officials reacted jubilantly. One later described the landmark nature of the 1977 consultation in terms of BC and AC – before the consultation, and after. Several strands of activity followed. For example, FAO's specifications group met again in 1979 and amongst other things agreed on guidelines for the treatment of confidential data submitted to the organisation by agrochemical companies.[57] Expert consultations on environmental criteria for registration of pesticides were convened in 1979 and 1981, likewise with GIFAP participating. The first of these defined the general principle that developing countries 'should be encouraged and supported in the initiation and/or development of pesticide registration schemes which include attention to potential environmental effects'. The second explored further the issue of agreed test procedures and the requirement for relevant environmental data, but emphasised the differences between each country's circumstances:

The balance between risk and benefit may differ greatly under different socio-economic systems. Under a highly developed well-resourced system harm to rare bird species may be sufficient reason to avoid or restrict the use of a particular chemical. In situations where vector-borne human diseases, starvation or malnutrition are possible factors, however, the risk/benefit analysis may lead to a different decision. Thus, each country undertaking registration must decide what aspects of its environment might be affected by proposed pesticide use.[58]

Preparations for the second government consultation in 1982 were accompanied by similar efforts on the part of industry representatives to ensure a receptive audience. There was industry participation in the various technical meetings that succeeded the 1977 conference. The coordinating of positions in GIFAP's agriculture committee and other bodies produced a fresh batch of submissions to FAO in anticipation of the 1982 sessions. More particularly, in the period since 1977 various industry forums had attacked with much greater vigour the issues surrounding the environmental criteria for registration of pesticides, since it was clear that on these kinds of points the industry was likely to be increasingly vulnerable to criticism from environmental groups and regulatory authorities.[59] As before, the confidentiality of proprietary data was the main rallying cry. There was already discussion of the need for some form of code of conduct to govern the international trade in pesticides. If any such code were to be drawn up, it should be FAO rather than any other international agency that should be tasked to undertake the consultative work. This view of GIFAP's was based not only on past experience with the organisation, but also on criticism of tendencies in other international bodies, for example of the implications for pesticides of some aspects of OECD recommended test methods for chemicals.[60]

The 1982 consultation adhered to the general form of the first. Four main working groups were established: on data requirements, registration procedures, effective national control of pesticides, and coordination of international activities. A couple of absences out of the 51 state delegations scheduled to attend marginally diminished the international impact of the consultation; Mexico, for example, had in recent years been following a path of active promotion by government and industry of harmonisation efforts in Latin America. As in 1977, the US delegation, which also included industry representatives, took up the theme of data confidentiality. Two of the final recommendations of the conference followed directly from US efforts. Amongst other things these affirmed the value of data to those companies responsible for generating it, and defended the principle that such companies had a right to a period of exclusive use to the data submitted in relation to new chemical compounds.[61] Sweden, however, as its delegation noted, was one of the countries that had more extensive definitions of the right of public access to government data. No way of resolving such differences of approach was found, but there was discussion of possible safeguards which might preclude use of data by competing companies.

One difference between 1977 and 1982 was discussion during the latter consultation of codes of conduct governing pesticide sales, particularly with respect to Third World countries. The second meeting, indeed, included a representative of one of the more vocal anti-pesticides environmental groups, the International Organisation of Consumer Unions. Thus debate on the allegations of dumping by western chemical companies of banned pesticides in developing countries, already prominent in UNEP approaches and in the 1981 and 1982 ECOSOC resolutions, also emerged in this arena. A measure of agreement was eventually reached on the desirability of such a code of conduct being negotiated. But those at the meeting sympathetic to industry concerns pointed out that if the goals of the consultation were progressively achieved, then such codes would be redundant; Third World countries with adequate and harmonised regulatory frameworks would be able to manage their pesticides and toxic chemicals policies themselves.[62]

THE POLITICS OF REGISTRATION

The two consultations of 1977 and 1982 did not, then, achieve the broad harmonisation goals defined by some participants. Taken in conjunction with some of the other developments discussed in this chapter, however, they indicate some expansion of the area of international agreement on pesticides registration. Confidentiality of proprietary information, for example, was more firmly set as a cornerstone of any future hypothetical regulatory regime. Some of the procedures agreed through the various OECD frameworks, for example on the content of pre-marketing data packages, represented substantial and relatively expeditious progress towards the objectives of greater uniformity. On the other hand, the handling of sensitive data by international bodies also remained a source of contention. Differences in national regulatory systems, in relation to pesticide chemicals or any other sector, are not caused primarily by the capacities of technical experts to reach divergent evaluations and recommendations. The element of irreconcilability in the differences is due to broader political interests. Regulations are a product of the interplay of political forces that shape policy. In them can be found the residues of the interests of the agricultural, industrial, governmental and other actors that had a hand in making them. Even in a setting in which states are committed in theory to a measure of harmonising change, as in the case of the member states of the European Community, negotiations can be difficult and protracted. The interests of the leading agricultural exporting nations in fostering greater uniformity have been noted in the last chapter, on the residues issue. A constraint distant from the pesticides area itself is likely to have increasing impact in the opposite direction. This is the trend towards possibly greater, rather than less, interest on the part of governments in various kinds of non-tariff barriers, as negotiated reductions of tariffs through GATT agreements in the 1970s and 1980s bring about protective scurryings for alternative devices.

6 Rational Use of Pesticides: Chemicals and the Environment

Among the wide diversity of environmental issues, pesticides have experienced periodic rises and falls of attention. In the early 1960s, discussion of the issues raised in Rachel Carson's book, *Silent Spring*, made pesticides the quintessential environmental problem. Later, however, pesticides were treated not so much as sources of hazard to the natural environment as of danger to human health. Consumers were at risk because of the presence of pesticide residues in foods. Users, including agricultural workers, could suffer potentially damaging consequences. Parallel with these kinds of public debates and linked to them, if at times only tenuously, has been a greater measure of continuity in the flow of scientific interest in the broader ecological consequences of pesticide use. As we saw in the last chapter, such questions form part of the standard criteria in determinations by regulatory bodies on the registration of particular compounds. It is not really possible in principle, or for that matter very useful, to separate out the various consequences of pesticide use and label some as falling under environmental headings. The working definition in this chapter stems in part from the perceptions and implicit classifications of types of hazard made by the various participants in pesticides debates. The environmentalist critique of pesticide use, however the term is defined, has been the most persistent and has had the most far-reaching consequences for agrochemical use. In brief, the critique has stressed the self-defeating aspects of the dependence of agriculture or forestry on pesticide chemicals, and has aimed to replace such controls with more appropriate and integrated – or, in a word, more 'rational' – long-term strategies.

The ebb and flow of public attention to these questions has been partly a function of the differing impact of scientific findings. During the 1960s it became evident that insecticides were in one form or

111

another widely distributed in the environment through interaction with soils, freshwater and seawater systems, and by way of global atmospheric circulation by wind.[1] At least since the 1940s a good deal has been known of the differing extent to which chemical compounds persist in the environment in toxic form. The policy implications are unclear, even assuming that scientific findings at any given time are adequate. Some critics have called, on the basis of this kind of evidence, for the banning or severe restriction of use of many pesticides. Particular attention focused in the 1960s and 1970s on organochlorine compounds on the grounds both of the high toxicity to mammals and birds of many of them, and their persistence. Various attempts have also been made to initiate a phasing-out of pesticide use, based, for example, on increasing reliance on biological control methods and on highly specific and relatively more environmentally safe chemical agents. Notions of integrated pest management, however, are notoriously open to many interpretations. While the key concept is the deployment of a variety of strategies, including where necessary the use of pesticide chemicals, industry critics have argued – rightly, in many cases – that behind some formulations can be found a hidden agenda of the progressive abolition of all such compounds.[2]

Because of the proliferation and power of myths in this area, however, it is often more expedient than fully accurate for manufacturers or agricultural users to portray sensible and traditional approaches as threatened in this fashion by the long march of the ignorant. Yet the conflicts over the use and environmental consequences of pesticides are real and profound. Discussion in this chapter focuses on the international level. We begin with an account of the non-governmental organisations which have often prepared the ground for the later involvement of more formal inter-governmental institutions, and which continue to act as the sharpest critics of pesticide use.

NON-GOVERNMENTAL NETWORKS

The profusion and diversity of these bodies makes generalisations difficult. Environmental groups are also usually preoccupied with several very different sets of issues, from nuclear power generation and pollution of the oceans to the extinction of wildlife species and the spread of desertification. The resources that can be devoted to any of these are likely to be slender. Choices of targets and strategies have to be made with some care. Only relatively few can mount major campaigns. In relation to pesticides some groups in the United States have emerged as significant players. The submissions made by the Audubon Society on pesticides issues to Congressional committees, for example, have revealed an impressive marshalling of evidence and arguments, and a skilful use of advisory scientific expertise. Similarly, not many of these groups, most of which have some form of transnational connections with broader networks, can be considered actors in the international regulatory debates on pesticides discussed in earlier chapters. Their political significance lies more in their capacity to shape and to respond to the changing moods of public debate on, and media accounts of, pesticides issues. We will take as an example an organisation which, while having consultative status as a non-governmental organisation (NGO) with various intergovernmental bodies, also belies this definition to some extent by comprising a mixed membership of states, government agencies, and environmental pressure groups.

This is the International Union for Conservation of Nature and Natural Resources (IUCN). It was set up in 1948 at around the time when discovery of the build-up of resistance among various insect species to DDT, following the earlier wartime dramatic successes of that compound in the public health field, was first beginning to have an impact on public opinion. Its primary concerns lay elsewhere, in such matters as the preservation of endangered species of wildlife and the promotion of national parks and protected areas. During the 1950s, this loosely structured grouping of national environmental protection bodies in a variety of countries sustained a continued interest in agrochemicals developments. Thus resolutions critical of insecticide use and development that were passed by several General Assemblies of the organisation fitted into a broader pattern of concern about threats from industrial pollution to the health of natural environments.[3] Several factors, however, including financial constraints and a lack of administrative facilities for encouraging liaison between sympathetic experts in different countries, limited IUCN capacities to press these concerns more forcefully. Even within the broad area of environmentalist concerns, moreover, articulation of these kinds of anxieties did not usually meet with a receptive audience.

Change came with the upsurge of public attention to pesticides issues that accompanied the *Silent Spring* atmosphere of the early and middle 1960s, particularly in the United States. More direct evidence could now be gathered on the hazards of the chemical economy by even the most ill-equipped environmental group, and more attentive ears were guaranteed. Threats from chemicals to wild birds, one of the main issues in US debates on the dangers of organochlorine insecticides in the 1960s, were increasingly studied by international bird protection organisations. The IUCN's Commission on Ecology set up a special group in 1961 and gave it the task of investigating the ecological effects of chemical methods of pest control.[4] As a result of this work a draft policy statement on pesticides was prepared by the organisation in 1966 and progressively revised during the rest of the decade. The thinking behind it gives a good indication of environmentalist approaches during these years. As a body which had aspirations to act as the leading member of the transnational network of environmental NGOs, however, IUCN's own approach was also marked by an appreciation of pesticide requirements. It was recognised that production of food was necessary, and that this, together with the need to eliminate the vectors of diseases, called for continued use of pesticides. But several factors had also to be taken into account: that the organism attacked by chemicals was actually the one doing the damage; that there were broader ecological consequences of pesticide use; that trends towards unnecessarily clean farming and monoculture contained inherent risks; that biological control methods presented alternative and long-term strategies; that chemicals should be applied at the minimum rate necessary to ensure effectiveness, and only at such places where control was necessary and at such times when application was effective; that more specific pesticides were needed; and, finally, that some pesticides were in some circumstances likely to be intrinsically more hazardous to wildlife than others.[5]

These kinds of points were not new. What was important was rather that growing attention was being paid to them. It was out of such formulations that more concerted anti-pesticides campaigns later grew. They also anticipated the diversity of later approaches by environmentalist critics. Pesticides for some became a crucial and symbolic issue in the battle to preserve healthy environments. Others were rather more prepared to acknowledge needs for agrochemicals, particularly on the part of developing countries. Conflicting approaches marked IUCN analyses. In the late 1960s, for example, some delegations to its annual meetings pointed out that though a ban had been imposed on DDT use in many temperate countries, this was not the case in the tropics where there was no alternative to its use for emergency human health purposes. The organisation's advisory experts on pesticide matters were critical of the anti-pesticides line increasingly being espoused by some members; at one point British officials and other delegates abstained rather than identify themselves with even more diluted anti-pesticides resolutions.[6] The resultant tension became more acute in the 1970s following the emergence of new environmental pressure groups in western countries, many of them eager to adopt more activist stances. Criticism of the impact of agrochemicals was still a regular feature of IUCN debates, but these tended to be secondary to more traditional concerns centring on endangered wildlife species and ecosystem conservation.[7]

Organisations with significant international elements were increasingly affected during the 1970s by developmental perspectives. Calling for outright bans on pesticides came to be viewed as ecologically unwise, though pressures were kept up against certain of the more notorious compounds. The argument instead was for the gradual development of alternatives and the spread of integrated pest management thinking. These kinds of compromises did not touch all groups equally; some elaborated critical attacks on older bodies such as IUCN on the grounds that agrochemicals posed urgent questions that required radically different approaches.

Pesticides occupied an important, but relatively low-profile, position in the *World Conservation Strategy*, drafted by IUCN, UNEP and the World Wildlife Fund in collaboration with FAO and UNESCO and published in its first version in 1980. The general position followed the reasoning which had evolved in the late 1960s:

The productivity of agricultural ecosystems depends not only on maintaining soil quality but also on retaining the habitats of beneficial insects and other animals, such as crop pollinators and the predators and parasites of pests. Effective pest control is no longer a matter of heavy application of pesticides, particularly because of the rising costs of petroleum-derived products but largely because excessive pesticide use promotes resistance . . ., destroys natural enemies, turns formerly innocuous species into pests, harms other non-target species, and contaminates food and feed. Instead pesticides should be used to supplement a battery of methods integrated in appropriate combinations: these methods include introduction of pest-resistant crop varieties, special planting combinations and patterns, mechanical methods, the use of repellants and hormones, and encouragement of natural enemies.[8]

The difference with the earlier period was more one of tone. By the 1980s environmental critics of pesticides were very much more confident that alternative approaches were practicable as well as desirable.

These kinds of probings by a large number of environmental groups have not usually had much direct influence over the policies of governments. They have, though, often served as sounding-boards and amplified the force of pressures from domestic groups. This has been particularly the case where a background of pesticide politics already existed, for example in relation to insect resistance to DDT and other compounds in the late 1940s and 1950s, or to threats to wild bird populations of excessive or careless use of agrochemicals in the early and middle 1960s, or to the atmospheric transport of pesticides to isolated parts of the planet in the 1970s, or to the carcinogenic and other dangerous properties of certain herbicide compounds in the 1980s. In addition some issues emerged initially in debates within such transnational groupings. A decade before the question became prominent in the United Nations and other inter-governmental forums, the General Assembly of IUCN passed a resolution in 1966 which not only drew attention to the hazards of toxic chemicals generally, but noted particularly the problem of the indiscriminate export and import of pesticides and urged controls over this trade by firms and governments in the leading exporting countries. There followed technical discussion of alternative control mechanisms, and of the problems surrounding export of organochlorine insecticides restricted by regulatory authorities for domestic use.[9]

Yet the ways in which pesticides issues tended to be framed were also constricting, particularly for activity at the international level. Domestically, a focus on health hazards of the use of pesticides, or on such arcane matters as the resilience of the egg-shells of wild birds, could be productive for an environmental group. This has been more particularly the case in the United States, where such groups have traditionally been more reluctant to accommodate the developmental issues that were increasingly of concern to some of their European counterparts. In dealings with international agencies in the UN system, however, this kind of perspective had limited staying power. Even for UNEP, as we shall see in a moment, the requirements of economic development in the Third World have constituted an evolving framework of attention within which appreciations of the hazards of pesticides have been set. Groupings such as IUCN have indeed emphasised that misuse of agrochemicals could be counter-productive in terms of economic development goals, for example in the case of threats to fish stocks near sprayed rice fields;[10] but for most environmental organisations the deployment of evidence has been dictated more by a visceral anti-chemicals approach. The issue of relations with industry, central to the international agency level, tended to be answered by default at the NGO level.[11]

AGROCHEMICALS AND UNEP

The UN's Environment Programme was launched in the aftermath of the world environment conference in Stockholm in 1972. Though UNEP was not the only actor in the UN system with an interest in environmental issues, it has been central in terms of the breadth of its objectives and the expectations surrounding it. Some of the activities of other international bodies were precursors of UNEP involvement in the agrochemicals field.

One of these arose indirectly out of the work of a variety of environmental and scientific NGOs on the classification and mapping of ecosystems, with a view to the compilation of authoritative listings of the planet's natural ecological regions and to the conservation of important, or representative, areas. The Man and the Biosphere (MAB) Programme of UNESCO became the most important vehicle of these concerns in the 1970s. It had its immediate origins in the 1968 biosphere conference held in Paris. The aim of the programme was the stimulation of relevant scientific and data-gathering activity on a wide front, and the concomitant raising of public awareness of threats to the natural environment. One of its major projects thus dealt with a series of topics woven together as the 'ecological assessment of pest management and fertilizer use on terrestrial and aquatic ecosystems'. At the first session in 1971 of the programme's coordinating body two broad categories of problems were identified as being of worldwide concern: the environmental consequences of widespread use of chemical pesticides; and the declining effectiveness of chemical con-trol in many areas. The aim of the research was thus directed 'towards enhancement of productivity with a minimum of adverse effects on non-target species and on the environment'.[12]

Structurally the MAB approach was divided into separate fertiliser and pesticides sections. The latter were clearly more germane to the environmental argument. Though the programme did not have aspirations of direct political influence, the kinds of research issues targeted were precisely those that other environmental organisations were urging should be treated more seriously by governments. These included the relationship between long-term soil contamination by pesticides and plant productivity, as measured by crop yield and quality; more intensive study of the causal links between such contamination and plant response; the consequences for fish production of pesticide disruption of freshwater ecosystems; the impact of pesticides generally in the context of programmes of pest control; the occurrence and distribution of pesticides in the tropical environment; the establishment of predictive models of pesticide–ecosystem interactions; the gathering of more reliable data on the ecological effects of pesticides; and the training of officials and technical experts.[13]

Even in 1968, when the scientific meetings in the Paris biosphere conference formulated general plans for this programme of research on a global basis, it was apparent that fragmentation and lack of coordination could provide significant checks on the potential for international environmental planning. The injection of greater cohesion into this system was one of the motivating factors behind the establishment of UNEP. Others arose from the lessons of earlier schemes. These pointed, firstly, to the importance of toxic chemicals as an environmental issue-area and, secondly, to the ambivalent responses of developing countries and of economic development actors in the UN system to these questions.

Attention to developing country requirements was a general feature of the early 1970s preparations for the 1972 environment conference. In attempts to specify the environmental costs both of traditional agricultural practices and of transitions to modern development strategies, a number of significant pesticides problems were detected. The application of fertilisers did not on balance pose serious environmental problems in the Middle East, one assessment concluded, though it was a contributing factor in the salinisation of water resources in Iran, Syria and Lebanon. However, the 'indiscriminate use' of pesticides in the region was regarded as a threat to man, fisheries and wildlife. Incidents were cited of fish kills due to contamination of water with chlorinated hydrocarbons in the Litani river in Lebanon and the Orontes and Barada rivers in Syria. Fish catches along the Lebanon coast were showing high levels of residues due to chemical pollution of coastal waters. The lack of regulatory standards on such matters, moreover, meant that agricultural exporting countries could face serious problems when trading with countries which had strict and enforced residues regulations.[14] In Africa, by contrast, the general conclusion was that levels of pesticide consumption had not by the late 1960s and early 1970s reached proportions where they could be seen as having serious ecological consequences.[15]

The activities of UNEP during the 1970s and 1980s were shaped in part, then, by prior definitions of the central place of pesticides and toxic chemicals generally. These definitions were brought to the 1972 Stockholm conference (UNCHE) by a number of delegations from western countries. The 'identification and control of pollutants and nuisances of broad international significance' thus formed a key part of preparatory approaches to the meetings.[16] Several major recommendations of the conference itself dealt with pollution. One of these (74) emphasised such matters as the need for more information and public awareness, together with the need to 'improve the international acceptability of procedures for testing pollutants and contaminants'. More particularly it called for the development of plans for an 'international registry' of data on chemicals in the environment, to be based on scientific data 'on the environmental behaviour of the most important man-made chemicals and containing production figures of the potentially most harmful chemicals, together with their pathways from factory via utilisation to ultimate disposal or recirculation'.[17]

Two issues assumed particular significance later. Firstly, phrases like 'most harmful' or 'most important' proved difficult to operationalise. The question of how best to define priorities for policy attention from among the huge numbers of toxic chemicals in common use was still plaguing UNEP endeavours at the end of the decade. Secondly, this approach contained implications for western notions of industrial property rights. Concerns about some of these kinds of questions on the part of the United States tended in the early 1970s to surface more as objections to the inherent difficulties of securing some data. Thus the United States did not oppose the 'registry' concept, the delegation stated, but rather the inclusion within this particular recommendation of the final phrase on the pathways of chemicals from factory to disposal. This, it was argued, would be unworkable.[18] It became clearer during the 1970s that many environmental questions, particularly those in the toxic chemicals area, touched on many sensitive issues for industry in western countries.

A full inventory of the points at which pesticides or pesticide-related issues emerged during the Stockholm conference, however, is very much lengthier. One of the 'principles' adopted by the conference, for example, referred very broadly to the environmental consequences of the discharge of toxic substances. Among pertinent recommendations were those relating to human malnutrition (13), a reflection of western sensitivities to developing countries' perceptions of the potential irrelevance of the exercise to their real needs; the strengthening and coordination of international programmes on integrated pest control 'and reduction of the harmful effects of agrochemicals' (21); coordination by FAO of work on pests and diseases (26); problems of pest outbreaks in forests (27); cooperation between governments in neighbouring or contiguous protected areas, in relation to plant and animal control and other matters (37); the need for development of varieties and breeds of crops giving higher yields and having higher resistance to local pests and diseases (45); pollution of the aquatic resources of other nations by a country, including that resulting from discharge of toxic chemicals (48); and the various pollution and marine pollution recommendations (70-85 and 86-94).[19]

Several constraints have affected UNEP agrochemical work. The first is of a more general character. As a programme, rather than an agency or other body within the UN system, it was inherently limited in its capacity to influence states. It could not, for example, project a visible presence through fieldwork in Third World countries. UNEP has also been the target of a number of general complaints by governments. Some objected to its pursuit of environmental conventions, on the grounds that these were best left to states. The terminology characteristic of UNEP approaches – on the 'urgency' or 'high priority' of a wide range of requirements, often with minimal discrimination and ordering – was argued to be counter-productive in terms of attempts to influence government policies.[20] Shifts of issues also affected UNEP's visibility and to some extent its funding levels. During much of the rest of the 1970s attention turned to energy questions, or to the more pressing sources of economic hardship in Third World countries. Environmentalist concerns took on a dated air.

Secondly, conflicting demands were placed on the world environment body. Statements at grand levels of synthesis on the planet's ecosystems, resources and human populations occurred regularly in UNEP documents, and were mutually resonant with alarums about the environmental hazards created by pesticides. These compounds, however, spanned a number of divergent policy areas. They were at the same time contributors to the defeat of malnutrition. Resolution of these dilemmas was not difficult to achieve in principle in the vocabularies of integrated pest management approaches, but in practice the choices of emphasis and resource allocation they posed were often more intractable.

Thirdly, pesticides, like many other aspects of UNEP work, were already in the early 1970s being handled by a variety of international organisations. The political momentum created by images of the newness of global environmental strategies could cut through this complex of activities, but not for long. During the 1972 conference a number of the basic approaches and specific recommendations were shaped in part by pressures from FAO participants. Together with WHO, as we have seen, this organisation also had a leading role in pesticides residues issues and their international regulation through the Codex Alimentarius machinery; while UNESCO, through the Man and the Biosphere Programme, was pushing forward on a broad scientific front on matters connected with the global environmental impact of pesticide use patterns. UNEP had few capabilities, even if it had had the terms of reference, to act as an overall coordinating mechanism.

The 'registry' work on toxic chemicals, however, provided the new organisation with a distinct niche. Despite this, and the emphasis on its importance at the 1972 conference, progress was relatively slow. The fact qualified the tone, but did not fundamentally alter the gist, of reactions by governments. And increasingly during the 1970s the rationale of development needs came to the fore. Several countries underlined the point in Governing Council sessions that toxic chemicals data were of particular value to developing countries, since most could not afford to set up research facilities of their own and were thus reliant on information supplied by manufacturers.[21] But there was also a chicken-and-egg problem. Governments urged that some basic choices were needed of those toxic chemicals which should be of most concern to them;[22] yet on scientific grounds it was frequently difficult to make such identifications until more comprehensive sets of data had been collected. And the question also arose, though somewhat later, of industry concerns that setting priorities could mean incipient blacklisting.

The search for data brought in train a mixture of organisational and political questions. A unit started operations at UNEP headquarters in Nairobi in 1976, but this moved shortly afterwards to the Programme's Geneva liaison offices because of the greater proximity to chemical data sources. A more precise listing of objectives was determined by the Governing Council in 1978. Staff of the International

Register of Potentially Toxic Chemicals (IRPTC) sought to compile data profiles for chemical compounds on the basis of information supplied by a developing network of correspondents in various countries and international bodies. By the end of the decade, information was on file in varying degrees of completeness for over 40 000 chemicals. Priority attention was being given to between 300 and 400, of which more than 160 were agrochemicals. The criteria for selection of compounds in this shorter list centred on identifiable concerns to health and environmental protection authorities in the participating countries.[23] The intrinsic difficulties of accumulating usable data on such a large number of compounds tended to be overlooked by governments critical of an apparent lack of expedition.[24] Several data banks containing information on chemicals were used, and resources such as the Environmental Chemicals Data and Information Network (ECDIN) of the EEC countries.[25] To be fully viable, however, the Register had to rest on an international network of direct contacts with organisations and individual experts active in research on chemicals.

While national correspondents of the system had been nominated in around 70 countries by 1980, the contacting of chemical manufacturers proved difficult. Some were responsive in cases involving specific compounds, but more generally the response was guarded or suspicious. The IRPTC aimed to evolve into a worldwide network of data collection and use on toxic chemicals, and to retain free access as a basic operating principle. These were not conditions reassuring to pesticide companies. Indeed the fact that there have been occasional approaches made to IRPTC to purchase data is an indication of the potentially sensitive commercial areas into which this kind of exercise inevitably strays. Ironically, despite the Geneva base, it has been the leading Swiss companies that have been among the most resistant to IRPTC overtures; whereas staff have been able to cite instances of cooperative responses to requests for information from US companies, including Dow Chemical and, to a lesser extent, Union Carbide.[26]

In terms of relations with industry, IRPTC has made somewhat more headway with representative chemical industry associations and more particularly, in the case of pesticide chemicals, with GIFAP. Even so, that grouping's own response has also been cautious, in part because of the constraints set by differing viewpoints held by member organisations and individual companies, many of whom have tended to see the IRPTC enterprise as a dubious scheme involving the compilation of blacklists of chemicals and the implicit assumption that those identified for priority attention should be banned or heavily restricted. Particular concerns focused on the advisory role to governments that might follow the consolidation and greater political acceptability of the Register. The capacity of IRPTC to issue warnings in relation to certain agrochemicals was taken as a signal of this possibility. However, if there was a chance that the exercise could become more prominent in the future, then clearly it was in the interests of the pesticide industry to forge potentially influential links at an early stage of its evolution. The resulting mixture of aims on both sides structured the exchanges that have taken place. GIFAP was originally 'not interested in cooperating with us', the IRPTC's Director, Jan Huismans, said later, 'but we told them we were going to go ahead with our register anyway, and now I think we have access to their data.'[27] This may have been an optimistic gloss, not least because the data of real interest were in the hands of the companies themselves. GIFAP's concern was to stress the need for respect of the principle of confidentiality of data, and particularly if there was to be any possibility in the future of the Register utilising unpublished company materials. It also pointed out that pesticide companies retained the right to make their own decisions about cooperation with the IRPTC system and whether or not to submit data to it.[28]

The concerns of some member-states were also relevant on this point. Though IRPTC aims have been restricted in scope to the level of data-gathering, it is possible to see in a more fully evolved scheme the presence of constraints on national regulatory options with regard to some compounds, especially those singled out for particular attention as priority chemicals. Thus states have in practice varied considerably in their degree of enthusiasm for the IRPTC. Some environmental authorities have been active in their support – officials have noted those of Sweden, the Netherlands, and Belgium – but this was less true of the EPA in the 1980s.[29] Use of alternative sources of US information, such as Chemline and Toxline, only partially made up for such deficiencies. Some governments, then, have in practice had to put more emphasis on their relations with domestic industry than with the international organisations in which they participate. Because of the sensitivity of much chemicals data, nurturing the first may imply a demoting of the second. A further source of unease, at least in the case of the United States, was the interest of the Soviet Union and east European countries in this kind of chemical data collection exercise, which has been reflected – in part also because of the non-convertibility of the rouble – in collaborative UNEP–USSR scientific translation and other technical programmes.

The result of these twin difficulties of securing good working relations with both governments and industry has been delay in the production of IRPTC materials. An initial set of data profiles was developed in 1978 and published the following year, but this project related specifically to marine pollution and was carried out at the request of another body within UNEP. Meeting the targets of data profile publication was then disrupted by internal UNEP developments, including lack of funds for staff for IRPTC work, and by the consequences of change in the UN's Geneva computer system in 1982. An intermediate step came with the publishing in 1980 of legal data profiles for some chemicals.[30]

These problems aside, the IRPTC has nonetheless survived UNEP's occasionally troubled history. It has not, however, achieved one of its main objectives of becoming a significant source of information for developing countries. The users of the data services have tended to be mainly from the advanced industrialised nations, just as distribution of the Register's regular information bulletin has in practice been concentrated on North America and western Europe. Making adequate use of its data profiles in practice presupposes an infrastructure of scientific and administrative attention to pesticides and toxic chemicals management issues.

Developing countries have, however, continued to exploit the opportunities provided by UNEP Governing Council sessions as a means of drawing attention to such requirements. Thus the IRPTC has been pointed to frequently as a mechanism with which developing countries could better structure their relations with multinational chemical companies. Information was urgently needed on the hazards posed by the pesticides, other chemicals and food products sold by enterprises based in western countries.[31] These meetings were significant points of transmission and amplification of the hazardous exports issue noted in the last chapter. As we have seen already, questions of the international trade in pesticides and other toxic chemicals had been debated in IUCN and other environmental forums in the mid-1960s. Pressures mounted during the following decade. A 1977 decision of UNEP's Governing Council urged governments 'to take steps to ensure that potentially harmful chemicals, in whatever form or commodity, which are unacceptable for domestic purposes in the exporting country, are not permitted to be exported without the knowledge and consent of appropriate authorities in the importing country'. Developing countries needed assistance on this matter from various international bodies, including the Codex Alimentarius Commission, 'in developing and strengthening their capacities for evaluating chemicals, foods, drugs, and cosmetics being distributed within their countries'.[32] This effort culminated in the development of a UNEP notification system on hazardous exports. By the time this began to come into existence, in the mid-1980s, the issue had worked its way through a number of other international arenas, notably in the form of the GATT trial scheme of 1982–84.

FRAGMENTATION OR COORDINATION

Different parts of the UN system have frequently been charged with failing to work well with other parts. Complaints about the costs of lack of effective coordination, duplication and wasted effort, and the commitment of energies to the defence of bureaucratic niches rather than the implementation of good programmes, have emerged with greater force during the 1970s and 1980s as western governments have attempted to focus greater political attention on budgets and the allocation of limited resources. UNEP came in for its share of the general criticism. Indeed, given the proliferation of various kinds of environmental activities among different organs of the UN system, it may have been shielded from still more by the political costs for western governments of targeting environmental cooperation for special attack. Significant pressures on UNEP operating budgets, however, forced reappraisals in a number of areas. In this political atmosphere, a demonstration of readiness and ability to collaborate with other organs was an asset.

A background of cooperative ventures in practice already marked the environmental areas with which FAO, WHO, UNEP and other organisations were involved. Many have been of limited duration and with specific operating goals. Collaboration between FAO and the International Atomic Energy Agency (IAEA) on pesticide residues monitoring is one example. In the period 1972–76 several major studies were supported by the two institutions in developing countries where increasing agrochemical dependence was thought likely to lead to future problems. Use was made of isotope tracer and other nuclear techniques for which nuclear energy officials could readily draw on expertise. Studies were carried out in Brazil, Ghana,

India, Israel, Lebanon, Mexico, Pakistan, Turkey and Uganda. The rationale for the approach was that the products concerned had considerable importance for the economies concerned; that certain conditions – such as differences in ecological circumstances, cultivation methods, or storage – tended to favour pest attack; that insect resistance to pesticides was a known problem affecting crop yields; and that products exported from these to developed countries were subject to pesticide residue regulations which could therefore have major implications for the agricultural sectors of many developing countries. The conclusion was that there was 'abundant evidence of trace contaminant and pollution problems in developing countries affecting food, soil and water of potential economic or health importance'.[33] While the report of the study acknowledged the infrastructure requirements of developing countries in this kind of monitoring exercise, the sophistication of the techniques employed also pointed by implication to the low probability that developing countries would in fact acquire them.

Other forms of inter-agency cooperation have already been discussed. The Codex enterprise itself constitutes a major example. One collaborative effort which had important implications for Codex activities was created amid some controversy early in the 1980s. The International Programme on Chemical Safety (IPCS) prompted fears on the part of participants in existing mechanisms, notably the Codex system and its technical infrastructure in the form of the Joint Meetings, that these were being jostled aside; and concern on the part of chemical companies that more of an anti-industry bias would as a result be built into the area of pesticides regulation.

The IPCS owed its origins to the lengthy background of WHO activity on pesticides and related health and occupational safety questions dating back at least to 1951. A more immediate factor was work during the 1970s in WHO's regional office for Europe. This focused on planning for emergencies and accidents involving the release of toxic chemicals. At the same time the International Labour Organisation (ILO) was evolving a health hazard alert system to be based on active participation by appropriate government agencies in member states. Part of this activity involved the identification of toxic chemicals likely to pose significant occupational safety or health hazards. The toxic chemicals data-gathering work of UNEP, then based in the European liaison offices, fitted in logically – and ideologically – with these approaches. The IPCS experiment could thus be portrayed in planning meetings in the late 1970s and early 1980s not as a radically new departure, but rather as an attempt to expand the area of collaboration between ILO, UNEP and WHO in the field of chemicals safety and the environment.[34] Data on toxic chemicals being collected by UNEP thus formed the main continuing information resource of the new programme.

The development tended to be viewed with some alarm by representatives of the pesticides industry. The reasons were partly historical and institutional. Industry dealings with WHO had had a history of being guarded, the organisation's staff and operating philosophies often being viewed as antipathetic to important industry concerns, and its general style as aloof. Criticism centred on the threats posed by this innovation to existing structures, more particularly the pesticide residues activities of the Codex machinery and the Joint Meetings. Despite its inter-agency collaborative aura, some regarded the proposed programme as little more than 'WHO in disguise'.[35] Some of the more ambitious early plans of WHO staff had to be restructured, in part because of industry arguments that some mechanisms would be inherently self-defeating since they would fail to elicit the active cooperation of industry on such key questions as the provision of data on toxic chemicals.

The risks to existing pesticides regulatory mechanisms were highlighted by the United States. The head of the US delegation to the Codex pesticide residues committee expressed concern in 1981 about the way the chemical safety programme was taking shape. The crucial issue was 'the security and unauthorised use of data'. This was raised by the proposals for integration of the programme with the joint FAO and WHO expert meetings on pesticide residues, which had been in operation since the mid-1960s and which formed the scientific and technical basis for the pesticides residues work of the Codex Alimentarius Commission. If this happened, the confidentiality and proprietary nature of industry data would be at stake, and in that event 'the data necessary for the setting of Acceptable Daily Intakes and tolerances will not be forthcoming from industry'. This in turn, by bringing into question the whole rationale for Codex operations, could entail the possibility that funding from member-states for this kind of international work could fall off.[36] FAO officials also expressed a marked lack of enthusiasm for the chemical safety programme. More formally, they took the position at first that the organisation was restrained constitutionally from joining in fully with this kind of activity. More pragmatically, it was pointed out that it did threaten the effective working of the Codex system as far as pesticide residues (and also food additives) were concerned, and that a programme which lacked industry confidence would not be viable.[37]

This atmosphere of criticism and doubt affected the formative period of the International Programme on Chemical Safety. The principle was agreed early in its life that the existing structure and working practices of the Codex pesticides residues and food additives bodies should not be modified, and indeed that funds should be earmarked to guarantee the continuation, and if possible the expansion, of these activities.[38] IPCS institutional arrangements were gradually put into place in the early 1980s. These involved use of the toxic chemicals register as a core data source, meetings of a Technical Committee of experts, and a Programme Advisory Committee consisting of member-state representatives. A network of leading institutions in various countries was projected. The one in Canada, for example, agreed to assume responsibility for work on the pesticides data sheets initiated and published regularly by WHO staff; while existing research efforts were adapted and incorporated into the system where appropriate and feasible, for example on the origins and pathology of Reye's syndrome in Czechoslovakia, and on toxicological data with regard to selected synthetic pyrethrins in the Federal Republic of Germany.[39] The character of the chemical safety programme, then, was in tune with the underlying goals both of the toxic chemicals register activity of UNEP and the occupational safety and environmental health concerns of ILO and WHO. More particularly the organisational objectives were primarily informational and educational, with emphasis being placed on the evaluation and dissemination of scientific data, the training of officials, and the encouragement of more effective use of the resource by developing countries. As such, the programme represented a divergent trend from that of Codex activities on pesticides and related chemicals, and the future evolution of relations among the various actors involved remained uncertain.

THE POLITICS OF RATIONAL USE

We have been able in this chapter to discuss only a few of the ways in which environmental consequences of pesticide use have entered the agendas of international organisations. Even so, the record reaffirms the magnitude of the constraints. Firstly, in relation to the compounds themselves, international bodies have been substantially limited in their capacity to secure adequate kinds of toxicological and other information. This is partly because of the potentially sensitive questions for companies involved in any regulatory efforts. As we saw in the previous chapter, national regulatory agencies in western countries confront significant hurdles when trying to probe for data required for purposes of regulation. The problem is compounded for international organisations. This is still more the case when, as in the example of the IRPTC, chemical companies may view some data-gathering attempts as early preludes to tougher regulatory moves, or as instruments which might be used for preliminary licensing or blacklisting schemes. At the same time there is a significant kernel of self-interest in the approaches of industry to such activities which points not towards confrontation or avoidance, but rather to a measure of active cooperation. Secondly, environmental definitions of pesticides problems tend to suggest the importance of focusing on questions of use as much as on the criteria for registration. Regulations which make unrealistic assumptions about the ways chemicals are used in practice can be seriously deficient. But here the regulatory difficulties are immense, and, ultimately, unresolvable in democratic societies. In developing countries, the uneven spread of regulatory frameworks is an indication, and reinforcement, of both kinds of gaps: information about the environmental, health and other hazards associated with use of pesticides, and the effective communication of sound guidelines on application practices.

Part III

Part III

7   The Politics of Regulatory Unevenness

Agricultural chemicals bestow similar kinds of benefits and bring in train similar kinds of problems wherever they are used. Insect and other pest populations may be reduced, though possibly only temporarily; agricultural or forestry workers applying them face some occupational risks and the consumers of food commodities may find themselves unknowingly ingesting pesticide residues; there are likely to be some ecological consequences; the species which is the focus of attack may develop resistance to a particular compound, or if it succumbs create room for another pest to flourish. There are several reasons, however, for paying special attention to conditions in developing countries.

Firstly, the ecological setting in many Third World countries is significantly different in many respects from that in the industrialised nations of the temperate zones. The conditions of climate, soils, and agricultural systems may make the transfer of lessons more risky and the consequences of expanded pesticide use less predictable. Compounds like DDT, for example, used effectively in malaria control, tend to be less persistent in the environment; others, such as many fungicides, may require many more applications in order to combat pests. Secondly, though it is easy to over-generalise about a large group of countries that range from the oil-rich to the chronically resource-poor, it is possible to identify certain traits of the economies and political systems of Third World countries that have policy implications in the agrochemicals area. More specifically, economic development goals assume priority over environmental protection objectives. The pesticides dilemma is likely to be essentially one of ensuring adequate supplies, whether by purchase from abroad or local production. Thirdly, as we saw in Chapter 3, the large multinational chemical companies of the western world have increasingly during the 1970s and 1980s turned their sights on developing country markets. And finally, in most developing countries the agricultural and administrative infrastructures required for effective handling of both the costs and benefits of agrochemical dependence are absent or else generally inadequately equipped for the task. The aim of this chapter is to review these issues in the light of the activities of international organisations. A detailed case study of regulatory politics and processes in Malaysia is presented in the chapter following.

PESTS AND PESTICIDES IN DEVELOPING COUNTRIES

A full assessment of the pest and pesticide problems encountered by developing countries is outside the scope of this study.[1] But it can readily be seen that the case for continued or expanded use of these chemicals rests on some impressive foundations. These have to do with the statistics on crop losses to pests in developing countries. Even so, they should be approached with some caution. A number of such estimates have been criticised as unreliable, unrepresentative, or based on dubious assumptions and extrapolations.[2] Agrochemical use is not necessarily the major factor likely to contribute to food productivity in Third World countries; and productivity cannot self-evidently be taken as the root of the food supply problem.

Estimates of crop destruction by pests vary from the specific to the general. A 1981 study calculated that the sugar industry in Tanzania was losing approximately $1.23 million annually because of sugar-cane smut.[3] Losses for 25 crops in India in the 1960s were put at 25 per cent for vegetables, 20 per cent for potatoes, 20 per cent for cotton, and 20 per cent for rice. Reductions in losses through the use of control measures were expected to be of the order of 50 per cent for castor and chillies, 25 per cent for sugar-cane, and 30 per cent for tobacco.[4] The cost of pest damage in Arab countries has been estimated at around $2 billion annually, with losses for particular sectors ranging from 25–72 per cent in the case of vegetables and 23–71 per cent in the case of various field crops.[5] Aggregating these kinds of figures has given estimates of total worldwide damage to agriculture of about $66 billion annually.[6] The US National Academy of Science published a study in 1977 which suggested that a reduction of only 20 per cent in losses resulting from pests attacking major food crops would be required to feed an additional 476 million or more people.[7] Worldwide post-harvest losses alone due to pests have been put at between 10–20 per cent, and estimates for pre- and post-harvest totals are approximately 45 per cent.[8] It bears repeating that the policy implications are not self-evident. Such figures can obviously be put to good use in the case for step-level increases in pesticide applications on major crops in developing countries. But other factors have to be taken into account. Pests can become resistant to chemicals; and the complex repercussions from expanded pesticide use can in some instances exacerbate crop loss problems.

The estimates are nonetheless important in policy terms because of the structures of national economies in many developing countries. One writer, K. H. Buechel, has cited examples such as the damage done to cocoa shrubs in Ghana and Nigeria by capsid bugs and swollen shoot disease, coffee berry disease in East African countries, and losses in coffee plantations in Latin America since the introduction of coffee rust disease. Failure to check the damage caused by pests and disease in such cases 'would not only have ruined the growers and those branches of trade and industry which depend on the crops, it would also have caused the economies of entire countries to collapse'. This, he argued, was because significant fluctuations in the output of cash crops, such as those caused by pests and disease, have marked adverse effects in economies with a high dependence on export sales.[9] The case for increasing agrochemical use in Third World countries cannot rest simply on the alleged benefits in terms of agricultural productivity; over-productivity, if it leads to depressed international markets for commodities, can also have costly implications for developing countries and may bring about difficult structural adjustment problems. This is not to deny the value of greater agricultural productivity and higher crop yields in some cases, such as fruits and vegetables grown for consumption in expanding urban areas. Generally speaking, pesticide use has beneficial effects if it can stabilise crop yields on a year-to-year basis, and in addition if this allows a more effective allocation of resources between the agrochemical and other sectors. There are, of course, various drawbacks associated with pesticide use. Balancing these against the advantages is not an easy task. But as one FAO expert group noted in 1970: 'While deaths from the misuse of pesticides in developing countries will undoubtedly be higher than in developed countries, they still may not be of primary importance to a health ministry which is stretched to capacity in attempting to deal with preventable and major causes of death, e.g. starvation and non-potable water supplies.'[10]

Such hazards from misuse of pesticides in developing countries have been well documented. Deaths resulting from the herbicide paraquat in Papua New Guinea have averaged 100 annually.[11] A wide variety of circumstances govern misuse. A study of problems in Sudan has observed that storage of pesticide containers in the open at the port of arrival can lead to metal deterioration from a combination of humidity and temperature, and that the compounds inside can be affected by rough handling as well as by oxidation and hydrolysis reactions. Lack of care during spraying operations has been described in a WHO study, also of Sudan. Agricultural workers were frequently in direct contact with insecticides, with no adequate protective clothing or nearby source of water; pesticide spillage was common; watching spraying at close quarters was a popular diversion for village boys; and since there was a drift of particles in the wind it was possible that people living in villages between fields could also be affected.[12] The high percentage of cotton field workers and their families living close to sprayed fields has frequently been cited as a factor leading to poisoning incidents in Latin America. Other factors include poor quality control practised by local formulators; inadequate or false labelling, poor storage conditions in retail outlets and contamination resulting from use of containers previously containing other chemicals; the widespread disregard of safe application practices, or the unavailability or high cost of appropriate protective clothing; lack of attention to problems of storage of seeds before planting or of crops after harvest; pesticide over-use by farmers with the objective of meeting local market deadlines or debt repayments; and, finally, the general unenforceability of whatever regulations do exist.

Pesticide residues in foods have also, for these kinds of reasons, been an important issue in some developing countries. We will return to this question later in this chapter. It is one part of a larger class of food standards problems in developing countries precipitated by various kinds of adulteration. Widespread contamination was revealed, for example, in checks by public health officers of soft drinks in different regions in Kenya in the early 1980s.[13]

Use of pesticides under some conditions can be self-defeating. Pest populations are not reduced significantly, or else develop resistance to compounds. In relation to cotton production in Latin America there have been instances of reductions in yields and increases in pest problems resulting from use of pesticides.[14] Similar examples have been described in the cases of cocoa and coffee in African countries and tea in Ceylon. Some forms of damage may in turn be a product of changes in approaches to agricultural development. Rubber diseases in Malaysia in the 1960s and 1970s have been attributed in part to wider use of budded clonal material, developed as a result of breeding and selection for higher yields, which was particularly susceptible to certain diseases.[15] Similar kinds of evidence comes from the public health field, for example that on increased vector resistance to DDT and other chemicals used in malaria control programmes in central America during the 1970s. The spread of monocultural agricultural development schemes has been seized on by many critics as a factor which increases the likelihood of major pest problems because of the elimination of species diversity and balance in those areas.

Relatively few developing countries have in practice paid much attention to some of the more obscure forms of environmental deterioration publicised by critics of pesticide use in western countries. Even so, a shift of attitude was detectable between the early 1970s and the early 1980s. In the meetings which preceded the UN Conference on the Human Environment in 1972 Third World delegations tended to reiterate their conviction that many types of environmental problems were concerns only of the richer nations, a penalty to be paid, perhaps, for over-indulgence in consumerism, economic success, or domination of the world economy. By the early 1980s there was on balance a greater readiness to treat seriously issues such as those presented by toxic chemicals. And pesticide issues in the western mould of the early 1960s do occasionally arise. An Indian study of 1981 noted high levels of organochlorine pesticide residues, particularly of benzene hexachloride, in the organs of certain wild birds such as the crow, pigeon and vulture.[16] Such questions are rarely located high on policy agendas, however.

DEVELOPING COUNTRIES AND THE INTERNATIONAL PESTICIDES ECONOMY

Pesticides are more of an economic development issue. Concerns have accordingly centred on matters such as the high cost of some pesticides, particularly the more specific compounds, short or unpredictable supply, problems of distribution, foreign exchange costs, and the various constraints which in practice set limits to the initiation or success of local manufacturing industries.

Even in the industrialised world, entry to the pesticides industry is not easy. The emphasis on heavy research and development investment costs is a significant deterrent to newcomers. Few developing countries, one western analysis has concluded, have the necessary raw materials and resources to develop an indigenous pesticides industry. Even leaving aside research and development, the design and operation of manufacturing processes can be expensive. Making parathion, for example, involves four separate major stages of production; one of the chemical groups involved in the manufacture of pirimicarb is expensive because it entails a protracted synthesis process from basic raw materials.[17] Hence a major dilemma. Domestic production, if it is embarked on, may mean essentially production only of first-generation kinds of compounds, such as DDT or BHC, so that the advantages of more sophisticated later chemicals are missed and the hazards associated with early compounds accentuated. Or production may have to rest heavily on the costly importation of the more complex chemical compounds used in the manufacturing of some widely used pesticides. In addition, local or regional markets may be inadequate to allow advantage to be taken of economies of scale, a factor which would itself tend to reinforce pressure to concentrate on the production of simpler products. Adequate technical manpower may not be available; indeed the presence of multinational companies may underscore this constraint by draining off local scientific and entrepreneurial expertise. The balance of the economic argument may thus be in the direction of the government of a developing country simply purchasing its pesticide and other chemicals requirements from abroad.

But this kind of conclusion has been generally an unsatisfactory one for developing countries for a combination of political and economic development reasons. There is in fact, now, considerable variety among Third World countries in their orientations to the international pesticide economy. Kenya and Tanzania, for example, have a traditional stake in the economy on the basis of local pyrethrum production. In the 1980s Rwanda embarked on a path aimed at significant expansion of its pyrethrum refining capacity. The project, funded by UN and European aid agencies, had as its rationale the potential of this kind of industry to generate employment and export growth. It was restricted in scope, however, to local processing and refining of the raw materials. Some insecticide manufacturing capacity was considered a long-term rather than a medium-term possibility.[18] This kind of enterprise was thus vulnerable to fluctuations in world markets, price changes, and the strength of competitive substitutes – in this case the highly successful synthetic pyrethroids. The pyrethrum industry in Kenya has for these kinds of reasons experienced periodic difficulties. Though traditionally a large foreign exchange earner, the industry was affected in the 1980s by a combination of low production levels in the mid-1970s, which had coincided with the initial marketing drives of synthetic substitutes in many western countries, followed by higher production levels by farmers' cooperatives which had had the effect of depressing prices and creating unsold stocks.[19] The availability of abundant raw materials for the production of botanical pesticides, then, does not appear in itself to be sufficient to lead to the establishment of viable manufacturing industries.

In order to overcome the foreign exchange costs of chemical imports a number of developing countries have officially encouraged the intermediate step of local formulation of imported active ingredients. With no background of a local pesticides industry, the government of Sudan in the mid-1950s initiated such a programme. One commonly used compound consisted of as much as 97.4 per cent inert and cheap materials such as talc or kaolin. The result was a reduction in local costs of pesticides by up to 50 per cent.[20] This kind of step depends, however, on the availability of formulation ingredients and technical resources. And if not sufficiently flexible local formulating plants can suffer from the obsolescence rate of pesticide active ingredients introduced by western manufacturers. Resources, moreover, may not match the quality control requirements of modern pesticide formulation methods.

The upshot is that few developing countries have much in the way of a pesticide manufacturing industry. Of these some, such as India, reached a level during the 1970s where transition to more sophisticated chemical production and a significant export trade seemed feasible. Locally produced pesticides were then accounting for up to one-third of Indian needs. In the early 1980s, though, there were some indications that production of technical-grade pesticides there had levelled off.[21] One factor was under-utilised formulation capacity; for a time the government even banned the sanctioning of new formulation plants. It is significant, too, that oil wealth in the 1970s did not set producing countries on a path of pesticide industrialisation, since many pesticides rely on inputs from petrochemical industries. Local down-stream petrochemical industries, for example in Arab countries, have in practice tended to be limited in their capacity to service the more complex requirements of a modern pesticides economy. If agricultural development has a high priority, then the best way to minimise costs is to rely on foreign agrochemical expertise and forego the possible advantages of a flourishing local pesticides sector.

Whether production is by local private or public sectors, or primarily by the branches of foreign chemical companies, the crucial pesticides issue is thus one of supply. Attention to the general question of pesticides supply in developing countries grew in the mid-1970s. Estimates during this period indicated that pesticide inventories for most products were depleted because of increased demand resulting from an expansion of areas coming under cultivation and manufacturing interruptions during the energy crisis of 1973–74.[22] The FAO calculated that past under-investment in the pesticides industry had led to demand exceeding worldwide capacity by between 10–30 per cent for some products. Other factors have contributed to supply problems. The rate of increase of use of herbicides on high-yielding varieties of cereals, for example, was often higher than anticipated in developing countries which had begun to turn to these compounds. A related factor was an increase in prices for products derived from some raw materials such as petroleum products and phosphorus. When shortages did occur, moreover, they tended to have greatest impact on developing countries since the allocation systems of the major manufacturers were frequently based on past purchase records – a factor which in turn led to higher spot prices.

REGULATORY CAPABILITIES

The situation had eased later in the decade, but its easing reinforced another set of obstacles to sound pesticide management policies and practices in developing countries. There is a pronounced lack of uniformity of approaches to pesticide regulation. Only during the 1970s did many countries begin to think seriously about regulatory requirements. Enforcement capabilities, moreover, often lagged behind laws and regulations. There were no laws on the subject in Nigeria at the beginning of the decade. A first step was the small one of production of a short guide for farmers on available compounds by the Ministry of Agriculture and Natural Resources and the Entomological Society of Nigeria.[23] Legislation on pesticides was introduced in Fiji for the first time in 1971, following recommendations made by the South Pacific Commission.[24] Where laws exist, their enforcement may be 'non-existent', to quote one account of the Philippines. Two older laws, of 1923 and 1963, on such matters as the labelling of insecticide and fungicide products or the setting of pesticide residues limits for foods, existed on paper only. A proposed new pesticides act of 1972 then fell prey to various mishaps. Martial law was declared, the operating budgets of government departments were scaled down, and a series of natural calamities directed attention towards more urgent policy matters.[25]

Some countries have put substantially more effort into the strengthening of their regulatory capabilities. Control machinery in India has grown out of earlier regulatory and advisory bodies set up to deal with broader issues of plant protection. Comprehensive legislation in this area arose in response to the situation brought about by the Bengal famine of 1943, one of the major causes of which was failure of the rice crop due to brown spot attack.[26] The main legislative instrument in India dealing specifically with pesticide chemicals came into existence in 1968. The regulations drawn up in the period since are extensive. The Central Insecticides Board, set up to advise both central and state governments, is empowered to deal with a large number of pesticides regulatory questions, including the setting of tolerance limits for residues, the minimum intervals between insecticide application and harvest, the details of labelling and packaging, the shelf-life of compounds, and, through a Registration Committee, with all applications from Indian and foreign companies for the registration and marketing of pesticides.

Significant constraints thus affect both the initial design and the subsequent implementation of pesticides regulatory schemes. Tough and enforced rules many deter foreign investors. Idiosyncratic rules may persuade some companies to steer clear of a particular market. Barriers against chemical companies may also in practice deprive some government officials in some countries of their unofficial side-payments for facilitating access; the figure has been put at around 10 per cent of the price of a compound.[27] Thus as developing countries began to devise a variety of regulatory frameworks during the 1970s, so international agency and industry criticism mounted of what has been called 'the problem of extreme stringency'.[28] Some regulations, it was argued, were just too complex ever to be implemented, even with the most favourable assumptions being made about government resources; and putting unenforceable laws on the books could only serve to undermine wider public and corporate confidence in government. Some criticism of schemes for excessively rigorous regulatory arrangements was directed at instruments inspired by procedures in the United States. 'Over-stringent' tended in this context to be a code-word for EPA-derived regulatory goals. FAO's own recommended standards on various aspects of pesticide control in developing countries have been more relaxed. As in the agency's 'model law' for pesticides control they have also been flexible, allowing a wide measure of adaptive variation to meet the requirements of different countries. In the 1980s the tenor of EPA approaches has shifted, though; officials then were more prepared to recognise that in general developing countries should not buy a Cadillac if all they needed was a Volkswagen.[29]

Chemical companies have their own reasons for criticising both the stringency and the variability of regulatory approaches. From the perspective of the pesticide manufacturer, developing countries also suffered if they set too much store on emulating regulatory schemes in the advanced industrialised nations. More specifically, measures which have the consequence of adding to the cost of pesticides to the consumer have been seen as self-defeating. Pesticide prices have traditionally been high in Chile; one factor has been high internal distribution costs, which reflect the relatively small size of the market.[30] Developing countries, the industry tends to argue, should not gratuitously add to such cost factors by interposing high or impenetrable regulatory hurdles between companies and users. In practice, of course, the hurdles may be more apparent than real because of lack of enforcement. In regions where smuggling is a tradition, as in South-east Asia and parts of West Africa, national borders may be more open to the flow of commerce than regulations on paper in national capitals might indicate.

Several factors, then, will determine whether or not a developing country moves far, if at all, along the regulatory path. First, other policy areas often have higher priority. The case of the Philippines was noted earlier. One reason why the regulations of 1963 on pesticide residues in food went largely unenforced was that greater emphasis was placed on regulation of the pharmaceutical trade and other food contaminants. The development of key sectors of the economy – cotton in Egypt, rice or rubber in Malaysia – may be viewed as having such a high priority that questions centring on the health and safety or environmental hazards of pesticides are at best secondary concerns. Further, within the pesticides area itself, limited resources mean that difficult choices have to be made. Deaths have resulted in many countries from faulty application practices or defective storage conditions. In general it has been thought more appropriate to try to develop regulatory thrust in such areas as these, rather than in the questions of pesticides residue levels emphasised in the approaches of many western countries. As in the early approaches to regulation in the United States in the nineteenth century, fraudulent or adulterated pesticide products also commonly have higher priority, and for reasons of their efficacy rather than their safety.

Secondly, patterns of policy-making vary. In some developing countries, particularly those with growing industrial and modernising agricultural sectors, pressures from middle-class city dwellers may force greater attention to be paid to residues or health hazards issues. Political systems also differ in the degree to which in practice they tolerate policy overtures from the private sector, or, indeed, in the degree to which industry is organised locally and able to present a case to government. The interplay of these various forces in the context of regulatory developments in one country, Malaysia, is studied in the next chapter.

Thirdly, the resources available for constructing effective regulatory structures are rarely present. The pesticides residues committee of the Codex system has argued that national infrastructures in African states require significant strengthening if knowledge about pesticide residues and their hazards is to be used.[31] Land tenure systems erect different kinds of obstacles. A multiplicity of small-holdings remote from national or regional administrative centres, as in the Philippines, may in practice make the work of agricultural extension officers impossible. But equally, a small number of very large estates may be immune to regulatory attempts because of the power of landowners. Divisions of responsibility between state and national levels of government compound these difficulties in some countries. Agriculture generally, and assessments of pesticide requirements more particularly, are in India the responsibility of the states. The main plant protection and pesticide regulatory structures, however, are at the federal level. Similar kinds of problems have been encountered in Malaysia, where the central government has in recent years been increasingly critical of administrative inefficiencies and corruption at local and state levels, where some of the main agricultural policy responsibilities lie. Plant protection capabilities generally take a long time to emerge. In the early 1950s only 14 out of 38 British overseas territories had even one entomologist in their departments of agriculture.[32] After three decades or so of political change in an unfavourable economic climate it is not surprising to find the pesticides field still overwhelmingly a western one. Some scientific and technical work is indeed carried out in Third World countries, for example at the Industrial Toxicology Research Centre in India, but the vast bulk of the effort in the area, as well as the productive capacity, lies in the advanced industrialised nations.

THE ROLE OF INTERNATIONAL AGENCIES

International organisations tend to form a more salient part of the external political environment of developing countries than they usually do for western states. They are viewed variously as forums for publicising views or issues, as central bases for establishing contacts with other governments, and as actors with a capacity to channel development funds into Third World countries. The operating goals of several agencies of the UN system intersect with those of developing countries at several points. In relation to pesticides we can look briefly at two: the role of several agencies and programmes in promoting the growth of industrial capacities; and in assisting the emergence of appropriate regulatory frameworks.

The first of these has followed from consideration by international agencies of the pesticide supply problems facing developing countries, particularly those which in some sectors reached crisis proportions in the aftermath of the 1973–74 energy price rises and disruptions. The economic development logic is that local formulation of pesticides saves foreign exchange and can lead to lower domestic prices while providing employment; it may also be a stepping-stone to the establishment of more fully-fledged industries manufacturing active ingredients. Most activity by the United Nations Industrial Development Organisation in this area has been at the pre-investment phase of pesticide development projects. Those supported have included the promotion of local pyrethrum industries, as in Rwanda, the setting up of pesticide formulation plants, and technical assistance with respect to the establishment of production plants.[33] The World Bank, by contrast, has tended to restrict its agrochemical interest to fertiliser plant development.

Development aspects of the various component parts of the international regulatory system have assumed growing importance since the mid-1960s. The increasing participation of delegates from Third World countries was greeted with approval by the Codex Commission at its 1981 meetings.[34] However, the weak and largely ineffective administrative and control infrastructures of many developing countries in practice had the effect of precluding them from any real participation in such debates. A number of attempts to break this pattern were made in the 1970s. Expanded imports by developing countries of toxic chemicals generally set the groundwork for such efforts. In the 1977 sessions of the Codex pesticides residues committee (the CCPR) Egypt reviewed a series of unfortunate experiences that developing countries had had with pesticides. These were attributed in part to misleading advice about the properties of chemical compounds provided by some companies. The delegation argued that there should be more supervision of pesticides entering international trade by the governments of the manufacturing countries.[35]

The airing of these kinds of complaints led to the formation of an *ad hoc* working group of the CCPR, chaired by Professor W. F. Almeida of Brazil. In its report the group stressed that many developing countries did not possess adequate facilities to undertake pre-registration trials in relation to pesticides and formulations, toxicological testing, pesticide residue analysis, or generation of appropriate data on the intake of pesticide residues and on the impact of pesticide use on the environment. In making recommendations on maximum residue limits, the report argued, consideration should also be given to the economic impact on the international trade of developing countries. The FAO and WHO in particular were urged to intensify their assistance to these countries. More specifically, the group proposed that national inter-departmental committees on pesticide residues were urgently needed; that there should be steps to ensure that pesticides were registered on the basis of appropriate data; that control should be exercised over the import, sale, distribution and use of pesticides; and that national Codex committees should be established to act as effective contact points in an international pesticides residues regulatory network.[36] The group continued to operate as a forum for debate on pesticides residues problems in developing countries. Special emphasis was put on the promotion of regional cooperation, for example in Latin America and the Caribbean, on such matters as registration, labelling, and education and training.

As a means of bringing toxic chemicals issues into greater international prominence, however, forums such as the Codex machinery were necessarily limited. Its character was viewed by some as compromised because of the active presence of industry representatives, either on member-state delegations or as observers. Delegates from western countries, moreover, were not always prepared to treat developing country concerns as central to their agendas. During the later 1970s and 1980s several Third World countries accordingly looked to better-known forums, such as the Governing Council meetings of UNEP, as a way of drawing wider international attention to pesticides and toxic chemicals issues of concern to them. The requirements of developing countries were already by then, as we have seen, a crucial part of the rationale for the toxic chemical registry (IRPTC), even though in practice it tended to be organisations in western countries that made more use of it. Group of 77 pressure nonetheless reinforced the point that the inventory should be regarded as particularly useful to developing countries since many could not set up research facilities of their own and had to rely instead on information supplied by manufacturers. Several countries – Indonesia, Mexico, Nigeria, Sri Lanka and Sudan – were among those in the early 1980s urging the speedy production of a list of priority chemicals.[37] Malaysia was among those countries which made use of Governing Council membership in order to call for greater funding from international agencies and programmes to aid the creation of more effective pesticides and chemicals regulatory schemes.

Despite the emergence of other organisations, periodic budgetary and personnel cutbacks, and political sniping from western countries, FAO has remained at the centre of the international pesticides regulatory system. More specifically, attempts by expert groups in the 1960s to design a basic pesticides control legislative package as a guide for developing countries have had a lasting impact. The 'model scheme' that resulted was based on a recognition that conditions in wet or dry tropical countries were different from those in which pesticide chemicals were originally developed, produced and tested. Further, and despite a leading role taken in FAO pesticides activities by British experts and seconded officials, the agency has tended to argue against adoption of any of the various voluntary schemes for registration or licensing of pesticides. Behind this approach was a dual objective of both contributing to individual developing country capabilities, while at the same time enhancing the degree of uniformity to be found in the international system. It would 'appreciably reduce costs and increase the efficiency of introducing a new chemical if some uniformity in official demands for information on the mode of behaviour of pesticides in any part of the world could be established.' Since countries varied in their capabilities as well as their objectives and requirements, the model was designed to have maximum scope within these limits for adaptation to national conditions. So 'the simplest possible scheme to achieve useful results' was defined and elaborated until a 'complex scheme suitable for a highly developed country' was arrived at. 'It should thus be possible for a country to enter the scheme at a point related to its economic resources and, as these expand, for the scheme to be expanded accordingly.'[38] Related to this approach has been that of WHO in devising classification schemes of pesticides by degree of hazard.[39]

AGRICULTURAL MODERNISATION AND INTEGRATED CONTROL

There are many intervening variables between calculations of food and other crop needs for growing populations on the one hand, and decisions on pesticide use and pest management strategies on the other. They include choice of overall agricultural development strategies by governments, patterns of land use and the prevalence of subsistence agriculture, the availability to farmers of capital and other inputs, and the state of evolution and coverage of government agricultural extension services. Subsistence farms are those that produce just enough for basic family requirements, including agricultural inputs such as seeds, fertiliser, manures, animal feeds and elementary equipment. Farming at subsistence level remains the norm in most developing countries; about 70 per cent of farmers produce at subsistence levels in Mexico, the impact of 'Green Revolution' seed and agricultural technology notwithstanding.[40] There are wider implications for national economies, in that limited economic interactions can occur between agricultural and other sectors; and for the use of agrochemicals, and for other aspects of modern agricultural practices generally, since resources for investment in such areas are unlikely to be present. An array of different methods of pest control have traditionally been practised. The most systematic use of traditional methods was developed in China. Even so, for farming at anything above subsistence levels the use of manual labour – checking entire fields to remove infested plants, examining plants individually to remove insect eggs, and so on – cannot be regarded as an adequate substitute for the deployment of chemical control strategies.[41]

There is room for considerable argument about the broader ecological consequences of different approaches to agricultural production in developing countries. The criterion here is not so much environmental protection, as these issues have tended to be presented in debates in Britain and other western countries on the impact of modern farming systems, but rather agricultural productivity. Viewed from one perspective, some agricultural development strategies necessarily entail increased reliance on pesticides, and in so doing reduce the area of choice within which decisions on pest management strategies can realistically be made. Some critics have argued that this tends to be the consequence of recent patterns of introduction of new crop strains: 'Better varieties selected for yield and not resistance, improved water management, richer fertilizers, larger monocultures, new cropping conditions creating favourable microenvironments, etc., etc., have favoured the development of pests where there were no pests before.'[42] New plant diseases and increased insect and other pest problems, that is, may be directly attributable to the inherent instability of the biologically simplified systems associated with agricultural modernisation processes in many developing countries.[43] On the other hand, it can be argued that increases in agricultural productivity in Third World countries require significant chemical inputs, and that these have minimal ecological disruptive effects compared with those associated with subsistence agriculture. One writer has criticised 'the propagation of the idea that an intensification of agriculture could have ecological consequences threatening the biological balance in tropical and subtropical regions. With some exceptions those who think along these lines are possessed by an environmental ideology which refuses to be influenced by facts. It is a fact, for example, that some of the disastrous environmental developments that have occurred in recent decades (in Africa, for instance) have resulted from extensive, as opposed to intensive, soil utilisation.'[44]

Wider agreement is possible on the principle, if not always on the meaning, of integrated pest management strategies. Use of pesticides cannot be eliminated, because of the crop losses and periodic disasters that would accompany their abandonment. The question therefore revolves around possible ways of ensuring effective use: of promoting productivity while minimising the health, ecological and other costs associated in particular with some of the organochlorine insecticide compounds. In theory, integrated controls can overcome the problems of reliance on chemical methods as the sole or primary method of attack: the development of insect resistance, the possibility of secondary outbreaks of pests after application, the problems of toxic residues, effects on livestock or economic fish species, as well as hazards for farmers, agricultural workers, and other users. Opting for control strategies that blend, in combinations appropriate to local circumstances, use of chemical, biological, cultural and other methods has considerable merit. There are obstacles, however, both of principle and practice. Firstly, the meaning of integrated control tends to be imprecise. The phrase can be used to defend and justify almost any mixture of pest control strategies. Definitions by environmentalist critics tend to be attacked within the industry as little more than anti-chemicals propaganda. Secondly, the practical and policy constraints are significant. Apart from the immediate evidence of their efficacy, the great virtue of agrochemical strategies is ease of implementation; planning for integrated controls consumes time and other resources and is intrinsically more complex. Thirdly, in most developing countries there is in practice a marked imbalance between the forces making for greater reliance on chemical methods on the one hand, and for integrated approaches on the other. The latter also require major allocations of technical and administrative resources into training and educational programmes and agricultural extension services by governments, and lack the employment effects of local pesticide production or formulation.

In the following chapter we examine the approaches to pesticide regulation in one country. Developing countries are characterised by considerable diversity. None is 'typical'. Similar kinds of regulatory dilemmas and constraints are encountered, however, in many different national contexts. Orientations towards foreign chemical companies, and responses to a wide variety of international organisations, represent fundamental choices about the external environment. The room for independent manoeuvre may in practice be significantly restricted. As a newly industrialising country, Malaysia's approach has tended to be more open to the activities of multinational enterprises, and the relevant parts of the government machinery more receptive to international agency inputs. The making of pesticides policy, however, has been set in a context of extensive public and media debate and group activity.

8 Regulatory Politics in Malaysia

Agricultural modernisation in Malaysia has entailed many changes. A growing dependence on more sophisticated agrochemicals has been one consequence. The more general strategies, as well as some of the more detailed policy implications, have been linked to a variety of international agencies. In the process Malaysia, and the South-east Asian region generally, has come to occupy an increasingly important place in the outlooks of leading western and Japanese chemical companies. Issues of pesticide use in agriculture became during the 1970s an important theme in criticism by a variety of domestic environmental and consumers' pressure groups of official economic development plans. The cause of the Malaysian environment, moreover, was taken up by external groups in western countries. The evolution of the government's policies in relation to pesticide regulation in part reflected the character of broader policy processes in Malaysia.[1] Emphasis is placed in this chapter on the interplay between the various domestic and external actors attempting to influence the main lines of development of pesticides regulation: the chemical companies themselves, both Malaysia and foreign, international agencies, and the more significant pressure groups inside the country. In examining the policy process the main focus of attention will be the construction and gradual implementation of the Pesticides Act of 1974.[2]

AGRICULTURAL DEVELOPMENT IN MALAYSIA

During the 1970s Malaysia's main crops were still the traditional ones of natural rubber and palm oil. In 1974 the country produced one-third of the world's palm oil. This together with rubber exports continued to form the chief export basis of Malaysian agricultural development.[3] But Malaysia is also fortunate in having a climate and resource base that has facilitated greater diversity in agriculture. Other sectors have traditionally included rice, particularly in the *padi* areas of the north-west of the Malayan peninsula; coffee and tea, particularly in the more temperate climatic conditions of upland areas such as the Cameron Highlands; vegetables and fruits, which have been of growing importance in relation to areas of urban development; and coconuts, tobacco and pepper.

By the early 1970s two sets of factors were bringing about fundamental change in this picture. The first was world economic recession after 1973–74, a condition which affected Malaysia as a country with important trading links with western nations. Inflation and recession in the OECD countries, or *stagflasi*, were significant background factors for any assessments of Malaysian agricultural development requirements and planning during the 1970s. Though high prices were maintained for palm oil, in general the economic restraints on Malaysia's traditional trading partners in the west led to a weakening of demand for its agricultural raw materials and a decline in export prices for most.[4] Similar problems being encountered in other export sectors led to a growing assertiveness and search for alternative arrangements on the part of the Malaysian government during the later 1970s, and encouragement to 'look east' in the early 1980s.

A second set of factors was already under way by the time the impact of world recession began to be felt. This was change in the underlying structure of the Malaysian agricultural economy. Several closely related aspects can be noted. First, rice was targeted with a goal of self-sufficiency. Already in the early 1970s around 85 per cent of rice consumed was grown in the country. The process entailed sometimes problematic and controversial changes in the traditional rice areas of the country, and was spearheaded by a large and ambitious modernisation scheme, the Muda programme in Kedah in the far north-west of peninsular Malaysia. This vast irrigation scheme was Malaysia's largest agricultural development project in the 1970s, and had as one central goal the widespread introduction to much of the *padi* land in Kedah of double cropping. A consequence was disruption of the traditional rice economy, giving rise to many of the pest control and pesticide related problems that will be taken up later in this chapter, including the poisoning of fish traditionally used by farmers as sources of protein and income, changes in the pest situation and a new dependence on heavier applications of chemicals, and incidents involving hazards to health for farmers in the area. This was related to a broader strategy of diversification of the agricultural economy away from over-reliance on the traditional export of such commodities as rubber and palm oil. Part of the basic rationale was growing population pressure and the limited area of land for new agricultural expansion. Malaysia's population in the 1980 census was 13.4 million.[5] Areas were available for expanded agricultural production in the future, but given the diversity of climatic, soil, and other conditions the choice of crop was seen to be clearly a crucial one. Expansion, in other words, implied some measure of diversification. It was also a means of protection against fluctuations in world market conditions for the traditional export commodities. Vegetables for urban markets, sorghum, maize, groundnuts and other annual crops thus appeared as attractive options for future development. This goal, too, had its implications for pest management, pesticide needs and pesticide control requirements if such development was not to be accompanied by unacceptable levels of crop losses or serious environmental deterioration.

While protection of the environment has been an important goal, it has necessarily remained secondary to that of economic development. The rubber industry is a major polluter, one of the largest sources of organic pollution of water in Malaysia along with palm oil and sewage. In 1977 the total load of the biological oxygen demand (BOD) discharged into Malaysian watercourses by the rubber industry was estimated at 227 tonnes per day.[6] But the industry was clearly vital. It was accepted by government departments, including those responsible for environmental protection, that operations must not be limited in such a way as to add significantly to the country's economic problems in a recessionary world economy. In this context pressures from environmentalist critics, whether Malaysian or external, could either be dismissed as marginal or irrelevant, or else deflected with the rebuke that priorities had to be ranked more responsibly. Nevertheless, weight was increasingly attached to the broad span of environmental problems being encountered during the 1970s. Demands for clean air and water had to be taken seriously, one newspaper argued in 1980; these were 'too often dismissed as the ravings of liberal do-gooders'.[7]

By the late 1970s the environmental and health hazards posed by pesticides had become a major ingredient in this larger debate. Use of chemicals to control pests attacking food and other crops, however, is by no means a new phenomenon in Malaysia. It was in the 1950s that resort to chemical control methods underwent a major expansion, parallel with developments in other countries and with greater emphasis on the research, development and marketing of new compounds by western companies. Before then, use of pesticides was localised and for the most part did not present difficulties. During the colonial period most work on questions of pest management was done in relation to the main plantation crops of natural rubber and palm oil. Indeed, expansion of the Department of Agriculture, founded in 1905 with a staff of three, paralleled expansions of rubber production in the early decades of the century. Discussion of pest problems was an inherent feature of the colonial agricultural economy. Recommendation of a diluted emulsion of phenyl as a spray against scales and mealy bugs on coffee was recorded as early as 1891.[8] This was combined with early experiments with biological control methods, as in the introduction of crows from Ceylon in 1903 for the control of coffee caterpillars.[9] The magnitude of the problems facing the authorities produced a generation of amateur entomologists and pesticide chemists. In *Derris elliptica*, or tuba root, the area had a substance well known historically for its insecticidal properties. Sold in bundles in most markets, it was a cheap and effective control agent used extensively by the Chinese in their vegetable gardens. There was considerable potential, one enthusiast argued in 1912, for it to be developed into a valuable export business for use in English orchards against the codling moth and gooseberry maggot. Several related poisonous plants were traditionally used as a poison for catching fish.[10] Greatly expanded use of chemical pesticides came only after World War II with the appearance of new insecticides and growing recognition by farmers and agricultural authorities of the value of already existing ones. In the 1950s some of these were either banned or restricted for general use in the Federation on such grounds as high mammalian toxicity. A number of field tests and research carried out during this period, particularly with respect to rice, added to continuing work on the area's major non-food sectors, notably natural rubber and palm oil.[11]

Criticism of over-dependence on chemical pest control methods emerged during the early 1960s. The main thrust of the attack was not on the more immediate dangers, but rather on the build-up of resistance on the part of pest populations as a result of exposure to pesticides, and the imbalances brought about in agricultural and other ecosystems by such uses. Malaya, the authors of one critical paper noted, was relatively free of accidental acute pesticide toxicity to man, though they added that deaths of cattle and game were quite common, as well as disturbance of wildlife on a local basis.[12] Towards the end of the decade problems were being encountered on a far larger scale both in rural areas and in the cities. These were magnified under the impact of the agricultural modernisation plans, particularly with respect to rice, implemented during the 1970s. At the most simple level problems arose because of the accelerating food and other crop needs of an expanding population, confined as it was to a relatively small area with restricted and finite possibilities for the opening up of new agricultural land. Without the use of pesticides, one specialist argued in 1982, some farmers would lose 70 per cent of their crop.[13] In part this was because expanded demand, particularly from growing city populations in the Kuala Lumpur area, was forcing up production of some crops in areas unsuitable for reliable yields. During the 1970s insect pests set a major limiting factor in production in both highland and lowland areas. Without heavy use of chemical control methods, production in some areas would not have been possible. Farmers might have to spray crops two or three times a week; and the need to spray with increased frequency constituted an economic limiting factor by making such farming unprofitable. *Sawi* was a good example of a vegetable widely used but particularly vulnerable. In one investigation in the late 1970s, carried out by the MARDI (Malaysian Agricultural Research and Development Institute) research station in Serdang, seedlings were completely destroyed by pests before maturity when no insecticide was applied.[14]

The basic rationale for deepening reliance on chemical pesticides was thus that agriculture could not otherwise meet the demands of the Malaysian population. This fostered complaints from farmers about the high cost of some products, particularly those needed for high frequency applications. In this economic milieu, incentives to universal quality control were diminished. A survey carried out in 1980 by the Malaysian Agricultural Chemicals Association (MACA), the main manufacturers' grouping, seized on the problem of adulteration as one highly detrimental to the interests of responsible pesticide manufacturers and formulators. In some instances, it was claimed, products might be either only mildly effectual or else totally ineffectual. The manufacture of imitation weedkiller was a thriving business in Johore, with paraquat being widely used as an ingredient in such products because of its ready availability. 'Due to the inadequacies of the law,' MACA's chairman complained, 'adulteration is becoming more rampant and widespread.'[15] As many as 12 per cent of smallholders, 11 per cent of the smaller estates, and 18 per cent of the larger estates were being affected through the marketing of adulterated herbicides and the failure of the authorities to halt the trade.

While manufacturers and formulators in Malaysia had an evident self-interest in bringing about a tighter regulatory system to check sales of cheap and adulterated products, they could also appeal to the broader public interest. Consumers' interests were poorly served by mislabelling and the lax storage and handling practices of retailers. In one case in 1981 the cooking oil used to prepare lunch for ten people in Sungai Besar was later found to be contaminated with a pesticide; three of the people died. Here, though, the Minister of Health maintained, following an investigation, the problem was due rather to bad storage in households, as no traces were found of pesticides in samples of the cooking oil taken from shops in the area afterwards.[16] The incidence of poisoning cases was difficult to monitor because of lack of appropriate control and record-keeping by health authorities. It was often difficult also, as in the Sungai Besar incident, to identify cause and effect in the cases that did arise. Information on pesticide poisoning was scanty, officials pointed out, but indicated an incidence on average of 72 cases a year in the period of 1968–74, and an average of an additional 52 cases of arsenical poisoning over the same period. Epidemics of accidental poisoning were attributable frequently to pesticide contamination of food. In one incident in Sarawak, for example, 120 people became sick following endosulfan poisoning; and five members of an Iban family died after eating rice contaminated with paraquat.[17] While lack of effective government regulation of the market in pesticide products was clearly at fault in at least some of these cases, enforcement requirements clearly outstripped administrative capacities.

Farmers were particularly at risk in this kind of situation, even where more careful controls were enforced on the kinds of products being used and on the conditions of their use. Incidents involving a death and 31 hospitalisation cases in the Muda scheme were attributed by officials of the Malaysian Agricultural Development Authority (MADA) to the fact that the victims had not followed directions for using pesticides. Officials emphasised that educational programmes had been carried out through the distribution to farmers of elementary rules and precautionary guidelines in relation to pesticides use, dealing for example with the use of masks and gloves, refraining from eating and smoking, washing hands, not standing near areas being sprayed, and boiling clothes following applications.[18] A survey carried out by one environmental group, however, suggested that 71 per cent of farmers were ignorant of the toxicity of pesticides, and that as many as 19 per cent were unaware of the fact that pesticides were dangerous.[19] A number of contributory factors were identified in accounts of hazards being met in this and other schemes. Even adequately labelled products could be misused if a farmer was unable to read instructions, even assuming inclination and a willingness to exercise patience in correct use. Unsafe practices in application continued: the use of backpack equipment by farmers clad only in t-shirt, shorts and slippers; or use only of a handkerchief or towel over the mouth as protection against inhalation when using powder sprayers and fogging machines. Agriculture officials for their part expressed some frustration: 'Our extension agents visit the farmers and demonstrate the proper techniques, but the farmers have short-term vision. They think that their present methods are more lucrative.'[20]

Since without pesticide use, production of some crops, particularly vegetables, was likely to be severely curtailed, residues left in food for the urban consumer became a significant issue. Lack of monitoring studies on residue levels was noted by officials as a gap in the government's regulatory system in 1974.[21] Traditionally it had been accepted that because of the difficulty and cost involved in detecting residues reliance would have to be placed instead on farmers themselves, and particularly on their observing stipulated time intervals between spraying and harvesting. But insect resistance to pesticides meant increasingly that much more of a product might have to be applied. Cases were reported in which 100 units of a compound were being required in the late 1970s for crops where 10 units would have sufficed in the 1950s, a practice which inevitably increased the risk to the consumer from pesticide residues in foods.[22] Apart from more effective farmer education or a fully-fledged monitoring system, a third policy option in the meanwhile was simply consumer education. Since laws to enforce residue limits on crops or food were not fully implemented, one researcher pointed out in 1980, consumers were 'always at risk when buying such crops'. They should therefore tolerate a little damage or blemishes on vegetables and properly clean them, and also remember that cooking helped to reduce pesticide residue levels.[23]

The argument that unless used with great care and discrimination pesticides could in the long run be inefficacious for ecological reasons had been developed in Malaysia in the 1960s by critics sympathetic to the anti-chemical case then gathering force in the United States and other western countries. Insects developed resistance; the natural predators of pests could be destroyed; and resulting ecological imbalances could produce fresh outbreaks of new pests. The weakness of this line of reasoning was that of convincingly demonstrating cause and effect. But impressive evidence could be presented, even if it was necessarily often of an isolated or anecdotal kind.[24] That problems of insect resistance or the destruction of natural pest predators or parasites were a product in part of pesticide misuse came to be increasingly recognised during the 1970s by agricultural officials and scientists in Malaysia. Use of insecticides since the 1950s was blamed at a major 1982 plant protection conference in Kuala Lumpur for the serious resistance problems being encountered in the Cameron Highlands; and one MARDI scientist in 1979 identified the liberal use of pesticides as a major cause of the sharp increase in rice-crop diseases.[25] Fish kills in *padi* areas focused public as well as scientific attention on this issue. Traditionally an important part of integrated *padi* development associated with rice growing and related irrigation networks, fish provided farmers with additional income from sales as well as a valuable protein source, especially in low-lying coastal areas in Northern Krian and Province Wellesley. Here fish provided up to 35 per cent of the income of farmers and constituted their main daily source of protein.[26] With the beginnings of large-scale modernisation and intensification projects in the 1960s, and particularly with double-cropping, the use of chemicals became widespread as more intractable pest and disease problems were encountered. The appearance of disease in various species of *padi* fish, referred to initially simply as *wabak kudis* by farmers and identified later as hæmorrhaging septicæmia, was traced in government investigations to the use of pesticides, though this was cited as only one of the factors involved.[27] Research carried out in the early 1970s suggested that the kinds of insecticides being used, thiodan and BHC, were likely to have these kinds of consequences. These two compounds were then the most widely used insecticides against stem borers in the Krian district. The first in particular was very toxic, one study noted, 'and it is doubtful whether it could be used effectively at a level which did not affect the fish in the field to which it was applied'. This presented a dilemma in an acute form. Farmers were 'faced with the question of whether to opt for a relatively pest-free paddy by using insecticides or to have fish in their fields by not using insecticides on their crops.'[28]

THE SOURCES OF REGULATORY CHANGE

In what kinds of ways did these problems give rise to demands and pressures on the Malaysian political system, and how were these handled? More particularly, how were the multiple sources of potential influence over the making of government policy, from domestic and external actors and from the variety of government and other organisations involved, dealt with in the policy process? There was a broad measure of agreement on the part of experts and the less well informed, both those with axes to grind and those without, that the questions here were indeed important ones affecting Malaysia's route towards modernisation and industrial and agricultural development.

At least three broad sets of actors outside the governmental system need to be considered. First, demands for tighter regulation arose from within the pesticide manufacturing and formulating sector, as smuggling within the South-east Asia region and the rise of markets in Malaysia for cheap pesticides made illicitly together constituted a threat to profit margins for locally-based companies. Secondly, agricultural officials of the government were in close and regular contact with the main international agencies with responsibilities in the pesticides area. This was a less publicised influence over government policy, but one of considerable importance when legislation was being framed in the period 1972–74 and implemented during the rest of the decade. And thirdly, various groups in Malaysia took up the issues involved in extended pesticide use. The grounds were varied, but the most vociferous grouping here was the broadly environmentalist one, itself a loose amalgam of different perspectives.

The companies had to try to avoid backing the government into a situation in which over-stringency in regulations relating to pesticide registration and marketing would be a likely consequence, while at the same time ensuring that sufficient regulatory controls over the market emerged to allow them to stay in business against competition from less scrupulous manufacturers more concerned with short-term profitability. A mix of indigenous and foreign-based companies shapes the Malaysian pesticide economy. Many of the major multinational chemical companies had established a stake in Malaysia by the middle or late 1970s. Production plants were being operated then by Bayer, Burroughs Wellcome, ICI, Monsanto, Nihon Nohyaku, Shell, and Takeda; and there was also participation by Boots, Ciba-Geigy, Dow, Fisons, Hoechst, and Rhone-Poulenc.[29] By the time the government's Pesticides Board completed its registration procedure in 1981, a total of 113 companies were listed as manufacturers or formulators of pesticide products.[30] Malaysia, in other words, was a focal point of interest in the South-east Asian region on the part of world chemical companies generally during the 1970s, sharing as it did many of the desirable attributes of agricultural development and modernisation schemes, access to foreign aid and international agency assistance, an infrastructure of farmer education, and a relatively buoyant economy.

In general the pesticides sector of the Malaysian economy was a foreign one simply by virtue of the complexity and sophistication of the product. Most pesticides in Malaysia are imported, or else imported as active ingredients and then formulated inside the country. In 1974–75 around 135 active ingredient chemicals were being sold in Malaysia, though these appeared on the market in a much larger number of formulations and trade names.[31] Protection of this market against the twin threats of government over-regulation and illicit trading was thus the main thrust of company representations to the agricultural authorities. Black markets and falsely labelled products were losing established manufacturers money. As it stood in 1980, the companies' main association stated, the law could not fully protect the pesticides market. A number of proposals were made by MACA: repeal of the Trade Description Act, and reinforcement of the 1950 Merchandise Trade Marks Ordinance with harsher penalties. It was the sheer difficulty of adequately monitoring the situation that called for more determined government action, particularly since adulterated pesticides were being sold to remote smallholdings. The nation's agricultural base could be sabotaged, MACA insisted, if this was allowed to continue unchecked.

Yet it was clearly against company interests for this kind of government action to become the thin end of a wedge leading to more comprehensive and stringent controls over all aspects of the pesticide economy in the country. The association formally expressed in 1980 its full support for government moves to implement the 1974 Pesticides Act, but added that it would be 'failing in its watchdog role if it does not remind the authorities that there will tend to be fewer [pesticide] registrations if the process is too costly or too cumbersome'.[32] Thus the criticism that emerged on the part of companies as the government began in October 1976 to implement procedures for registering all pesticides marketed in Malaysia was that this contained the danger of excessive requirements for information and a potential for too stringent regulation. The official gazetting of the rules for registration did follow consultation between the government and MACA, as well as other bodies,[33] but many companies thought this practice should be extended and regularised. A six-point plan prepared by the association in 1981 called for the setting up by the Pesticides Board of a consultative body with three representatives each from the Board and from MACA, designed to replace the existing practice of *ad hoc* consultation. This was intended in part as a device to ensure that information being called for in registration procedures would not be so demanding as to constrain profitability significantly. The Pesticides Board was also urged to involve itself directly in eradicating the adulteration problem.[34]

A second source of influence, sometimes in conflict with the approaches taken by companies, was the network of international agencies, particularly those of the United Nations system, and the often closely connected links between these and technical experts and organisations in western countries. For Malaysia in the late 1960s and early and middle 1970s, Britain continued to be the more significant of the western countries carrying out these kinds of functions. External evaluations of Malaysian agricultural development requirements generally had been appearing regularly since the early 1960s. These tended to dwell on Malaysia's needs for institutional expansion and technical education and agricultural extension. The significance of these kinds of activities for the shaping of evolving official policies is threefold. Firstly, they contributed to a growing framework within which the foreign graduate training of pesticides officials in Kuala Lumpur took place; secondly, they brought technical assistance for the design and implementation of plant protection, agricultural extension, pesticides registration and other programmes; and, thirdly, but not least, they gave exposure to the kinds of thinking about pesticides laws and policies that had been emerging in various international settings since the early 1960s. It was from this source that there emerged in Malaysia in the early 1970s the detailed inspiration for the nuts and bolts of pesticide legislation and regulations that were fitted into place subsequently, primarily through the vehicle of the Pesticides Act of 1974. Two reports helped lead the way. The first was prepared in 1970 by an official of the Ministry of Agriculture, Fisheries and Food in Britain who also served for a time as chairman of one of FAO's key technical committees in the pesticides regulation field. This report dealt with Malaysian requirements with respect to pesticides registration and approval. Its author later returned to Kuala Lumpur on assignment in the mid-1970s for eighteen months following passage of the 1974 Pesticides Act.[35] A second was prepared for FAO in 1972, also by an official of the ministry in Britain with extensive international agency experience. This recommended amongst other things that 'control of the manufacture, importation, formulation, storage, transport, supply, sale and use of pesticides should be introduced by way of effective legislation as soon as possible'.[36] This should rely mainly on a licensing scheme, and primary responsibility for the control of pesticides should be given to a special section of the Crop Protection Branch of the Ministry of Agriculture in collaboration with designated colleagues in the Ministry of Health. A variety of other detailed recommendations were listed on registration and licensing, cooperation between government and industry, sale and labelling, research and so on.

This kind of interaction became more regularised during the decade as Malaysian officials for the first time took up places on FAO and other international pesticides regulatory technical committees and attended the growing number of specialised conferences and consultative exercises of the period. Indeed, the government emphasised in 1981 that the registration exercise then nearing completion had been based on communications with other national bodies and international organisations such as FAO, WHO and the Council of Europe.[37]

A third source of demands for change came from the consumers of agricultural produce and the environmental and consumer groups claiming to represent them. While consumers, storekeepers, small farmers, environmentalists and others had to some extent different interests and approaches, one common threat was a sense of unease, bordering on acute anxiety at times in the middle and later 1970s, about the state of the pesticides world. The complexity of the issues involved, and the multiplicity of organisations which seemed to have some stake in the matter, served to enhance this unease. 'The public is equally doubtful of the claims of producers and distributors of agricultural chemicals about the efficacy or harmlessness of their products because of vested interests,' as one commentator put it in 1981.[38] Newspapers were themselves active in publicising various aspects of the pesticides question, and gave considerable attention during the second half of the 1970s to the eminently newsworthy calamities involving death, severe illness, fish poisoning, wildlife disruptions and adulteration. While the early initiative was taken by a small number of environmental groups, which took up pesticides issues as an offshoot of the interest in environmental issues that began to attract Malaysians in the early 1970s, the publicity surrounding the question produced a two-way relationship in which the news media could also be considered influential participants in the domestic political process. Interest in environmental issues generally, indeed, constituted an important background to debate on pesticides during this period, particularly where the questions intertwined, as with water pollution or food quality. A rash of incidents involving foreign objects found in soft drinks and other food items, for example, tied in well with other current fears of urban consumers concerning pesticide residues in vegetables from local markets.

The groups that pressed pesticides questions with particular vigour tended to be creations of the 1970s. Older and more established groups tended to be less active. The Malayan Nature Society, for example, had been reconstituted after the end of Japanese occupation and, except for sporadic discussions in the 1960s of pesticides and other questions, tended for the most part to interest itself in more traditional questions of flora and fauna in the country – though there was inevitably some overlap of personnel, concerns and membership with the newer groups of the following decade. Two of these deserve particular attention. They are the local Malaysian group attached to the wider international, though predominantly western, Friends of the Earth network, or Sahabat Alam Malaysia (SAM); and the Environmental Protection Society of Malaysia (EPSM).

The EPSM can in the longer run be regarded as the more influential, though the other grouping attracted for a time considerably more publicity on the pesticides question. Several looser environmentalist groups that had emerged in Malaysia in direct response to western and United Nations developments, notably the Stockholm conference of 1972, merged in 1974 to form the EPSM. Based in Kuala Lumpur, it pressed for action from the government on a wide front of issues. There was in Malaysia at the time, and particularly in the capital, a good deal of diffuse and unfocused sympathy for environmental causes that helped to foster such a group, but a large measure of its success was due to the energies and enterprise of its founder, Gurmit Singh. A small budget, raised from local membership and some external funds, was concentrated on a combination of research on environmental problems, publications, and attempts to influence publics and government. The first was obviously constrained by lack of funding. An investigation into the impact of toxic chemicals on the Malaysian environment was clearly beyond its capabilities. Reliance was placed instead on gathering of information from a variety of scientific, public and official sources. Bilingual publications centred on the journal *Alam Sekitar*. Attempts to influence publics and the government naturally encompassed a broader span than pesticide misuse. The argument was that the government was not devoting sufficient resources to protection of the environment. The Fourth Malaysia Plan was criticised for the inadequate coverage given to the environment (though in practice by then environmental conservation responsibilities had been institutionalised in government). Many specific questions were raised and given wide media coverage at different times: the prevention of Concorde flights over Malaysia, elimination of all consideration of nuclear options, an overhaul of urban transportation systems, noise pollution, or the overgrowth of weeds on street fire hydrants. The theme of 'development without destruction' was one that could be readily applied to a number of environmental threats. A leading example was provided by the Batu Caves, where quarrying for more than 25 years had brought this important cultural and ecological site to a point of near destruction and which became a symbol of environmental irresponsibility. The decision by the state authorities in Selangor to halt this activity was a major achievement for the EPSM and other groups.[39]

Pesticides constituted an issue that fitted neatly into this growing environmentalism. At times questions became the leading edge of EPSM and other groups' concerns. Over-use of chemicals because of modernisation plans in the Muda project, with its associated poisoning, pest outbreak and resistance problems, offered a ready-made target.[40] Dangers presented by residues on vegetables from pesticide misuse, or applications too close to harvesting, provided another, and one closer to the immediate concerns of the largely middle-class city residents who constituted the main potential supporters of environmental groups. The EPSM in particular was able to make skilful use of newspapers in Malaysia reporting on hazards to farmers and consumers from pesticides, and also to play a significant role in attracting wider international attention to this and other environmental problems in Malaysia. In general the line of EPSM criticism tended to be well informed rather than rhetorical, with detailed and constructive criticism of policies or of allegedly slow responses on the part of government departments.[41]

A more activist and radical stance was taken by SAM, which had its main office in Penang. It took its cue on pesticides questions far more than did other groups from the relatively more strident anti-chemicals stand taken by a number of environmental groups in western countries in the 1960s and 1970s. Moreover, it pressed forward with the pesticides issue far more single-mindedly. Its main argument and evidence were presented in a small book.[42] This developed the case that pesticides banned elsewhere were still being used in Malaysia. A lack of public information and good education was blamed for the over-use of pesticides, given their ease of application, availability and the labour saved. The absence of effective regulation of pesticides was sharply criticised; the need for this was argued to be underscored by the wide range of pesticides, some highly toxic, then available in the country. The government, it maintained, had to provide adequate education for farmers, otherwise they were entirely reliant on shopkeepers, the sales personnel of chemical companies, or trial-and-error experience; and what legislation there was, in the form of the 1974 act, was just not being implemented.

POLICY-MAKING: SCIENTIFIC UNCERTAINTIES AND POLITICAL COMPLEXITIES

The Malaysian government was thus faced with multiple pressures for change. While there were some matters on which agreement was possible – for example, that adulterated products should be banned – there was clearly also much ground for disagreement. The company case, and much of that from farmers themselves, was built upon the need for expanded pesticide use; the ultimate goal of many of the environmentalist or consumer protection groups was a diminishing of reliance on chemicals with a view to their replacement ultimately by alternative strategies of pest control. Many of these arguments were being echoed, though in more muted form, inside government in Malaysia and within the range of official and semi-official institutions dealing with agricultural policy. Differences of opinion within this set of institutions were reduced, however, by the shared commitment to the priority given to development objectives in Malaysian economic planning. In the wider public arena, a major aim was essentially to secure broader support for pesticides regulatory policies already embarked upon. Some points of view could be accommodated; proponents of more critical ones could with patience be argued out of them; and the expression of some environmentalist viewpoints was seen in some parts of the government machinery as being positively useful, as it allowed steps to be taken which would otherwise be impossible or else delayed.

At the termination of the pesticides registration exercise in 1981, the governmental machinery for handling these kinds of questions was considerably altered from that existing in 1971 when the first try was made at such a procedure.[43] The decisive change was the passing of the Pesticides Act of 1974. This established a Pesticides Board, under the chairmanship of the Director General of Agriculture and with representations from various agricultural, health and research bodies.[44] It was designed as the official body responsible for registering pesticides and for various other functions specified in the act.

The act went a long way towards rationalising policy formulation in the pesticides area. This process of change and adaptation continued during the decade. Different parts of the government carrying out activities related to pesticides and the use of agricultural chemicals generally tended in the early 1970s to be fragmented, with little liaison between them. Lack of chemical analysis facilities continued to be a major problem into the 1980s because of lack of funds, and the small chemistry section of the agriculture ministry responsible for checking soil samples and other tasks was not well integrated with other parts of the official machinery handling related chemical use or residue questions. Inadequate liaison affected both policy-making and the general advisory and educational functions of agricultural officials in the early 1970s. Three organisations – the ministry itself, MARDI, and the Farmers' Association established by the government in 1967 – could pursue quite independent policies in relation to pesticides and these often conflicted. Advice might be given to farmers on the use of pesticides by their association without crop protection officials in the ministry being consulted.[45]

In the evolution of pesticides policy, the fundamental policy link, especially in the early formative stage of the first half of the 1970s, lay in the relationship between Malaysian officials responsible for agricultural development policy on the one hand, and representatives of the major international agencies on the other. Some of the reports made on behalf of external bodies were noted earlier. The detailed provisions of the 1974 act followed along the general lines laid out by FAO and WHO in the 1960s in their initial approaches to pesticides legislation requirements in developing countries. The official Malaysian response to these policy ideas tended to be positive, though coupled with the reservation that in a developing country like Malaysia far more needed to be done and for this added funds from agencies and governments abroad were needed. In the pesticides area this meant such things as the construction and running of a good laboratory without which residue analysis and monitoring could not be carried out.

Domestically, the government had to engage in consultation with appropriate organisations while ensuring some continuity in policy. The noisy demands often put to the authorities never really threatened this. Provided criticisms were being voiced in a manner thought reasonably responsible, and were couched in terms well based in scientific facts, some were valued and encouraged by the government. The right kind of environmental criticism being expressed in a leading newspaper, or by a broadly-based group at a public conference, could facilitate measures being taken inside government or being accelerated that otherwise might not be possible. But when things became particularly heated in relation to pesticides misuse the combination of citizens' groups, companies and others in a highly visible public setting could give officials headaches: 'And in between the Government goes "ding-dong ding-dong"', as one environment official said in 1978.[46] From an official point of view public groups could usually be divided into different categories of legitimacy. On the pesticides question, some were obviously 'hysterical'.[47] In general the government's strategy was one of patient dialogue. Pesticides officials themselves made good use of public forums and newspapers to explain government policies at length, and to deal with particular criticisms in detail. In the background lay potential instruments of control through the government's powers relating to group registration,[48] but for the most part the search on the part of government was for a slowly emerging consensus.

More difficult questions were posed by the pesticides industry and the need of the government to secure cooperation on matters such as pesticides registration. The 1971 attempt failed not least because of the reluctance on the part of companies to accept a wider regulatory role for government. This experiment was voluntary, designed to obtain data and compile a comprehensive record of the pesticides market. While some firms showed a 'cooperative and sensible attitude in the data supplied', it was noted shortly afterwards, 'one or two firms, representing or backed by large international chemical manufacturers, had returned a questionnaire containing a derisory amount of data, although considerable data on the products was available'.[49] The importance of effective collaboration between companies and government was emphasised in all official reviews of the situation.[50] The 1971 experiment with voluntary registration was one factor leading to agreement on the part of many agricultural chemical firms in Malaysia later that year to form their own association. This body, later MACA, gradually became the focal point of negotiation and consultation between government and the pesticide industry. But companies remained critical of many aspects of government policy, and called at various times for direct representation on the Pesticides Board itself. The rules for registration were officially gazetted in October 1976 after consultation with this association and other bodies. Though essentially completed by April 1981 an eight-month grace period until 1 January 1982 was allowed to give dealers and shopkeepers a chance to clear remaining stocks.[51] Earlier pressures from the industry for still more time were rejected.

Official consideration of the need for a new legislative framework had begun in desultory fashion in the early 1960s.[52] Work on the act was finalised in the period 1972–74, following extensive consultation with FAO and other outside specialist organisations, a growing appreciation after the 1971 trial of the inherent weakneses of a voluntary scheme, expanding pesticide use, and the emergence of a Malaysian pesticides manufacturers' association. As the government's chief pesticides official observed later, there was a 'need for a comprehensive control of pesticides especially as a result of the rapid introduction of a wide range of active ingredients in various formulations, containing different ingredients, packed by a large number of companies and sold under different trade names'.[53] Three initial factors constrained the shape of the legislation. Firstly, in line with general FAO thinking pesticides were to be treated as an inherent feature of agricultural rather than health policy, and their use as well as avoidance of hazards an integrated part of agricultural development. Secondly, the route taken by some other countries, of regulating residue levels in foods, was not a realistic option. Absence of residue monitoring during the 1970s continued to be a weakness in the pesticides regulatory system in Malaysia. At the centre of the legislative strategy, accordingly, was a licensing system for pesticides actually on the market. Thirdly, it was accepted that implementation of the legislation, even given the most favourable circumstances, would be a slow process; the 1974 act was a framework covering all aspects of pesticide regulation, with some parts designed as a guide for detailed measures at a later stage.

The key administrative and institutional provision of the act, then, was the creation of a Pesticides Board. Part III of the act then dealt with the registration and permit of pesticides, whether manufactured in Malaysia or imported. Information required of manufacturers or importers was itemised under ten headings, including toxicological information, matters proposed to be included in the label, proposed packaging, reports on efficacy and safety, statements of methods of analysis and sources of information, and a statement of the methods of determining the residue of a pesticide on plants or crops on which it was intended to be used.[54] A successful registration was initially for a three-year period only, after which a fresh application would have to be made. Registration could be cancelled, for example if the Board considered it 'undesirable that the pesticide should continue to remain registered owing to its toxicity or inefficacy' or if it did not conform to the claims made for it on the label.[55] The fundamental principle was then defined in Section 20: 'No person shall manufacture, sell, or store for sale a pesticide unless he is licensed to do so under this Act or otherwise than in accordance with the conditions of a licence to do so issued to him under this Act.'[56] It was clearly the goal of the act to set a tight ring around the pesticides market and to ensure, so far as this was practicable, that only registered compounds were sold and that only licensed manufacturers, importers or storekeepers dealt in them.

It was several years before even the main provisions on registration could finally be implemented. Rules on registration were published by the government on 1 October 1976, following detailed consideration in the Pesticides Board of matters related to the registration, labelling and classification of pesticides. These were also studied by MACA, and discussions were held between industry representatives and Board officials to reach agreement on the various requirements, particularly in relation to the application procedure and identification of information needed. Toxicological data requirements, the government noted, were 'very much in line with those in developed nations'.[57] The registration process was no rubber-stamp operation. In investigations by officials during the process, approximately 21 per cent of samples analysed were found to have an active ingredient content lower than that declared. Examples were cited of certain endosulfan products which contained only about a half of the declared content.[58] By mid-1981 the ministry had received a total of 1912 applications. Of these 1087 had been registered and about 600 not, with 319 being withdrawn by dealers or manufacturers.[59] The deadline as well as the procedure itself continued to irk many companies. Industry representatives claimed that firms were working overtime to comply with labelling requirements, adding that this was going to result in consumers having to face a lot of small print.[60]

Progress was also made in relation to various other parts of the framework instrument. Here, too, the influence of international agency thinking can be seen. Classification of pesticides for labelling purposes, for example, was based on WHO categories.[61] Similarly, while the registration authorities did not themselves dictate packaging requirements, it was emphasised that all manufacturers were expected to pack their products in impervious containers made of material which did not affect or react with the pesticide. A group of officials in a paper in 1978 stated that the containers of some pesticide products 'leave much to be desired. Almost every bottle of a commonly used herbicide marketed by one local firm had its label stained with the contents although the seal had not been broken . . . Poor packaging can cause serious accidents especially in countries like Malaysia where pesticide items are often transported and sold alongside food items. In addition, poor packaging may also affect the pesticide product within and render it ineffective.'[62] The provisions of the act relating to advertising were also brought into force in 1981, with the aim of ensuring that misleading or false claims were not being made.[63] Preparations were being made as early as 1975 for construction of a new pesticides analytical laboratory, but capabilities continued to lag behind requirements both in this area and in monitoring for pesticide residue detection and measurement in foods, and a full laboratory was still awaited in the early 1980s. Partly for this reason, and partly to respond to pressures from local industry, the act provided also for importation of pesticides specifically for research or educational needs.[64] Finally, as accidents involving pesticides continued to occur, as well as suicides by weedkiller,[65] the Ministry of Health gradually increased its ability to prepare comprehensive lists of different types of poisoning cases, together with basic data on antidotes and the tabulation of signs and symptoms. In 1981–82 no such proper list existed, and a variety of treatments were in operation. The list was to be distributed to all hospitals and clinics in the country as an aid to the medical services.[66]

CONSTRAINTS AND PERFORMANCE

The political system of Malaysia should not be viewed in the light of pluralist models used by political scientists for the study of western advanced industrialised states. An unwieldy competitive pluralism has tended to be regarded in official and leading party circles in Malaysia as either an undesirable or an inappropriate western phenomenon. The rise of *bumiputra* (Malay) nationalism as both a political and economic force may have acted to reinforce such a tendency, as may continuation of a security-oriented political atmosphere with continuation of low-level anti-guerrilla operations in the central border areas with Thailand. Only a fine line may distinguish at times the 'irresponsible' but tolerated critic of government policy from the destabilising agent. In identifying three sources of extra-governmental influence over policy-making in this specific area – companies, both indigenous and transnational, inter-governmental agencies, and domestic environmental and other pressure groups – this chapter has not assumed that the government was a mere arena for the interplay between competing forces.

At least three major constraints set limits to the government's room for manoeuvre. Firstly, the openness of the pesticides economy created problems. The market in cheap products, usually based on paraquat formulations, persisted even after the beginning of 1982. These appealed to small farmers, for whom cost was a paramount concern. Smuggling through both major ports and smaller coastal towns meant that the economy was also open to illicit trade from other parts of the region. Enforcement by way of monitoring of all land crossings and points of entry by customs authorities was simply not feasible. It is evident that a greater measure of harmonisation in the pesticides registration and control policies of Malaysia and of other ASEAN (Association of South-east Asian Nations) states, together with tighter regulation of intra-regional commerce, would be a pre-requisite for more effective regulatory systems within any single country in the region. Further, it was accepted that the pesticides sector was dominated by private enterprise. It was not a part of official thinking to bring about conditions that would lead eventually to the creation of a state-run pesticides production and formulation industry in Malaysia. While some steps were taken to encourage locally-owned enterprises, for example through research, the general assumption remained that the technical sophistication of this particular industry implied dependence on compounds developed and marketed primarily by the Malaysian branches of foreign multinational companies. Thus it was several years (1974–82) before the registration exercise attempted first in 1971 and planned more systematically during 1972–74 came to fruition. Industry had to be persuaded to take part in this regulatory experiment, and the government gave many indications of being reluctant to attempt to speed up the process by adopting a tougher line with recalcitrant companies.[67]

Secondly, the emergence of a pesticides control policy took place in the context of prior decisions on agricultural modernisation and development. These tended to assume greater reliance on agrochemicals generally. Agricultural development planning thus rested on the anticipated availability of large and increasing quantities of foreign pesticide chemicals. A switch to mass labour techniques was not a practical alternative to herbicide use, nor in practice was greater reliance on biological control methods, though research on such alternatives expanded in Malaysia during the 1970s. Definitions of these prior goals also had implications for pesticides policy considered as part of a broadly environmental issue-area. As with pollution from the rubber industry, questions such as pesticides run-off into water-courses could be tackled by the government only in a limited and marginal manner; and the diminished space given environmental matters in the Fourth as opposed to the Third Malaysia Plan may indicate a more committed pursuit later in the 1970s of core economic development goals and strategies.

Thirdly, the government suffered from significant administrative and enforcement weaknesses. This general problem frequently took the particular form of tensions in centre–state relations. In the early 1980s there was renewed emphasis generally on greater dynamism from Kuala Lumpur in the battle against corruption in certain states. These efforts tended to revolve around the composition and policy directions of the 'Excos', the leading groups in various State Assemblies. Relations between the two levels showed signs of becoming more fractious in some cases as disagreements surfaced over the pace of deepening Islamic codes and practices. While the matters discussed in this chapter fall within the competence of the central authorities, much work had also to be done through state administrations because of the general constitutional provision giving authority in certain land-use matters to state governments. This was necessarily a slow and time-consuming process. At the central level, too, absence of effective pesticide residue analysis and monitoring capabilities in relation to foods continues, in the mid-1980s, to be a significant constraint limiting the government's area of choice in pesticide regulation and control. As in other areas, such as weaknesses in the agricultural extension services or staffing of inspectorates to monitor stores or the trade in adulterated products, the root problems were often lack of funding. Malaysia pressed in the UNEP Governing Council in 1981 for more funds to be allocated to the region for environmental and developmental goals by international agencies.

The argument put by EPSM, SAM and other groups, and some leading newspapers, that Malaysia was being used as a dumping ground by multinational chemical companies for toxic chemicals which they could not market elsewhere, had both strengths and weaknesses. It pointed directly to gaps in the national regulatory system, but failed to take adequate note either of the progress of governmental initiatives in this area or of the countervailing arguments derived from Malaysia's underlying commitment to economic development goals. That the point was developed with such force is an indication of the links – more those of mutual attentiveness than of organisation – between some groups and their counterparts in western industrialised nations. Those charges with most appeal in the latter, such as the 'Agent Orange' controversy surrounding dioxin contamination of herbicide mixtures, tended to be those that also received publicity inside Malaysia, whether or not the grounds were realistic. The government's longer-term approach of building on a slowly-emerging consensus, and using dialogue in a succession of public forums to defend its more gradualist strategy, was ultimately a successful one. This facilitated the relative insulation of two relationships regarded from the outset as more crucial: that with the companies and their representative associations on the one hand, and that with the major inter-governmental agencies on the other.

Part IV

9 Pesticides and the Politics of International Regulation

Agricultural technologies have continued to change. While a number of developments in areas of biological control and other methods for attacking agricultural pests appear to have significant potential for the future, it also seems to be the case that the more traditionally conceived chemical strategies of the last half-century will remain well into the next. These form a corner-stone of modern agribusiness practice in the developed countries. Agricultural progress in developing countries is inconceivable without them. Despite technical and practical difficulties in evaluating crop losses due to pests, and the willingness of statistics to allow themselves to be manipulated by any passing vested interest, there is clear evidence that such losses are proportionately large, would be still greater without the availability of pesticide chemicals, and will continue to constrain the rate of growth of food productivity. Regulatory dilemmas arise because of the costs associated with the widespread use of toxic chemicals in terms of human health and environmental conservation. Sporadic outbreaks of pests are also reminders of the limits to efficacy set by problems of insect resistance, or, as in the re-emergence of citrus canker in Florida in 1984, of the restricted area of protection afforded by any form of defence.

Regulation, and regulatory politics of one kind or another, is thus an intrinsic feature of the chemical economy. Industrial society, in the sense in which the term was used by Raymond Aron,[1] is by its nature a regulated society. This is an arena of political interaction because it is unlikely that agreement can be reached easily on such questions as the extent, type, cost, or procedure for determining the content of regulatory instruments. Conflict is not necessarily more prevalent at the international level, since the actors in international regulatory forums may not be fully representative of the range of participants in confrontations and negotiations within countries. Some of the international bodies studied in earlier chapters have been successful, by their own criteria, in part because access to them is limited by a variety of formal and practical obstacles. The absence of an indisputably central forum for tackling regulatory questions, however, is what gives the international level its distinctive character; the fact that others exist, and that still others can be created, hovers over the activities of each. In this final chapter we will first review some of the regulatory choices generated by technological change in the chemical industry, then turn to discuss developments in the pesticides area and their significance for the politics of international regulation.

TECHNOLOGY, CHOICE AND REGULATION

There is some irony in the definition of pesticides problems. Here, after all, are substances which seem to contain the key to the visions of pestless abundance that have accompanied the history of agriculture. One of the most vivid was given by Homer in his description of Odysseus' approach to the palace of Alcinous, and the orchard 'where trees hang their greenery on high, the pear and the pomegranate, the apple with its glossy burden, the sweet fig and the luxuriant olive. Their fruit never fails nor runs short, winter and summer alike. It comes at all seasons of the year. . . so that pear after pear, apple after apple, cluster on cluster of grapes, and fig upon fig are always coming to perfection.'[2] In solving some problems, changing technologies and scientific discoveries create others. The choices that emerge are central to the politics of regulatory change and adaptation.

One consequence of developments in the area of pesticide chemicals – such as those of the 1860s and 1870s, and of the major transformations that followed the research and development of organochlorine and organophosphorus compounds in the 1930s and 1940s – has been to restrict the range and type of pest control strategies employed in agriculture. A reliance on chemicals has come to occupy a more prominent place in the repertoire of control responses. While productivity has benefited, this has usually been at the cost of some loss of diversity in approaches. A mixture of biological, cultural, chemical and other control strategies formed part of traditional practices. A 1912 report of the Imperial Department of Agriculture in India, for example, following research on the economic status of various species of resident and migratory wild birds, concluded that these played a significant role in the control of some agricultural pests.[3] Advice written at the same time for gardeners in England noted different categories of controls against pests, including manual removal, cultural controls, the use of tobacco water and flowers of sulphur, and reliance on toads, birds and ladybirds; these were to be employed variously against 'all evil things that infest the garden' and 'the multitudinous pests which are always springing into life to prey upon sickly subjects'.[4] A similar diversity marked traditional approaches on small farms in Japan. On a criterion of agricultural productivity, or even of environmental protection, many chemically based strategies are incontestable winners. Their sheer efficacy, though, has carried with it a momentum of use patterns that in practice constrain the area of choice, so that some forms of biological control options may be difficult to implement successfully and the problems of integrated pest control strategies may appear intractable.[5]

A second consequence also has implications for political choices. The universe of discourse on agrochemical regulation has been affected by the fact that some regulatory options have come to be identified with the preferences of large industrial sectors with significant roles in the workings of modern economies. Regulation has real economic consequences. It may also, as representatives of pesticides industries have maintained, exert a deterrent effect on technological innovation and applied scientific research. The making of regulatory judgements in both industrialised and developing countries involves processes that touch on many complex areas of economic and social policy. The other side of this coin is a tendency on the part of some actors in regulatory politics to discount industry inputs because of the manifest interests that lie behind them. Technological change, then, not only gives rise to difficult regulatory questions; more particularly it refocuses attention on policy processes and regulatory procedures, on questions of rights of access to decision-making arenas and of the extent to which technical advances can be relied upon to resolve regulatory conflicts.

A third aspect emerges from the connections between policy areas. In this study we have looked at issues of regulation affecting pesticide chemicals, particularly with reference to agriculture rather than to other major domains such as public health or forestry. Questions of regulation in this narrowly defined area, however, cannot usefully be viewed in isolation from the wider contexts of varied sets of agricultural policy issues. Productivity is not a simple function of agrochemical use. Apart from other immediate inputs of resources and expertise, the wider economic environment is also important. Indeed according to one kind of approach to economic development questions, an environment of high prices for agricultural products in a developing country, rather than of subsidies in the interests of urban consumers, is one of the crucial ingredients of agricultural productivity. Where regulation of the food sector is practised by price controls and quotas for basic commodities, the system may be resistant to change, as shown by the riots in Egypt in 1977 which followed the announcement of price increases for some regulated staple products.[6] Similarly, it is an oversimplification to equate world food problems with questions of productivity and to neglect consideration of such factors as security of supply, distribution, or the organisation of international agricultural commodity trade. The interrelatedness of these questions, however, means that regulatory politics in a particular area often entails adoption of simplifying assumptions. In practical terms pesticides are a component part of the agricultural modernisation package; approaches to regulation fit into this broader perspective. Attempts to disaggregate these and other parts of the package, for example by research into different varieties of food or pasture crops or cropping patterns that might lead to diminished small-farmer reliance on high-cost agrochemical inputs,[7] are unlikely to achieve much short- or medium-term impact.

The policy choices generated by technological change are also dependent on levels of economic development, political cultures, ecological settings, and, in general, on those circumstances which make states different from each other. The major divide tends to be between developing countries and those of the advanced industrialised world, with policy choices resting on development criteria for the first and, increasingly, on health and environmental criteria for the second. The effective use of agrochemicals in developing countries depends to a large extent on the availability of government expertise and advice to farmers through agricultural extension services, rather than on any significant additions to knowledge. Misuse of pesticides can be counter-productive, as well as hazardous. Misapplication of fertiliser can promote lush plant growth and accordingly create conditions favourable to the growth of pests and pathogens.[8] Attention to supply problems in developing countries thus points also to requirements in terms of administrative resources and regulatory and educational infrastructures.

By contrast, security of supply of both agrochemicals and agricultural products has shifted the ground of policy debates in developed countries towards consideration of the costs of pesticide use. The internationalist aspect of these debates has also become more pronounced since the early 1960s. It includes both global considerations – how big a mass of organochlorine pesticides or their metabolites has accumulated in the biosphere, and what risks are involved in this process – and others at the level of inter-state relations, as in approaches to the international toxic chemicals trade or to questions of pesticide residues in agricultural imports from Third World countries. Clashes of competing values have also become sharper. Wetlands, for example, can be viewed either as areas for ecosystem preservation for scientific or other purposes, or as regions for agricultural expansion – 'most uninteresting, all sky, and thistles, and buttercups', as one farmer described part of the Halvergate Marshes in Norfolk in one controversial herbicide spraying case in England in 1984.[9] The issues involved in land-use planning are accordingly more complicated. In the more litigious setting of the United States, the development and refining of legal principles has accompanied the politics of pesticide regulation, and attempts have been made to define more precisely the location of responsibility in cases of damage resulting from pesticides or other toxic chemicals.[10]

Yet a bifurcation of the range of policy choices into those confronting developing countries on the one hand, and the advanced industrialised nations of the western world on the other, is obviously too simple. First, developing countries during the 1970s became increasingly interested in the policy issues surrounding toxic chemical use. Pesticides, because of their key role in agricultural modernisation strategies, played a significant role in highlighting the importance of the environmental dimension of processes of economic development. Similarly, environmentalist pressure against over-use of pesticides in Western Europe and North America did not lead to any significant diminution of industrial society's dependence on them. In the United States, a broader ideological emphasis on de-regulation in the first half of the 1980s served to accentuate, but did not itself create, concern for the costs of stringent pesticides regulatory frameworks on agricultural and other users. Secondly, in an interdependent economy regulatory issues form a web; small changes at one national point can set up vibrations which are felt more widely. This has been particularly noticeable in relation to questions of agricultural exports from developing countries, such as vegetables from Kenya to Britain, oranges from Mexico to Canada, or beef products from El Salvador to the United States. Pesticide rules and use patterns, and the efficacy of enforcement procedures, can have consequences for residue levels in products which cross national borders. The setting of regulations on these levels may in turn have significant effects in the form of non-tariff barriers to trade. It was this concern that prompted some of the leading western nations with interests in international agricultural trade to support the moves which led in the 1960s to the initiation of the Codex pesticides residues machinery.

In this respect the evidence points back to a central theme of functionalist logic in international relations: that states cooperate in technical areas because the dynamics of domestic policy issues leave them little choice in the matter. This has to be qualified, though, by consideration not only of broader national interests, but also of the mainsprings of diversity in national regulatory systems. The record of OECD chemicals meetings on such questions as good laboratory practice or the pre-marketing data requirements for the registration of compounds indicates that many technical issues in disputes between governments can indeed be resolved expeditiously, provided, however, that the underlying factor of political will is present. Many aspects of the regulation of pesticides lead to divergence in the practices of governments because of the interests of domestic actors and the ways in which these are accommodated in national regulatory processes. So long as such differences exist, questions of pesticide regulation will retain significant international dimensions, if only because companies have the capacity to propel them on to policy agendas.

REGULATORY FUNCTIONS AND THE PESTICIDES REGIME

How are these international dimensions handled? The proliferation of international bodies implies in practice a dispersal of effort on the part of states and other actors. Many groups active at the national level in regulatory debates lack the resources to take part in international deliberations. The structuring of international institutions around the principle of member-state representation and the sovereign equality of states creates special problems for industry and other non-state participants. An absence of enforcement power on the part of international agencies is likely to deter some governments or other groups from engaging in these processes, or from doing so in anything more than a minimalist fashion. While the fractured sprawl of the world of international organisations has been a perennial source of frustration to those taking part, a lack of coordination also serves some useful purposes. Governments or international bodies unhappy with the policy trends in one set of institutional arrangements can turn to, or even create, others; similarly, the accumulated weight of a resolution or recommendation as it moves in different forms through different organisations – as did those on the international trade in toxic chemicals during the late 1970s and early 1980s – compensates to some extent for any inherent lack of political visibility each may have.

A variety of regulatory functions are carried out by international bodies in the pesticides area. Only a small number have more strictly regulatory or quasi-regulatory roles, in the sense of a relatively direct link with the processes and outcomes of rule-making activity inside states. On this continuum more directly regulatory functions are evident in the processes of the European Community. There, as we have seen, the broad goal, or visionary slogan, of harmonisation set down in the Treaty of Rome and promoted by the European Commission is echoed in the declared objectives of the pesticide industry and its representative bodies – though these have tended to be critical of slow rates of progress towards the successful negotiation of Directives. The provisions of those that emerged during the 1970s indicate the complex groupings of interests that play some role in shaping these regulatory outcomes. The European Parliament, for example, emerged during the late 1970s as a significant forum for the articulation of competing environmental and agricultural viewpoints. Some member-states, such as Denmark and Britain, have been particularly uneasy with the regulatory trend of these years on the grounds than an ultimate transfer of regulatory authority – on key matters such as the registration of new compounds, and the designing of tests and requirements for data at the pre-marketing stage – from member-states individually to the Community collectively might be the eventual upshot. European Community developments also highlight the importance of the inter-departmental regulatory and consultative arrangements inside each country. In Britain, for example, the beginnings of a Community impact on pesticides regulation, in the late 1970s, coincided with attempts on the part of some actors to effect a shift in the balance of authority from the traditional organs associated with the agriculture ministry to newer ones with wider health and occupational safety responsibilities, and with more broadly-based decision-making structures. This kind of division, as well as the character of Community processes more generally, also facilitated approaches to pesticides questions by environmental groups. Many of these were successful in increasing the visibility of pesticides issues on political agendas. This changing political environment in the late 1970s and the first half of the 1980s sharpened the focus on a number of specific questions, such as the exclusion of pesticides exported to third countries from EC Directives, or the detailed listings of compounds or permitted pesticide residue levels in technical annexes.

Compared with other international groupings that have dealt with pesticides regulation, however, the European Community is a special case. Such intensive forms of regional cooperation between states are not practised elsewhere. Of UN bodies, only the Codex Alimentarius Commission's pesticides work can be described in quasi-regulatory terms. The design of procedures for evaluating the risks associated with different compounds has blended scientific and political criteria. While some issues move swiftly through the machinery, others seem amenable only to protracted examination at best. The main determining factor here seems to be not the presence of tangible economic or industrial interests, but rather the controversial nature of some of the compounds involved; the use of DDT, for example, which is still important in public health programmes in developing countries, despite the sporadic emergence of vector resistance problems, continues to raise delicate political and regulatory questions in western countries. The process from its inception has been constrained, at times seriously, by issues of data availability and confidentiality. Here, as in European Community and OECD approaches to toxic chemicals regulation, firms have often reacted with extreme caution to proposals involving the wider international dissemination of toxicological and other data on pesticides. Industry concerns have centred on the possible use of data supplied initially to regulatory bodies by competing companies for registration purposes. Governments have varied in their readiness to assist the workings of forums such as the joint pesticides meetings of experts associated with the Codex machinery; their own acquisition of data from domestic firms is not guaranteed, as the record of chemicals regulation in the United States shows, and their capacity to persuade firms to be more open may be diminished by too active a degree of support for international regulatory activities. Data gaps have not, however, forced the Codex enterprise to a halt. Its capacity to affect national regulatory determinations has been due in large measure to the design and structure of the acceptance system. By the time an issue reaches the latter steps of Codex procedures, governments have already had several opportunities to exert influence. The availability of a sliding scale of 'acceptance' categories then allows for considerable flexibility in government responses to internationally recommended Codex standards.

Less fully institutionalised have been the provisional and largely experimental hazardous exports notification schemes, to the extent that these involved the pesticide chemicals trade, operated in the early and middle 1980s by the GATT and UNEP. These hinted at the possibility of the eventual negotiation of an international convention on the subject, with monitoring by an international secretariat following its entry into force, but at the time of writing it is too early to speculate on the likelihood of such a development. Some of the approaches to toxic chemicals regulation in the OECD have had a similar quasi-regulatory flavour, particularly the agreements reached on such matters as pre-marketing data requirements and the elaboration of guidelines on good laboratory practice. Partly as a result of the OECD's own structures, and its definitions of the weight attached to different categories of resolutions agreed to by member-states, these instruments have been more significant additions to the international inventory than have recommendations from many of the UN organs.

Several other functions linked to regulatory activity can be distinguished. For the reasons just noted, the data-gathering efforts of several bodies, notably the International Register of Potentially Toxic Chemicals, have been subject to powerful constraints. The UNEP scheme has been more vulnerable to industry criticism of a limited capacity to assure adequate protection for sensitive data. Its attempts to cut corners by securing more elusive data direct from governments have also had mixed results. While its role became more central as a result of the establishment and work of the International Programme of Chemical Safety in the early 1980s, the Register experiment has underlined the difficulties confronting developing countries, in particular, in making effective use of toxic chemicals data. The requirement of developing countries for reliable information on the efficacy and hazards of agrochemicals and other compounds used in agriculture, forestry, industry and public health programmes has formed a consistent and major part of the IRPTC rationale, yet in practice the main users of the system have been from western Europe, Canada and the United States. Other data-gathering programmes connected with pesticides regulation at the international level include the pesticides use pattern and residue intake surveys carried out through the Codex pesticides machinery, and the international trade analyses of the UN's Economic Commission for Europe.

Most inter-governmental organisations perform a mixture of consultative and exhortative functions. The meetings organised by FAO on pesticides registration and held in 1977 and 1982 constitute the most prominent instance of inter-government consultation in this area. The results were not directly influential in terms of government policies, and the consultations were not designed with this immediate objective in view. Consensus was reached on a number of points, however: on the desirability of a greater measure of uniformity among national regulatory schemes; the need to avoid excessive stringency in such schemes, especially where developing countries are concerned; the requirements for heavier investments in regulatory and extension infrastructures in developing countries; and, by implication, the importance of collaboration between the world pesticide industry on the one hand, and governments and international organisations on the other. Some of the more specific developments associated with this longer-term consultative sequence were also significant. These include broad agreements in technical forums on the handling of sensitive industry data with commercial implications, and FAO's related exploratory probes into the environmental criteria for pesticides registration. To characterise many of the attempts by international bodies to devise guidelines for pesticides regulation as exhortative is not to deny them practical significance. The UNEP, ECOSOC and other resolutions on hazardous exports controls, for example, focused attention on these issues and, by helping to sketch out the broad outlines of the principle that importing countries should be alerted to the risks inherent in specific toxic chemicals, played an important part in governmental approaches to various notification schemes in the early and mid-1980s. They also reinforced tendencies within European Community institutions to deal with export questions in the context of pesticides directives. Some instruments – FAO's model pesticides law, for example, or the guidelines of the Council of Europe on pesticides registration, of the Codex machinery on good agricultural practice, or of the OECD on good laboratory practice – have had more direct policy repercussions at the national level, though in more of a random or sporadic way than a predictable and regularised fashion.

We have examined three broad categories of non-governmental

actors. Two have broadly representational functions, in that the targets of their international activities are usually inter-governmental bodies whose policies their members seek to influence. These are business groups, and more particularly associations representing pesticide industry interests, and environmental groups. The first are interest groups, and fit the familiar pattern of group activity inside states. Their members, that is, share common outlooks and aims by virtue of the objective criterion of being firms in the same industry.[11] The range of the common interests of these members is not coextensive with their activities, since competition characterises all pesticides sectors, even where, as in synthetic pyrethrins, the high costs of entry can restrict drastically the number of competing companies. The objectives pursued by GIFAP, for example, have related to shared definitions of industrial property rights, patent protection, the dilution of regulatory burdens, checking the regulatory demands of environmental groups, and greater uniformity and harmonisation among national pesticides regulations. Access to some international forums has been facilitated by the relatively more sympathetic position on issues of government–industry cooperation adopted by the Codex pesticides systems, FAO consultative and expert meetings, and some of the scientific and technical non-governmental bodies active in the pesticides area. Some international organisations, such as UNEP and occasionally WHO, have been perceived by industry representatives as either indifferent or actively antipathetic to industry goals. As inter-governmental organisations are shaped and constrained by the interests and policies of their member-states, so industry associations are limited in their freedom of manoeuvre by their own member companies or sectoral groupings; some firms, particularly in the United States, have in the past been uneasy with the costs of this kind of international activity, but the growing complexity and demonstrable effects of international regulation have ensured continued support for it.

Transnational environmental groups, by comparison, aspire to be representative not of identifiable interests but rather of broader movements of attitudes and ideologies. Their resource bases, too, tend to be different. While organisational and financial capabilities may be weak, they have nonetheless been able to operate within a nutrient milieu of receptive publics and media amplifiers. Pursuit of the aim of publicising the hazards of pesticide use, of regulation by revelation, has had varied results. As the 2,4,5-T case shows, regulatory determinations made in different countries can often diverge. In the United States environmental group activity and influence in relation to Congressional bodies and public opinion formed a supportive, if not always uncritical, atmosphere for the maintenance of EPA pressure on chemical companies in this kind of case. On the other hand, group activities in Britain and in Canada, whether targeted on administrative, legislative, or judicial bodies, tended to have minimal, short-lived or ambiguous results. The more intensely emotional the level of media attention, the more it could be accommodated by companies by resort to more effective public relations devices. A greater measure of regulatory stringency appeared to be the trend in West Germany for a time, but the case developed by industry in relation to the requirements of domestic agriculture and the importance of the pesticides export market, together with the policy momentum of federal health and agriculture regulatory agencies, set limits to this process of change. The transnational aspect, though, has been far from negligible. Regulatory politics in Malaysia during the 1970s were shaped in part by links between local consumer protection and environmental groups and those in some western countries; and the emergence of pesticides policies in the European Community was itself a factor which stimulated the growth of links between environmental groups in different member-states. The approaches and goals of these groups, however, have not been uniform. Some organisations more alert to world development issues have tended to be constrained in their criticism of the forces making for agrochemical dependence by a greater appreciation of the pesticides supply requirements of Third World countries.

The third kind of non-governmental organisation in the international pesticides area is that engaged in scientific or technical tasks. The number and variety of these bodies is a reflection of the diversity in the ways that pesticide issues can be interpreted and attacked. By reaffirming the point that an appeal to science cannot in itself resolve regulatory dilemmas, this diversity has a wider policy significance. Judgements have still to be made on such issues as the methods of testing compounds, the amount and type of information needed to decide on the registration and approved uses of chemicals, the levels of residues in foods that can be regarded as acceptable, or the degree to which environmental criteria such as the effects on wildlife populations should enter the calculations. Scientific findings influence these kinds of judgements, but determine regulatory outcomes only when certain prior assumptions have been made by the deciding bodies. A number of organisations have incorporated scientific work within the range of their own activities, a process which both smooths the connections between the setting of questions, the making of assumptions and the pursuit of findings, and also alleviates the costs of dependence on autonomous bodies. These costs were thrown into vivid relief by the discovery in the United States in the mid-1970s of major failings in the practices of one independent laboratory which had performed tests for the EPA and provided data used by the pesticides residues committees of the Codex system.

Two final functions should be mentioned. Several of the United Nations bodies operate technical assistance programmes which have a direct bearing on the workings of pesticide sectors and the course of pesticide regulation in developing countries. Particularly in the 1960s and early 1970s use was made of the FAO guidelines on legislation by a number of countries, and, as we have seen, experts using these and other instruments played an important role in the evolution of Malaysian laws and regulations during the 1970s. The activities of UNIDO and the UN Development Programme in relation to pesticide production and formulation in developing countries are also part of this picture. In some instances the impact of this work is challenged by bilateral programmes, as in the case of British technical assistance to developing countries on pesticides use and management matters, or by some of the multilateral development activities of the OECD. The OECD was also the vehicle chosen for conflict resolution in relation to the divergent toxic chemicals schemes adopted in the late 1970s by the United States in the Toxic Substances Control Act and by the European Community in the form of the Sixth Amendment.

Whether or not these various developments add up to the elements of an international pesticides regime is in part a semantic question. From the perspective of some actors it is an imperfectly structured and organised regime at best. Yet some of the more far-reaching goals that we have met during the course of the study should be recognised as unrealisable, though important nonetheless because of the manner in which they shape the approaches and strategies of participants. Harmonisation in its fullest sense is perhaps best regarded as a mobilising slogan for industry. Too many competing domestic interests play a part in structuring national regulatory systems for these to be brought into alignment through international negotiations. It is conceivable that trends in the international trade regime towards the progressive erosion of tariffs will undermine such moves because of the incentive they give to the retention of alternative means of shielding domestic markets. Similarly, calls for the more effective protection of industrial property rights are likely to be unevenly heeded, particularly with the rise of Third World chemicals producers and exporters; indeed patents in some industrial sectors, according to the more cynical industry viewpoint, may serve only to guarantee that a company will not be legally prevented from selling its own products.

A fully-fledged and comprehensive international regulatory regime is also not a realistic possibility. Criticisms of the fragmented character of the present system, and of the limited extent of government acceptance of internationally-agreed regulatory standards, occasionally provoke calls for its strengthening into a more centralised scheme.[12] The record of UN politics in this as in a number of other economic and social areas does not provide much evidence for the viability of such proposals. We should expect to see rather a continuation of the process by which new bodies are occasionally created and existing ones compete or coexist, while states, the central actors, either agree to be courted, walk off in a huff, or try to work out ways to alter rules and relationships. There are elements of a working regime in the form of the arrangements set up through the Codex system on pesticides residues questions, through WHO on the classification of pesticides by degree of hazard, and through UNEP in the form of the chemicals register. Others have already been noted: the UNEP and GATT attempts to regulate international, and more particularly North–South, trade in toxic chemicals; the regional schemes of the European Community and, to some extent, the OECD; the emerging practice of consultation on registration and harmonisation questions under FAO auspices; those aspects of government policies, for example in the United States, which have implications for international pesticides issues; and, finally, the emergence and spreading acceptance of a number of working principles or assumptions, such as the desirability of greater uniformity in national approaches to pesticides regulation, the need for more regularised inter-governmental consultations on basic regulatory issues, and the special requirements of developing countries for assistance in the management of toxic chemicals.

It is also evident, however, that the degree of internal cohesion and organisation within this overall system is somewhat stunted. Pesticides entered international agendas slowly. The activities of WHO and FAO from the early and middle 1950s were followed a decade or so later by their establishment and consolidation of the Codex residues machinery. Growing attention to pesticides issues on the part of environmental organisations of various types marked the late 1960s and early 1970s, and culminated in the setting up of the UN Environment Programme; it was the end of the decade before its toxic chemicals data gathering exercise began to show concrete results. The European Community's pesticides directives also started to appear during the 1970s, a period which coincided with several of the key developments associated with FAO's pesticide programmes. In some of these events longer-term cycles can occasionally be glimpsed, as in the protracted several-year gestation periods for EC directives, or the still longer time taken for the debates in environmental bodies of the 1960s on the pesticides trade to find more concrete expression in the form of the international notification schemes of the early and middle 1980s. There is no easy formula for successful regime construction, whether in relation to pesticides or to any other complex international problem. 'Here', as one early geological observer wrote in 1695, 'is such a vast variety of phenomena and these many of them so delusive, that 'tis very hard to escape imposition and mistake.'[13]

Select Bibliography

Arnon, I. *Modernization of Agriculture in Developing Countries: Resources, Potentials and Problems* (New York: Wiley, 1981).

Balaam, D. N. and M. J. Carey (eds), *Food Politics: The Regional Conflict* (Totowa, NJ: Littlefield, Adams, 1982).

Bates, J. A. R. 'The Evaluation of Pesticide Residues in Food: Procedures and Problems in Setting Maximum Residues Limits', *Journal of the Science of Food Agriculture*, vol. 30 (1979) pp. 401–16.

Brickman, R., S. Jasanoff and T. Ilgen, *Chemical Regulation and Cancer: A Cross-National Study of Policy and Politics* (Washington, DC: National Science Foundation, 1982).

Brown, A. W. A. *Ecology of Pesticides* (New York: Wiley, 1978).

Bull, D. *A Growing Problem: Pesticides and the Third World Poor* (Oxford: Oxfam Publications, 1982).

Buyckx, E. J. and L. Ling, 'International Cooperation in Plant Protection and the Role of FAO', *Mededelingen Faculteit Landbouwwetenschappen Gent*, vol. XXXVIII (1973) pp. 613–25.

Carson, R. *Silent Spring* (Greenwich, Conn.: Fawcett Publications, 1962).

Chattopadhyay, S. *Principles and Procedures of Plant Protection* (New Delhi: Oxford and IBH, 1980).

Cockerill, C. 'Agricultural Pesticides: The Urgent Need for Harmonization of International Regulation', *California Western International Law Journal*, vol. 9 (1979) no. 1, pp. 111–38.

Corbett, J. R. 'The Future of Pesticides and Other Methods of Pest Control', in T. H. Coakes (ed.), *Applied Biology* (London: Academic Press, 1978) pp. 229–330.

Cox, G. W. and M. D. Atkins, *Agricultural Ecology* (London: W. H. Freeman, 1980).

Cramer, H. 'Plant Protection and World Plant Production', *Pflanzenschutz Nachrichten Bayer*, vol. 20 (1967) pp. 1–524.

Dahlberg, K. *Beyond the Green Revolution: The Ecology and Politics of Global Agricultural Development* (New York: Plenum Press, 1980).

Dethier, V. G. *Man's Plague? Insects and Agriculture* (Princeton, NJ: The Darwin Press, 1976).

Edwards, C. A. (ed.), *Environmental Pollution by Pesticides* (New York: Plenum Press, 1977).

Elliot, M. 'Progress in the Design of Insecticides', *Chemistry and Industry*, 17 Nov. 1979.

Elliott, D. A. E. and R. H. Elliott, *The Control of Technology* (London: Taylor & Francis, 1976).

189

Flint, M. L. *Introduction to Integrated Pest Management* (New York: Plenum Press, 1981).

Fletcher, W. W. *The Pest War* (Oxford: Blackwell, 1974).

Geissbuehler, H. (ed.), *Advances in Pesticide Science* (Oxford: Pergamon, 1979).

George, S. *How the Other Half Dies* (Harmondsworth: Penguin, 1978).

Graham, F., Jr, *Since Silent Spring* (London: Hamish Hamilton, 1970).

Green M. B. *Pesticides: Boon or Bane?* (London: Paul Elek, 1976).

Green M. B., G. S. Hartley and T. F. West, *Chemicals for Crop Protection and Pest Control* (Oxford: Pergamon, 1977).

Gunn, D. L., and J. G. R. Stevens (eds), *Pesticides and Human Welfare* (Oxford University Press, 1976).

Hadwiger, D. F. *The Politics of Agricultural Research* (University of Nebraska Press, 1982).

Hardie, D. W. F. and J. Davidson Pratt, *A History of the Modern British Chemical Industry* (Oxford: Pergamon, 1966).

Hassall, K. A. *The Chemistry of Pesticides: Their Metabolism, Mode of Action and Uses in Crop Protection* (Weinheim: Verlag chemie, 1982).

Hay, A. *The Chemical Scythe: Lessons of 2,4,5-T and Dioxin* (New York: Plenum Press, 1982).

Hill, D. S. *Agricultural Insect Pests of the Tropics and Their Control* (Cambridge University Press, 1978).

Howard, L. O. 'A History of Applied Entomology', *Smithsonian Misc. Publications*, vol. 84 (1930) pp. 1–564.

Huismans, J. W. 'The IRPTC: Its Present State of Development and Future Plans', *Ambio*, vol. 7 (1978) pp. 275–7.

Huismans, J. W. 'The IRPTC', *Ecotoxicology and Environmental Safety*, vol. 4 (1980) pp. 393–403.

Ilgen, T. '"Better Living through Chemistry": The Chemical Industry in the World Economy', *International Organization*, vol 37 (1983) no. 4, pp. 647–80.

Kimbrell, E. 'Codex Alimentarius Food Standards and Their Relevance to US Standards', *Food Technology*, June 1982, pp. 93–5.

Kucherenko, A. I. and J. W. Huismans, 'The IRPTC of UNEP', *Environmental Conservation*, vol. 9 (1982) no. 1, pp. 59–63.

Leive, D. M. *International Regulatory Regimes: Case Studies in Health, Meteorology, and Food* (Lexington, Mass.: Lexington Books, 1976).

Levi, J. and M. Havinden, *Economics of African Agriculture* (London: Longman, 1981).

Melrose, D. *Bitter Pills: Medicine and the Third World Poor* (Oxford: Oxfam Publications, 1983).

Ordish, G. *Untaken Harvest* (London: Constable, 1952).

Ordish, G. *The Constant Pest: A Short History of Pests and Their Control* (London: Davies, 1976).

Perkins, J. H. *Insects, Experts and the Insecticide Crisis: The Quest for New Pest Management Strategies* (New York: Plenum Press, 1982).

Perring, F. H. and K. Mellanby (eds), *Ecological Effects of Pesticides* (New York: Academic Press, 1977).

Pimentel, D. (ed.), *CRC Handbook of Pest Management in Agriculture* (Boca Raton, Fla.: CRC Press, 1981).

Pimentel, D. and J. H. Perkins (eds), *Pest Control: Cultural and Environmental Aspects* (Boulder: Westview, 1980).

Regenstein, L. *America the Poisoned* (New York: Acropolis, 1982).

Reuben, B. G. and M. L. Burstall, *The Chemical Economy: A Guide to the Technology and Economics of the Chemical Industry* (London: Longman, 1973).

Schwartz, B. *Pesticides: Mist of Death* (West Haven, Conn.: Pendulum Press, 1971).

Sheets, T. J. and D. Pimentel (eds), *Pesticides: Contemporary Roles in Agriculture, Health and Environment* (Clifton, NJ: Humana Press, 1979).

Shorey, H. H., *et al.* (eds), *Chemical Control of Insect Behavior: Theory and Application* (New York: Wiley, 1977).

Shreve, R. N. and J. A. Brink, Jr, *Chemical Process Industries* (New York: McGraw-Hill, 1977).

Silverman, M., P. R. Lee and M. Lydecker, *Prescriptions for Death: The Drugging of the Third World* (University of California Press, 1982).

Smith, A. E. and D. M. Secoy, 'Forerunners of Pesticides in Classical Greece and Rome', *Journal of Agricultural and Food Chemistry*, vol. 23 (1975) pp. 1050–5.

Trauberman, J. 'Statutory Reform of "Toxic Torts": Relieving Legal, Scientific and Economic Burdens on the Chemical Victim', *Harvard Economic Law Review*, vol. 7 (1983) no. 2.

Turner, B. A. *Man-Made Disasters* (London: Taylor & Francis, 1978).

Van Den Bosch, P. T. *The Pesticide Conspiracy* (New York: Doubleday, 1978).

Van Heemstra, E. A., and W. F. Tordoir (eds), *Education and Safe Handling in Pesticide Application* (Amsterdam: Elsevier, 1982).

Vettorazzi, G. *International Regulatory Aspects for Pesticide Chemicals* (Boca Raton, Fla.: CRC Press, 1979); vol. 2, with B. M. Radaelli-Benvenuti (1982).

Vettorazzi, G. (ed.), *Handbook of International Food Regulatory Toxicology*, 2 vols. (Lancaster: MTP Press, 1980).

Watson, D. L., and A. W. A. Brown (eds), *Pesticide Management and Insecticide Resistance* (New York: Academic Press, 1977).

Weir, D. and M. Schapiro, *Circle of Poison: Pesticides and People in a Hungry World* (San Francisco: Institute for Food and Development Policy, 1981).

World Conservation Strategy: Living Resource Conservation for Sustainable Development (IUCN-UNEP-WWF, 1980).

Wurster, C. F. 'Effects of Pesticides', in N. Polunin (ed.), *The Environmental Future* (London: Macmillan, 1972) pp. 293–310.

Notes

CHAPTER 1

1. D. L. Gunn and J. G. R. Stevens, (eds), *Pesticides and Human Welfare* (Oxford University Press, 1976) p. v; and GIFAP *Bull.*, vol. 7 (1981) no. 2, p. 4.
2. V. G. Dethier, *Man's Plague? Insects and Agriculture* (Princeton, NJ: Darwin Press, 1976) p. 100.
3. G. W. Ivey *et al.*, 'Natural Toxicants in Human Foods', *Science*, vol. 213 (1981) pp. 909–10.
4. 'About Chemicals and Chemophobia', IRPTC *Bull.*, vol. 6 (1983) no. 1, p. 2.
5. On the 'biocide' debate see *Chemical and Engineering News*, 2 Nov. 1981, p. 4.
6. Cited by M. D. W. Jeffreys, 'The Spider in West Africa', *Nigeria*, vol. 41 (1953) p. 60.
7. See T. R. E. Southwood, 'The Insect/Plant Relationship: An Evolutionary Perspective', in H. F. van Emden (ed.), *Insect/Plant Relationships* (Oxford: Blackwell, 1973) p. 21; and P. Harris 'Insects in the Population Dynamics of Plants', ibid., pp. 201–4.
8. C. Johansen, 'Principles of Insect Control', in R. E. Pfadt (ed.), *Fundamentals of Applied Entomology*, 2nd edn (New York: McGraw-Hill, 1971) p. 171.
9. K. C. Barrons, in *Wall Street Journal*, 13 Jan. 1984.
10. J. Krummel, 'The Economic Consequences of Abandoning Pesticide Use', *Ecologist*, vol. 10 (1980) no. 3, pp. 98–101. More generally see the major study by H. Cramer, published as 'Plant Protection and World Plant Production', *Pflanzenschutz Nachrichten Bayer*, vol. 20 (1967), pp. 1–524; and L. Chiarappa, *Crop Loss Assessment Methods* (Rome: FAO, 1971).
11. Cited in *Control of Pesticides: A Survey of Existing Legislation* (Geneva: WHO, 1970) p. 4.
12. *Chemical and Engineering News*, 11 May 1981, p. 26.
13. IRPTC *Bull.*, vol. 5 (1982) no. 1, p. 23.
14. A. A. Saad, *Pesticide Chemicals in the Sudan* (Khartoum: Agricultural Research Council, 1975) pp. 102–3.
15. *Chemistry and Industry*, 19 Jan. 1980, p. 51.
16. See *Pesticide Regulatory Program Study. Hearings before the Subcommittee on Department Operations, Research, and Foreign Agriculture of the Committee on Agriculture, House of Representatives, 97th Cong., 2d Sess., Dec. 17, 1982* (Washington, DC: USGPO, 1983) p. 131.

17. Mr Justice Nunn, in the *Chronicle Herald* (Halifax), 16 Sept. 1983.
18. *Manchester Guardian Weekly*, 26 Dec. 1982, p. 8.
19. For a recent evaluation see *DDT and Derivatives (Environmental Health Criteria No. 9)* (Geneva: WHO/UNEP, 1982).
20. A recent study is reported by R. Frank *et al.*, 'Removal of Captan from Treated Apples', *Archives of Environmental Contamination and Toxicology*, vol. 12 (1983) no. 3, pp. 265 ff.

CHAPTER 2

1. C. K. Webster and S. Herbert, *The League of Nations in Theory and Practice* (London: Allen & Unwin, 1933) p. 26; cited by G. Goodwin, 'International Institutions and International Order', in A. James (ed.), *The Bases of International Order: Essays in Honour of C. A. W. Manning* (Oxford University Press, 1973) p. 162.
2. *Government Regulation. What Kind of Reform?* (Washington, DC: American Enterprise Institute for Public Policy Research, 1976) p. 4.
3. R. E. Smith, 'Protecting Workers' Health and Safety', in R. W. Poole, Jr (ed.), *Instead of Regulation: Alternatives to Federal Regulatory Agencies* (Lexington, Mass.: Lexington Books, 1982) p. 318.
4. T. A. Murphy, 'The Distressing Relationship Between Government and Business', in J. F. Gatti (ed.), *The Limits of Government Regulation* (New York: Academic Press, 1981) p. 136; M. L. Weidenbaum, *The Future of Business Regulation: Private Action and Public Demand* (New York: Amacom, 1979) p. 12.
5. See the discussion in J. F. Weston, 'International Competition, Industrial Structure, and Economic Policy', in I. Leveson and J. W. Wheeler (eds), *Western Economies in Transition: Structural Change and Adjustment Policies in Industrial Countries* (Boulder: Westview, 1980) pp. 258–9.
6. See Chapter 3.
7. L. J. White, *Reforming Regulation: Processes and Problems* (Englewood Cliffs, NJ: Prentice-Hall, 1981) p. 214.
8. P. J. Quirk, *Industry Influence in Federal Regulatory Agencies* (Princeton University Press, 1981) p. 179. More generally, see B. M. Mitnick, *The Political Economy of Regulation: Creating, Designing, and Removing Regulatory Forums* (New York: Columbia University Press, 1980); and C. E. Lindblom, *Politics and Markets* (New York: Basic Books, 1977).
9. Weidenbaum, op. cit., p. 12.
10. A. Smith, *The Wealth of Nations*, cited in J. W. Grove, *Government and Industry in Britain* (London: Longman, 1962) p. 4.
11. R. H. Tawney, in a 1943 article cited ibid., p. 39.
12. T. G. Weiss, *International Bureaucracy* (Lexington, Mass.: Lexington Books, 1975) p. 90.
13. M. Hill, *The United Nations System: Coordinating its Economic and Social Work* (Cambridge University Press, 1978) pp. 1–2.
14. See the chapter by A. Judge and K. Skjelsbaek in A. J. R. Groom and P.

194 *Notes*

Taylor (eds), *International Organisation: A Conceptual Approach* (London: Frances Pinter, 1978) p. 215; and K. Skjelsbaek, 'The Growth of International Nongovernmental Organisation in the Twentieth Century', in R. O. Keohane and J. S. Nye, Jr (eds), *Transnational Relations and World Politics* (Cambridge, Mass.: Harvard University Press, 1970) pp. 70–92.

15. *Review of Overseas Representation. Report by the Central Policy Review Staff* (London: HMSO, 1977) para. 5.4, p. 34.

16. L. T. Farley, *Change Processes in International Organisations* (Cambridge, Mass.: Schenkman, 1982) p. 9.

17. For a critique of assumptions underlying analyses of international organisations along these lines, see J. A. Conybeare, 'International Organization and the Theory of Property Rights', *International Organization*, vol. 34 (1980) no. 3, pp. 307–34.

18. D. M. Leive, *International Regulatory Regimes: Case Studies in Health, Meteorology, and Food* vol. I (Lexington, Mass.: Lexington Books, 1976) p. xxiii. On 'quasi-legislative' processes in international agencies see C. Alexandrowicz, *The Law-Making Functions of the Specialised Agencies of the United Nations* (Sydney: Angus & Robertson, 1973) p. 152.

19. See for example E. B. Haas, 'Regime Decay: Conflict Management and International Organizations, 1945–1981', *International Organization*, vol. 37 (1983) no. 2, especially pp. 191–2; and R. Boardman and J. F. Keeley (eds), *Nuclear Exports and World Politics: Policy and Regime* (London: Macmillan, 1983) Chapters 9 and 10.

20. R. Boardman, *International Organization and the Conservation of Nature* (London: Macmillan, 1981) Chapter 5.

21. For an attempt to model the processes see J. A. Vasquez and R. W. Mansbach, 'The Issue Cycle: Conceptualizing Long-Term Global Political Change', *International Organization*, vol. 37 (1983) no. 2, pp. 257–80. In relation to environmental issues see A. Downs, 'Up and Down with Ecology: The Issue Attention Cycle', *Public Interest*, vol. 28 (1972) pp. 38–50.

22. Some of the interlocking economic and political processes here have been integrated in attempts to define the logic of product cycles. See for example R. Vernon, '*Sovereignty at Bay* Ten Years After', *International Organization*, vol. 35 (1981) no. 3, pp. 517–30; and J. R. Kurth, 'The Political Consequences of the Product Cycle: Industrial History and Political Outcomes', *International Organization*, vol. 33 (1979) no. 1, pp. 1–34.

23. See for example M. S. Rajan, 'The United Nations and Sovereignty over Natural Resources', in R. Jütte and A. Grosse-Jütte (eds), *The Future of International Organisation* (London: Frances Pinter, 1981) pp. 37–50; and W. J. Feld, *Multinational Corporations and UN Politics: The Quest for Codes of Conduct* (New York: Pergamon, 1980).

24. For an emphasis on autonomy of the political sphere, see W. Grant and D. Marsh, *The Confederation of British Industry* (London: Hodder & Stoughton, 1977) pp. 187–8.

CHAPTER 3

1. *The Book of Songs* (transl. Arthur Waley) (New York: Grove, 1960), pp. 169, 171.
2. Psalm 105. Cf. Haggai, 2, 16–17, and II Chronicles, 6, 28.
3. W. Don Fronk, 'Chemical Control', in R. E. Pfadt (ed.), *Fundamentals of Applied Entomology*, 2nd edn (New York: McGraw-Hill, 1971) p. 191.
4. M. Elliot, 'Progress in the Design of Insecticides', *Chemistry and Industry*, 17 Nov. 1979, p. 761.
5. M. B. Green, G. S. Hartley and T. F. West, *Chemicals for Crop Protection and Pest Control* (Oxford: Pergamon, 1977) p. 29.
6. K. A. Hassall, *The Chemistry of Pesticides: Their Metabolism, Mode of Action and Uses in Crop Protection* (Weinheim: Verlag chemie, 1982) p. 47.
7. For convenience we are omitting older inorganic compounds, more specialised products such as nematicides, and different classes of control agents such as growth modifiers.
8. *New Generation Insect Control* (Fernhurst: ICI Plant Protection Division, 1979).
9. Elliot, op. cit., pp. 758–9.
10. Hassall, op. cit., p. 120.
11. Ibid, p. 67; and Green *et al.*, op. cit., p. 5.
12. D. Schwartzman, *Innovation in the Pharmaceutical Industry* (Baltimore: Johns Hopkins University Press, 1976) p. 9, and Chapter 3 passim.
13. A. Woodburn, cited in GIFAP *Bull.*, vol. 9 (1983) no. 9, p. 4.
14. J. T. Braunholtz, 'Techno-economic Considerations', *Chemistry and Industry*, 17 Nov. 1979, p. 790.
15. For an estimate of around two million compounds screened since the late 1940s, see J. R. Corbett, 'The Future of Pesticides and Other Methods of Pest Control', in T. H. Coakes (ed.), *Applied Biology*, vol. III (London: Academic Press, 1978) pp. 233–4.
16. Green, *et al.*, op. cit., pp. 5–6.
17. C. A. I. Goring, 'Prospects and Problems for the Pesticide Manufacturer' *Proc. 8th British Insecticide and Fungicide Conf. (1975)*, vol. 3, pp. 920–1.
18. J. R. Corbett, 'Technical Considerations Affecting the Discovery of New Pesticides', *Chemistry and Industry*, 17 Nov. 1979, p. 772.
19. Green, *et al.*, op. cit., p. 12; and C. H. Gilbert, in *Farm Chemicals*, April 1978, p. 20.
20. *Chemistry and Industry*, 1 Dec. 1979, p. 802.
21. R. N. Shreve and J. A. Brink, Jr, *Chemical Process Industries*, 4th edn (New York: McGraw-Hill, 1977) pp. 420 ff. and Chapter 26.
22. Green, *et al.*, op. cit., p. 16.
23. *Chemical Week*, cited in the *Encyclopedia of Chemical Technology*, 3rd edn, vol. 18, p. 302.
24. B. G. Reuben and M. L. Burstall, *The Chemical Economy: A Guide to*

the Technology and Economics of the Chemical Industry (London: Longman, 1973) pp. 111–2, 121.

25. GIFAP *Bull.*, vol. 7 (1981) no. 10, p. 4, citing Wood, Mackenzie estimates. See also the IAC report quoted in *Chemistry and Industry*, 1 Nov. 1980, p. 839; and that by Predicasts Inc., in GIFAP *Bull.*, vol. 9 (1983) no. 11, p. 8.
26. A. Woodburn, cited in GIFAP *Bull.*, vol. 9 (1983) no. 9, pp. 2, 5.
27. Green, *et al.*, op. cit., p. 2.
28. W. J. Reader, *Imperial Chemical Industries: A History*, vol. 2 (Oxford University Press, 1975) pp. 12, 318, 335, 455.
29. P. Erni, *The Basel Marriage: History of the Ciba-Geigy Merger* (Zurich: Neue Zürcher Zeitung Pubns, 1979) pp. 32–58, 137, 332.
30. W. J. Storck, in *Chemical and Engineering News*, 28 April 1980, pp. 10–13.
31. F. Bradbury and J. Russell, 'Technology Change and its Manpower Implications . . . Pt.2: Agrochemicals and Pharmaceuticals', *Chemistry and Industry*, 5 April 1980, p. 255. See also A. Hayes, 'What Can the Agrochemical Industry Learn From the Pharmaceutical Industry?', *Agrochemical Monitor*, vol. 18 (Sept. 1981).
32. Reader, op. cit., p. 479.
33. J. D. Early, in *Proc. National Conf. on the Codex Alimentarius International Pesticides Residue Limits, Washington, DC, May 5, 1976* (NACA, 1976) pp. 59–60.
34. One Indian association (ABMP) was also a full member, and New Zealand joined as an associate at the 1983 General Assembly.
35. R. C. Back, in *Proc. National Conf. Codex Alimentarius* (NACA, 1976) pp. 56–8. There are also associations for the chemical industry generally. The main body in western Europe is the Conseil européen des féderations de l'industrie chimique (CEFIC).
36. Early, op. cit., p. 58.
37. GIFAP *Bull.*, vol. 8 (1982) no. 1, p. 9.
38. For a criticism of proliferation trends from an industry perspective, see GIFAP *Bull.*, vol. 9 (1983) pp. 3–4.
39. On the last, see *Cooperation in Science and Technology* (Moscow: CMEA, 1979) pp. 24, 52, 58–9.
40. GIFAP *Bull.*, vol. 7 (1981) no. 2, pp. 6–7.

CHAPTER 4

1. See for example G. Taksdal, 'The Insecticide Residue Problem in Export Production of Vegetables and Fruits in East Africa', *Acta Horticulturae*, vol. 33 (1973) pp. 123–9.
2. J. A. R. Bates, 'The Evaluation of Pesticide Residues in Food: Procedures and Problems in Setting Maximum Residues Limits', *Journal of the Science of Food Agriculture*, vol. 30 (1979) pp. 409–10.
3. *Codex Alimentarius Commission. Procedural Manual*, 5th edn (Rome: FAO/WHO, 1981) p. 1.
4. Bates, op. cit., p. 409.

5. GIFAP *Bull.*, vol. 7 (1981) no. 11, p. 7.
6. *Codex Procedural Manual* (1981) pp. 33 ff., 59 ff., 81 ff.
7. Ibid. For a general evaluation of Codex workings see D. M. Leive, *International Regulatory Regimes* vol. II (Lexington, Mass.: Lexington Books, 1976) Chapter 17.
8. The WHO body is the Expert Committee on Pesticide Residues. That of FAO was variously designated during the 1960s as the Panel of Experts in the Use of Pesticides in Agriculture, the Committee on Pesticides in Agriculture, and the Working Party of Experts on Pesticide Residues. The last designation was that at the commencement of the Joint Meetings in 1966. In 1976 this became the FAO Panel of Experts on Pesticide Residues and the Environment. FAO's position is also complicated by the fact that in the early 1960s other expert groups in agriculture also dealt with residues questions.
9. See for example *Report of the 1967 JMPR* (Rome: FAO, PL/1967/M/11, 1968) p. 4.
10. See for example, 'Good Analytical Practice in Pesticide Residue Analysis', *Report of the 12th Session of the CCPR* (ALINORM 81/24, App. II, Annex II); the chapters by J. A. Burke and W. Horwitz in H. Geissbuehler (ed.), *Advances in Pesticide Science* (Oxford: Pergamon, 1979); and IUPAC, 'Development and Evaluation of Simplified Approaches to Residue Analysis', *Pure and Applied Chemistry*, vol. 53 (1981) pp. 1039–49.
11. G. Vettorazzi, with B. M. Radaelli-Benvenuti, *International Regulatory Aspects for Pesticide Chemicals*, vol. II (Boca Raton, Fla.: CRC Press, 1982) p. 6. Cf. Bates, op. cit., p. 406.
12. Vettorazzi, op. cit., pp. 5–6.
13. Ibid.
14. Bates, op. cit., pp. 405–6.
15. See the discussion in the IRPTC *Bull.*, vol. 5 (1982) no. 2, p. 2.
16. Though this did not prevent work continuing. See *Report of the 2nd Session of the CCPR* (ALINORM 68/24, 1968) p. 10.
17. *Report of the 13th session of the CAC* (ALINORM 79/38, 1980) p. 35; and *Report of the 14th session of the CAC* (ALINORM 81/39, 1981) para. 252.
18. *Report of the 2nd Session of the CCPR* (ALINORM 68/24, 1968) p. 10.
19. *Report of the 12th Session of the CAC* (ALINORM 78/41, 1978) p. 35; and documents ALINORM 76/44–389 and 78/24–6. See also *Report of the 14th Session of the CAC* (ALINORM 81/39, 1981) and the *Codex Procedural Manual* (1981) p. 81; and *Report of the 12th Session of the CCPR* (ALINORM 81/24, 1981) pp. 6–7.
20. See *Pesticide Regulatory Program Study. Hearings before the Subcommittee on Department Operations, Research, and Foreign Agriculture of the Committee on Agriculture, House of Representatives, 97th Cong., 2d Sess., Dec. 17, 1982* (Washington, DC: USGPO, 1983) p. 131. The implications were discussed by the JMPR and the CCPR (ALINORM 81/39, para. 225, and ALINORM 83/24A, p. 32).
21. *Report of the 1974 JMPR* (Rome: FAO/WHO, 1975) p. 19; *Report of the 1977 JMPR* (Rome: FAO/WHO, 1978) pp. 3–4; and *Report of the 1978 JMPR* (Rome: FAO/WHO, 1979) p. 2. The problems are

discussed in the paper by G. Vettorazzi in *Impact Monitoring of Agricultural Pesticides. Proc. FAO/UNEP Expert Consultation, Rome, 1975* (AGP: 1976/M/4) (Rome, 1976) pp. 39–41.

22. For example *Report of the 1969 JMPR* (Rome: FAO/WHO, 1970) pp. 4–5, and *Report of the 1974 JMPR* (Rome: FAO/WHO, 1975) p. 15.

23. *Report of the 12th Session of the CCPR* (ALINORM 81/24, 1981) pp. 6–7.

24. *Report of the 1977 JMPR* (Rome: FAO/WHO, 1978) p. 4.

25. *Report of the 9th Session of the CAC* (ALINORM 72/35, 1973) p. 38.

26. 'Report of an *Ad Hoc* Working Group of the CCPR, Copenhagen, Oct. 1971', pp. 1–3; and *Report of the 9th Session of the CAC* (ALINORM 72/24, 1973) pp. 14, 15, and (ALINORM 72/35, 1973) pp. 11, 38. On 1969 discussions in the JMPR and CCPR on good agricultural practice see 'Report of the *Ad Hoc* Drafting Group on Principles for Establishing and Enforcing Pesticide Residue Tolerances, Ottawa, June 1969', in *Report of the 4th Session of the CCPR* (ALINORM 70/24, 1970) App. II, p. 5.

27. *Report of the 5th Session of the CCPR* (ALINORM 71/24, 1972) App. VIII; and ALINORM 72/24A, para. 19 (document CX/PR 72/7); *Report of the 7th Session of the CCPR* (ALINORM 74/24, 1974) p. 20 (document CX/PR 74/9); *Report of the 8th Session of the CCPR* (ALINORM 76/24, 1976) pp. 24–5; and 'Summary of Replies to the Questionnaire on Good Agricultural Practice . . .' (document CX/PR 79/16) in *Report of the 11th Session of the CCPR* (ALINORM 79/24–A, 1979) p. 30.

28. Document CX/PR 74/10, ALINORM 74/24, p. 21; document CX/PR 75/8, in ALINORM 76/24, p. 6; and document CX/PR 77/11, in ALINORM 78/24, pp. 25–6, and App. VII, pp. 78–83. See also the *Codex Procedural Manual* (1981) pp. 29–30 ('Definitions for the Purposes of the CAC').

29. *Report of the 14th Session of the CCPR* (ALINORM 83/24A, 1983) pp. 14–15.

30. There has been variation over time in the adaptation of the general Codex scheme. See 'Procedure for the Elaboration of Codex Maximum Limits for Pesticide Residues', in the *Codex Procedural Manual* (1981) pp. 31 ff.; and the summary in Bates, op. cit., pp. 410–1.

31. *Report of the 4th Session of the CCPR* (ALINORM 70/24, 1970) p. 31; and ALINORM 78/41, p. 33. On the 1966 and 1967 discussions see *Report of the 2nd Session of the CCPR* (ALINORM 68/24, 1968) pp. 1–2.

32. *Report of the 7th Session of the CCPR* (ALINORM 74/24, 1974) p. 24. The conclusion of these reappraisals was that major change was not needed in the relationship between the CCPR and the JMPR.

33. See 'The FAO/WHO Joint Programme on Residues of Pesticides in Foods', Ad Hoc *Govt. Consultation on Pesticides in Agriculture and Public Health, Rome, April 1975* (AGP: PEST/PH/75/B 40) (Rome: FAO, 1975).

34. GIFAP *Bull.*, vol. 8 (1982) no. 8, pp. 5–6. See also C. Feldberg, 'Industry Views on Codex', *Seminar on US Participation in the Codex*

Alimentarius Food Standards Program, Sept. 1981 (Washington, DC: Department of Agriculture, 1981) pp. 28–37.

35. *Report of the 14th Session of the CCPR* (ALINORM 83/24A, 1983) App. I, pp. 44 ff., and App. IX, p. 100.

36. Ibid., pp. 33–4.

37. *Proc. Seminar US Codex Alimentarius* (Washington, DC: Department of Agriculture, 1976); *Proc. National Conf. on the Codex Alimentarius International Pesticide Residue Limits, May 5, 1976* (NACA, 1976); and *Seminar on US Participation in the Codex Alimentarius Food Standards Program, Sept. 1981* (Washington, DC: Department of Agriculture, 1981).

38. See the chapter by L. E. Miller in D. L. Watson and A. W. A. Brown (eds), *Pesticide Management and Insecticide Resistance* (New York: Academic Press, 1977).

39. J. M. de Man, *Principles of Food Chemistry* (Westport: Avi, 1980) p. 394; and *Report of the 12th Session of the CCPR* (ALINORM 81/24, 1981) p. 6.

40. *The Times*, 16 April 1984.

41. For a full description of the categories see the *Codex Procedural Manual* (1981) pp. 21 ff., especially at (6) 'Acceptance of Codex Maximum Limits for Pesticide Residues'. For debates and the US position on the so-called two-tolerance system (with distinctions between imported and domestic agricultural commodities) see *Report of the 3rd Session of the CCPR* (ALINORM 69/24, 1969) p. 12.

42. *Report of the 4th Session of the CCPR* (ALINORM 70/24, 1970) p. 25.

43. *Report of the 12th Session of the CAC* (ALINORM 78/41, 1978) pp. 4–5.

44. Data from S. N. Fertig, 'Codex Committee on Pesticide Residues', in *Seminar on US Participation* (1981) pp. 3–5.

45. E. F. Kimbrell, 'Codex Alimentarius Food Standards and Their Relevance to US Standards', *Food Technology* (June 1982) p. 93.

46. *Report of the 13th Session of the CAC* (ALINORM 79/38, 1980) pp. 34–5.

47. *Report of the 7th Session of the CCPR* (ALINORM 74/24, 1974) p. 24.

CHAPTER 5

1. National Research Council, *Regulating Pesticides: A Report Prepared by the Committee on Prototype Explicit Analyses for Pesticides . . .* (Washington, DC: National Academy of Sciences, 1980) p. 20.

2. Ibid., p. 21.

3. Ibid., pp. 22–3.

4. Ibid., pp. 28–30. See also *Decision Making in the Environmental Protection Agency* (Washington, DC: National Academy of Sciences, 1977); and *Pesticide Decision Making* (Washington, DC: National Academy of Sciences, 1978).

5. *Pesticide Regulatory Program Study. Hearings Before the Subcommittee on Department Operations, Research, and Foreign Agriculture of the*

Committee on Agriculture, House of Representatives, 97th Cong., 2d Sess., Dec. 17, 1982 (Washington, DC: USGPO, 1983) pp. 176, 199.

6. Ibid., pp. 56, 65.
7. Ibid., p. 83, and 155 ff.
8. For example the Audubon Society, cited ibid., pp. 74–5.
9. *PSPS Agreed Between Government Departments and Industry* (London: Pesticides Branch, MAFF, 1979) p. 1.
10. Ibid.
11. Ibid., pp. 2–8.
12. BAA, Press release, 2 March 1982.
13. *Chemistry and Industry*, 5 April 1980, p. 249; and 20 Sept. 1980, p. 703.
14. See R. F. Glasser, 'Pesticides: The Legal Environment', in D. L. Gunn and J. G. R. Stevens (eds), *Pesticides and Human Welfare* (Oxford University Press, 1976) pp. 234–5.
15. I. Yamamoto, 'Pesticide Regulation in Japan', in P. S. Motooka (ed.), *Proc. Conf. on the Impact of Pesticide Laws, December 1976* (Honolulu: East–West Center, 1977) p. 74.
16. Summarised from the account in A. Hay, *The Chemical Scythe: Lessons of 2,4,5-T and Dioxin* (New York: Plenum Press, 1982) Chapter 1.
17. Ibid., pp. 147, 163, 165, 177–8.
18. See further R. Brickman, S. Jasanoff, and T. Ilgen, *Chemical Regulation and Cancer: A Cross-National Study of Policy and Politics* (Washington, DC: National Science Foundation, 1982) pp. 236–9.
19. J. Crocker, '2,4,5-T: Contradictions Continue', *Chemistry and Industry*, 1 Dec. 1979, p. 803.
20. See comments by C. Kaufman, NUAAW, ibid.
21. *Report on Phenoxy Acid Herbicides* (London: Advisory Committee on Pesticides, MAFF, 1982).
22. GIFAP *Bull.*, vol. 8 (1982) no. 8, p. 7.
23. The Partial Agreement in question is Resolution (59)23, adopted by the Committee of Ministers, 16 Nov. 1959. The Sub-Committee on Pesticides was until 1965 known as the Working Party on Poisonous Substances in Agriculture (set up in 1956 by the Sub-Committee on Health Control of Foodstuffs).
24. Council of Europe, Committee of Ministers, Resolution AP (79) 1, adopted 6 Feb. 1979, p. 2 and App.
25. Council of Europe, Committee of Ministers, Resolution AP (81) 3, adopted 11 Feb. 1981; Resolution AP (81) 1, adopted 11 Feb. 1981; Resolution AP (77) 4, adopted 28 Sept. 1977; and Resolution AP (81) 2, adopted 11 Feb. 1981.
26. 76/895/EEC, *Official Journal of the European Communities*, No. L 340/26–28/9.12.76. Annex I lists 29 products or product categories, and Annex II identifies maximum levels in 43 cases.
27. *Official Journal of the European Communities*, No. C 56/14/6.3.80.
28. 79/117/EEC, *Official Journal of the European Communities*, No. L 33/36 ff./8.2.79. For the 1976 proposals for a Directive on regulation by way of a system of 'EEC-accepted' plant protection products, see *Official Journal of the European Communities*, No. C 212/3/9.9.76. The

Scientific Committee on Pesticides was set up in 1978 (see 76/894/EEC, OJ No. L 340/25/9.12.76, and 78/436/EEC, OJ No. L 124/16/12.5.78). It has since provided the Commission with scientific evaluations, for example in the 'Communication from the Commission to the Council Concerning the Marketing and Use of Plant Protection Products Containing 2,4,5-T', 8 July 1982.

29. *Official Journal of the European Communities*, No. L 196, 16 August 1967, p. 1.
30. 79/831/EEC, *Official Journal of the European Communities*, No. L 259/10 ff./15.10.79.
31. 78/631/EEC, *Official Journal of the European Communities*, No. L 206/13 ff./29.7.78.
32. For the background to these developments see Brickman, *et al.*, op. cit., pp. 354–6.
33. GIFAP *Bull.*, vol. 7 (1981) no. 9, p. 3. See *The Notification of New Substances Regulation, 1982* (London: HMSO, 1982).
34. GIFAP *Bull.*, vol. 8 (1982) no. 4, p. 4; also vol. 8 (1982) no. 8, p. 2, and vol. 8 (1982) no. 11, p. 10. CEFIC concerns, also put to Commission officials, centred on the treatment of confidential data, in light of the Sixth Amendment provisions for exchange of information between governments and the Commission (see GIFAP *Bull.*, vol. 9 (1983) no. 4, p. 4).
35. M. Trowbridge, 'Government–Industry Interface: A European Industry View', *Chemistry and Industry*, 20 Oct. 1979, p. 700.
36. GIFAP *Bull.*, vol. 7 (1981) no. 2, p. 7; and vol. 9 (1983) no. 2, p. 3. The document at that stage was the Commission's proposal of January 1980 (*Official Journal of the European Communities*, No. C 56/14/6.3.80). Later the plant protection products Directive (79/117/EEC at note 28 above) was amended and new restrictions put on several mercury-based and organochlorine compounds (83/131/EEC, *Official Journal of the European Communities*, No. L 91/35/9.4.83).
37. See comments by G. Dominguez, *Chemistry and Industry*, 17 Nov. 1979, pp. 752–3. One US applicant was reported to have claimed confidentiality for everything, including the name of the company; the application was rejected. See also Brickman *et al.*, op. cit., pp. 356–9.
38. OECD, *Decision of the Council Concerning the Minimum Pre-Marketing Set of Data in the Assessment of Chemicals*, C(82)196 (Paris: OECD, 1982). See also *Good Laboratory Practice in the Testing of Chemicals* (Paris: OECD, 1982).
39. See the report in IRPTC *Bull.*, vol. 5 (1983) no. 3, pp. 11–12.
40. Ibid. ToSCA had not authorised the EPA to require any standard package of test data.
41. See further *Better Regulation of Pesticide Exports and Pesticide Residues in Imported Food Is Essential. Report of the Comptroller-General to the Congress* (CED–79–43) (Washington, DC: US General Accounting Office, 1979) p. 53; and, in general, B. Vagliano, 'Any Place but There: A Critique of US Hazardous Export Policy', *Brooklyn Journal of International Law*, vol. 7 (1981) pp. 329–63; the comment in the

Harvard International Law Review, vol. 20 (1979) pp. 368–73; and C. A. O'Connor *et al.*, 'Regulating Export of Toxic and Hazardous Chemicals', *Chemical Times and Trends*, vol. 4 (1981) pp. 57–61.

42. See the report 'Reagan Opens the Door to a Dangerous Trade', *New Scientist*, 17 Sept. 1981, p. 707. On the Carter policies see the *Federal Register*, vol. 45, (28 July 1980) no. 146 and vol. 46 (19 Jan. 1981) no. 12. The subject was tackled at length by Congress. See for example *Export of Hazardous Products. Hearings Before the Subcommittee on International Economic Policy and Trade of the Committee on Foreign Affairs, House of Representatives. 96th Cong., 2d Sess., June 5, 12, and Sept. 9, 1980* (Washington, DC: USGPO, 1980); and *US Export of Banned Products. Hearings Before the Commerce, Consumer and Monetary Affairs Subcommittee of the House Committee on Government Operations, 95th Cong., 2d Sess., July 11, 12, 1978* (Washington, DC: USGPO, 1978).

43. G. E. Brown, Jr (Chairman of the Sub-Committee of the House Agriculture Committee which had been examining pesticides issues), *Congressional Record*, E 2528, 27 May 1982.

44. GIFAP *Bull.*, vol. 9 (1983) no. 10, pp. 10–11.

45. 'Report of the Secretary-General', A/36/255 (1981). Pressure also mounted in GATT during the early 1980s for some kind of regulatory system, and a trial scheme was tested out in advance of the 1984 GATT meetings.

46. See in particular D. Bull, *A Growing Problem: Pesticides and the Third World Poor* (Oxford: Oxfam Publications, 1982).

47. UN, *Report of the World Food Conf., Rome, Nov. 1974* (E/CONF. 65/20, 1975) pp. 11–12.

48. UN, Preparatory Committee of the UN World Food Conf., 2nd Sess., 'Preliminary Assessment of the World Food Situation, Present and Future' (E/CONF. 65/PREP/6, 1974) p. 7.

49. 'The World Food Problem. Proposals for National and International Action' (E/CONF. 65/4, 1974) pp. 49 ff. On the background of FAO Council and ECOSOC interest in the supply issue, see 'Information System on Pesticide Supply and Demand', Ad Hoc *Govt. Consultation on Pesticides in Agriculture and Public Health, Rome, 1975* (AGP:PEST/PH/75/W5) (Rome: FAO, 1975). A consultation on fertilisers was held in October 1973.

50. 'International Registration Requirements', AGP:PEST/PH/75/W9, p. 2. See also 'Need for International Standardisation of Basic Pesticide Registration: Requirements, Testing, and Environmental Rules and Procedures', AGP:PEST/PH/75/B 50.

51. H. F. Metzger, 'Will Harmonization be Achieved in Rome?' *Farm Chemicals* (International edn) vol. 141 (1977) no. 9, pp. 14–16.

52. Ibid., p. 15.

53. The key background document was by J. T. Snelson, head of the Australian delegation, and long active in Codex activities. See 'Need for and Principles of Registration', AGP: PRR/77/BP17. See also 'Need for International Standardisation of Pesticide Registration Requirements', AGP: PRR/77/BP 15; and 'Legal Aspects of International Standardisa-

tion', AGP: PRR/77/WP 10. Industry submissions (by the BAA and GIFAP) on data and registration are documents AGP: PRR/77/BP 9 and 31.

54. *Report of the* Ad Hoc *Govt. Consultation on International Standardisation of Pesticide Registration Requirements, Rome, Oct. 1977* (AGP: 1977/M/9) (Rome: FAO, 1977) pp. 26–8.
55. Ibid., para. 93, p. 29.
56. Ibid., para. 90–1, pp. 28–9.
57. *Report of the FAO Panel of Experts on Pesticide Specifications, Registration Requirements, and Application Standards (Group on Specifications), Rome, Oct. 1979* (AGP/M/1979/M) (Rome: FAO, 1979).
58. An FAO expert consultation on pesticides and the environment was also held in 1977 (AGP: 1977/M/7). On the 1979 and 1981 sessions see documents AGPP: MISC/34 (Rome: FAO, 1979), p. 12; and FAO, 'Second Expert Consultation . . .', *Plant Production and Protection Papers*, vol. 28 (1981). The 1975 FAO/UNEP consultation on impact monitoring of residues has been referred to already.
59. These matters were pursued primarily through the GIFAP agriculture committee. See in particular *Environmental Criteria for Registration of Chemicals* (GIFAP, Technical Mono. No. 3, 1980). There had been a number of industry criticisms of specific developments such as the treatment of wildlife questions in the Council of Europe's Pesticides guidelines.
60. GIFAP *Bull.*, vol. 8 (1982) no. 9, pp. 1–2; and vol. 8 (1982) no. 5, p. 6.
61. *Report of the Second Govt. Consultation on International Harmonisation of Pesticide Registration Requirements, Rome, Oct. 1982* (AGP: 1982/M/5) (Rome: FAO, 1983). See for example 'A Phased Registration Scheme for Pesticides', AGP: PEST/RR/82/BP 11.
62. GIFAP *Bull.*, vol. 8 (1982) no. 10 pp. 1–3.

CHAPTER 6

1. See for example M. S. Sharom, F. L. McEwen and C. R. Harris, 'Movement of Pesticides in the Environment and Biodegradability', in D. Pimentel (ed.), *CRC Handbook of Pest Management in Agriculture*, vol. III (Boca Raton, Fla.: CRC Press, 1981) pp. 143 ff.
2. *NACA White Paper. The IPM Issue* (NACA, 1981) p. 1.
3. IUPN, *Proc. 4th General Assembly* (IUPN, 1955) p. 64; IUCN *Proc. 5th General Assembly* (IUCN, 1957) pp. 31, 85; and *Proc. 6th General Assembly* (IUCN, 1960) p. 154.
4. IUCN, *Proc. 8th General Assembly* (IUCN, 1964) pp. 67, 102.
5. IUCN, *Proc. 9th General Assembly* (IUCN, 1967) pp. 129, 134–7; and *Proc. 10th General Assembly*, vol. II (IUCN, 1970) pp. 99–100, 101–2.
6. IUCN, *Proc. 9th General Assembly* (IUCN, 1967) p. 168; and *Proc. 10th General Assembly* (IUCN, 1970) pp. 23, 160.
7. Document GA. 72/11, IUCN, *Proc. 11th General Assembly* (IUCN, 1972) p. 129.

8. *World Conservation Strategy: Living Resource Conservation for Sustainable Development* (IUCN-UNEP-WWF, 1980) Sections 2–5.
9. IUCN, *Proc. 9th General Assembly* (IUCN, 1967) pp. 199–200; *Proc. 10th General Assembly*, vol. II (IUCN, 1970) p. 97.
10. IUCN *Bull.*, vol. 3 (1972) no. 6, p. 23; and *Proc. 11th General Assembly* (IUCN, 1972) p. 114.
11. Industry has also been critical of environmental NGO approaches to integrated pest control. See GIFAP *Bull.*, vol. 7 (1981) no. 8, pp. 2–3.
12. UNESCO, *Man and the Biosphere Programme. Expert Consultation on Project 9. Final Report* (MAB Report Series, No. 24) (1975) p. 7.
13. Ibid., pp. 9–10.
14. UNESOB, *Regional Seminar on Development and Environment* (ESOB/DE/1, 1971) pp. 39–40.
15. ECA, *Seminar on the Human Environment in Africa* (1971) Annex 1, pp. 1–2.
16. *Preparatory Committee for the UNCHE, 1st session* (A/CONF.48/PC/6, 1970) p. 6; *3rd session* (A/CONF. 48/PC/13, 1971) p. 25.
17. UNGA, *Report of the UNCHE held at Stockholm, 5–16 June 1972* (A/CONF.48/14, 1972) pp. 40–1.
18. 'Results of the UNCHE at Stockholm', (US Department of State, Bureau of Public Affairs, 1972) p. 34. The United States made proposals for a more restricted programme in 1970; the more immediate origins lay in discussions in the Scientific Committee on Problems of the Environment (SCOPE) of the International Council of Scientific Unions (ICSU) during 1971 in connection with the work of the UNCHE Preparatory Commission.
19. *Report of the UNCHE*, pp. 4, 13, 18, 20–1, 24, 29, 32.
20. UNEP, *Report of the Governing Council on the Work of Its 4th Session* (UNEP/GC/85, 1976) p. 25.
21. UNEP, *Report of the Governing Council on the Work of Its 2nd Session* (UNEP/GC/26, 1974) p. 13 and Annex I, p. 61.
22. 'Report of Sessional Committee I', ibid., Annex III, p. 94; and UNEP/GC/14, Add. 2, Ch. II, Sect. 1.24.
23. UNEP, *The International Register of Potentially Toxic Chemicals*, (n.d.); and UNEP, *Report of the Governing Council on the Work of Its 3rd Session* (UNEP/GC/55, 1975) Annex I, p. 96.
24. UNEP, *Report of the Governing Council on the Work of Its 6th Session* (UNEP/GC.6/19, 1978) p. 34.
25. J. W. Huismans, 'The International Register of Potentially Toxic Chemicals', *Ecotoxicology and Environmental Safety*, vol. 4 (1980) pp. 393–403.
26. J. W. Huismans, cited in the GIFAP *Bull.*, vol. 9 (1983) nos 7–8, p. 7.
27. Ibid., pp. 7–8.
28. 'The IRPTC', GIFAP *Bull.*, vol. 7 (1981) no. 3, pp. 4–5.
29. J. W. Huismans, in GIFAP *Bull.*, vol. 9 (1983) nos 7–8, p. 7.
30. IRPTC, *Data Profiles for Chemicals for the Evaluation of Their Hazards to the Environment of the Mediterranean Sea* (Geneva, 1979); and IRPTC *Bull.*, vol. 6 (1983) no. 1, p. 3.
31. UNEP/GC/85, p. 30; and UNEP, *Report of the Governing Council on the Work of Its 5th Session* (UNEP/GC/96, 1977) Annex, p. 27.

32. Decision 85(V) ibid., p. 116. On the obligations of exporting countries, see also UNEP/GC.6/19, p. 129 (Decision 6/4).
33. IAEA, *Trace Contaminants of Agriculture, Fisheries and Food in Developing Countries. Final Report and Conclusions* (STI/PUB/454) (Vienna: IAEA, 1976) pp. 97–8, 102–3.
34. *IPCS. Report of the 1st Meeting of the Programme Advisory Committee, April 1980* (EHE/80.10) pp. 1–2; and UNEP, *Report of the Governing Council on the Work of Its 8th Session* (UNEP/GC.8/10) para. 221, p. 50.
35. For an industry perspective on the origins and character of the programme see GIFAP *Bull.*, vol. 7 (1981) no. 3, p. 3, and vol. 7 (1981) no. 5, p. 11.
36. Comments by S. N. Fertig (USDA) and S. Miller (FDA), as cited in GIFAP *Bull.*, vol. 7 (1981) no. 10 p. 2.
37. For the FAO emphasis on Codex procedures see UNEP, *Report of the Governing Council on the Work of Its 8th Session* (UNEP/GC.8/10) para. 256, p. 56.
38. *IPCS. Report of the 2nd Session of the Technical Committee, Feb. 1981* (EHE/81.21).
39. Ibid. On the aims of this work see *IPCS. Report of the 1st Meeting of the Programme Advisory Committee, April 1980* (EHE/80.10) p. 4; and the summaries in the IRPTC *Bull.*, vol. 5 (1982) no. 1, pp. 10–11; vol. 5 (1983) no. 3, pp. 8–9; and vol. 6 (1983) no. 1, pp. 11–13.

CHAPTER 7

1. See for example A. V. Adam, 'The Importance of Pesticides in Developing Countries', in D. L. Gunn and J. G. R. Stevens (eds), *Pesticides and Human Welfare* (Oxford University Press, 1976) pp. 115–30; M. B. Green, G. S. Hartley and T. F. West, *Chemicals for Crop Protection and Pest Control* (Oxford: Pergamon, 1977) Chapters 1, 2 and 3; and F. H. Tschirley, 'The Role of Pesticides in Increasing Agricultural Productions', in T. J. Sheets and D. Pimentel (eds), *Pesticides: Contemporary Roles in Agriculture, Health and Environment* (Clifton, NJ: Humana Press, 1979) pp. 3–20.
2. On FAO approaches see L. Chiarappa, *Crop Loss Assessment Methods* (FAO, 1971). The pioneering study is H. Cramer, 'Plant Protection and World Plant Production', *Pflanzenschutz Nachrichten Bayer*, vol. 20 (1967).
3. C. L. Keswani and Z. E. Msechu, 'Economic Importance of Sugar-Cane Smut in Tanzania: Crop/Food Loss Appraisal Report', *FAO Plant Protection Bull.*, vol. 29 (1981) nos. 3–4, pp. 67–70. See also the study by P. T. Walker, 'Survey of Losses of Cereals to Pests in Kenya and Tanzania', *FAO Symposium on Crop Losses*, vol. 2 (Rome: FAO 1967) pp. 79–88.
4. D. B. Reddy, 'The Importance of Pesticides in Indian Food Production', in *Proc. Royal Society, Series B (Biological Sciences)*, vol. 167 (1967) no. 1007, p. 146.

5.   A. A. Hussain, 'Arab Coordination in the Field of Pest Control', *Proc. 3rd Pest Control Conf.* (University of Ain Shams, 1978) pp. 81–2.
6.   *Encyclopedia of Chemical Technology*, 3rd edn, vol. 18, p. 302.
7.   National Academy of Sciences, *World Food and Nutrition Study. Supporting Papers*, vol. I (Washington DC, 1977) pp. 102–5.
8.   National Academy of Sciences, *Post-Harvest Food Losses in Developing Countries* (Washington DC, 1978); D. Pimentel (ed.), *CRC Handbook of Pest Management in Agriculture*, vol. I (Boca Raton, Fla.: CRC Press, 1981) p. 3. See also 'The World Food Problem. Proposals for National and International Action', *UN World Food Conf., Rome, 5–16 Nov. 1974* (E/CONF. 65/4, 1974).
9.   K. H. Buechel, 'Impact of the Agrochemicals Industry on the Third World', *Chemistry and Industry*, 17 Nov. 1979, pp. 794–5.
10.   FAO Working Party of Experts on the Official Control of Pesticides, Section A (Legislation), *A Model Scheme for the Establishment of National Organisations for the Official Control of Pesticides* (AGP: CP 28) (Rome: FAO, 1970) pp. 12–13.
11.   *WHO Drug Information Bull.* (Oct.–Dec. 1980) discussed in IRPTC *Bull.*, vol. 5 (1982) no. 1, p. 23.
12.   A. A. Saad, *Pesticide Chemicals in the Sudan* (Khartoum: Agricultural Research Council, 1975) pp. 92–5, 102–3; and Y. Osman, *et al.*, 'Exposure to Pesticides of Workers Loading Planes for ULV Aerial Spraying in the Gezira Scheme, Sudan', (WHO/VBC/78.684) (Geneva, 1978) pp. 2–3, 5. For a study of effects on cholinesterase activity in a group of 94 Korean farmers, see H. I. Ree, *et al.*, 'Epidemiological Study on Occupational Exposure to Pesticides in Korea', (WHO/VBC/82.866) (Geneva, 1982).
13.   *Daily Nation* (Nairobi) 14 May 1982.
14.   *An Environmental and Economic Study of the Consequences of Pesticide Use in Latin American Cotton Production. Final Report*, 2nd edn (Guatemala: ICAITI, 1977) pp. 98, 176.
15.   B. Sripathi Rao, 'Changing Aspects of Rubber Diseases in Malaysia', *FAO Plant Protection Bulletin*, vol. 20 (1972) no. 1, pp. 1–8. On public health problems see G. Chapin and R. Wasserstrom, 'Pesticide Use and Malaria Resurgence in Central America', *Ecologist*, vol. 13 (1983) no. 4, pp. 115 ff.
16.   B. S. Kaphalia, *et al.*, 'Organochlorine Pesticide Residues in Some Indian Wild Birds', *Pesticides Monitoring Journal*, vol. 15 (1981) no. 1, pp. 9–11.
17.   'The Manufacture of Pesticides in Developing Countries', Ad Hoc *Govt. Consultation on Pesticides in Agriculture and Public Health, Rome, 1975* (Rome: FAO, 1975) document AGP: PEST/PH/75/B 46, 5–6, 9, 10–12.
18.   J. Omo-Fadaka, 'The Sweet Smell of Success for Rwanda', *New African* (May 1982) p. 22.
19.   P. Mungai, 'Threat to Kenya's Pyrethrum Industry', *Sunday Nation* (Nairobi) 9 May 1982.
20.   Saad, op. cit., pp. 84–5. On the problems generally see 'The Formulation of Pesticides in Developing Countries', AGP: PEST/PH/75/B 47,

pp. 4, 8; UNIDO, *Industrial Production and Formulation of Pesticides in Developing Countries* (1972; and revised version centring on formulation, 1983).
21. GIFAP *Bull.*, vol. 8 (1982) no. 7, p. 9; and vol. 8 (1982) no. 10, p. 10. See also J. C. Marshall, 'New Producers: The Far East', *Chemistry and Industry*, 5 Jan. 1980, p. 45.
22. 'FAO Preliminary Report on the Pesticide Supply/Demand Situation', AGP: PEST/PH/75/B 42, pp. 2–6. In 1971–73, consumption of pesticides in developing countries increased by 23 per cent (herbicides 32 per cent, insecticides 21 per cent, fungicides 25 per cent), whereas earlier industry estimates had been for a steady 10 per cent expansion. See 'Pesticide Requirements in Developing Countries', AGP: PEST/PH/75/B 44, p. 3.
23. J. Donnelly (comp.), *Handbook of Agricultural Insecticides Available in Nigeria*, 2nd edn (Lagos: Ministry of Agriculture and Natural Resources, and Entomological Society of Nigeria, 1970) p. 1.
24. I. D. Firman, *Pesticide Handbook* (Noumea: South Pacific Commission, 1976) p. iii.
25. E. D. Magallona, 'Pesticide Regulation in the Philippines', in P. S. Motooka (ed.), *Proc. Conf. on the Impact of Pesticide Laws, 1976* (Honolulu: East–West Center, 1977) pp. 47–8.
26. S. B. Chattopadhyay, *Principles and Procedures of Plant Protection* (New Delhi: Oxford and IBH, 1980) pp. 340–5, 371–7.
27. Figures vary, as do estimates of the extent of the practice. This estimate was given to the author by an official of an international agency active in pesticides questions.
28. V. H. Freed and J. T. Snelson, 'Need for International Standardisation of Basic Pesticide Registration: Requirements, Testing, and Environmental Rules and Procedures', AGP: PEST/PH/75/B 50, p. 4. See also *Impact of Pesticide Laws*, report and recommendations, p. 5.
29. N. Chandler, *Pesticide and Chemical News*, 15 April 1981; noted in GIFAP *Bull.*, vol. 7 (1981) no. 5, p. 7.
30. P. R. Crosson, *Agricultural Development and Productivity: Lessons from the Chilean Experience* (Baltimore: Johns Hopkins Press, 1970) p. 26.
31. *Report of the 14th Session of the CCPR* (ALINORM 83/24A, 1983) para. 7, p. 2.
32. T. Wallace and J. T. Martin (eds), *Insecticides and Colonial Agricultural Development* (London: Butterworth, 1954) p. 8.
33. 'Review of UNIDO Pesticide Programmes', AGP: PEST/PH/75/B 41, pp. 3, 8–10, and the references at note 20 above. Collaboration with FAO staff has been a central feature of this activity, as in the major inter-agency consultation on formulation plants held in 1983.
34. *Report of the 12th Session of the CAC* (ALINORM 81/39, 1981) para. 223, p. 37.
35. *Report of the 9th Session of the CCPR* (ALINORM 78/24, 1978) pp. 25–6.
36. *Report of the 11th Session of the CCPR* (ALINORM 79/24–A, 1979) App. VIII, pp. 77–8. It was recognised that some facilities for residue

analysis existed in Third World countries. See also *Report of the 12th Session of the CCPR* (ALINORM 81/24, 1981) App. V, pp. 87–90; and *Report of the 14th Session of the CCPR* (ALINORM 83/24A, 1983) pp. 72–80.

37. UNEP, *Report of the Governing Council on the Work of Its 9th Session* (UNEP/GC.9/15, 1981) p. 28; and 'List of Dangerous Chemical Substances', UNEP/GC.9/L.11.

38. FAO Working Party of Experts on the Official Control of Pesticides, Section A (Legislation), *A Model Scheme for the Establishment of National Organisations for the Official Control of Pesticides* (AGP: CP 28) (Rome: FAO, 1970) pp. 2–3, 5.

39. See resolution WHA 28.62, in *WHO Handbook of Resolutions and Decisions*, Vol. II, 3rd edn (1979) p. 75.

40. See for example I. Arnon, *Modernization of Agriculture in Developing Countries: Resources, Potentials and Problems* (New York: John Wiley, 1981) Chapters I, III.

41. H. C. Chiang, 'Pest Management in the People's Republic of China', *FAO Plant Protection Bull.*, vol. 25 (1977) no. 1, p. 2.

42. V. G. Dethier, *Man's Plague? Insects and Agriculture* (Princeton, NJ: The Darwin Press, 1976) p. 91.

43. K. Dahlberg, *Beyond the Green Revolution: The Ecology and Politics of Global Agricultural Development* (New York: Plenum Press, 1980) pp. 81–2, 149–66.

44. K. H. Buechel, 'Impact of the Agrochemicals Industry on the Third World', *Chemistry and Industry*, 17 Nov. 1979, p. 795.

CHAPTER 8

1. See for example G. P. Means, *Malaysian Politics*, 2nd edn (London: Hodder & Stoughton, 1976); M. J. Esman, *Administration and Development in Malaysia: Institution Building and Reform in a Plural Society* (Ithaca: Cornell University Press, 1972); and D. R. Snodgrass, *Inequality and Economic Development in Malaysia* (New York: Oxford University Press, 1980).

2. *Laws of Malaysia, Act 149. Pesticides Act, 1974.*

3. A. Balasubramaniam, 'Environmental Problems Arising from the Use of Pesticides in Malaysia', in *Impact Monitoring of Agricultural Pesticides. Proc. FAO/UNEP Expert Consultation* (AGP: 1976/M/4) (Rome: FAO, 1976) p. 23.

4. See comments by Lew Sip Hon, in *Malaysia. Penyata Rasmi Parlimen. Dewan Rakyat. Parlimen Keempat: Penggal Pertama* (Jilid I. Bil. 16) 27 Nov. 1974, pp. 1470–1.

5. *New Straits Times*, 12 Feb. 1981.

6. A. Maheswaran, 'Prohibition and Control of Pollution in the Rubber Industry: Promulgation of Regulations', in *Proc. RRIM Planters Conf., 1977*, pp. 189–200.

7. 'Let's Clean Up Our Acts', *New Straits Times*, editorial, 1 June 1980.

On the 'total transformation' taking place in the environment in Malaysia see also Goh Hock Guan, *Malaysia. Penyata Rasmi Parlimen. Dewan Rakyat. Parlimen Ketiga: Penggal Parlimen Keempat* (Jilid IV. Bil. II.) 30 April 1974, p. 1333.

8. A. Balasubramaniam *et al.*, 'Pesticide Legislation in Malaysia', in L. L. Amin, *et al.*, (eds), *Proc. Plant Protection Conf., 1978* (Kuala Lumpur, 1978) p. 243.

9. A. C. Peter Ooi *et al.*, 'Biological Control in Malaysia', in Lim Tong Kwee *et al.*, (eds), *Strategies in Plant Protection. Proc. Malaysia Plant Protection Conf.* (Kuala Lumpur, 1979) p. 5.

10. W. L. Wood, 'Tuba Root', *The Agricultural Bulletin of the Federated Malay States*, vol. 1, (August 1912) no. 1, pp. 164–6.

11. See for example Ahmad Yunus, 'Review of Work on Major Insect Pests of Rice in Malaysia. Part I: Malayan Region', *Malaysian Agricultural Journal*, vol. 45 (1965) no. 1, p. 33.

12. C. R. Conway and B. J. Wood, 'Pesticide Chemicals – Help or Hindrance in Malaysian Agriculture?' *Malayan Nature Journal*, vol. 18 (1964) p. 111.

13. Professor K. I. Sudderuddin, University of Malaya, cited in the *New Straits Times*, 5 March 1982. In general see K. G. Singh, 'Losses in Food Crop Production', *Food and Agriculture – Malaysia 2000. Proc. Conf. Universiti Pertanian* (1977) p. 291.

14. Cited by M. S. Sharom, 'Frequency of Insecticide Application on *sawi (Brassica juncea)* Production', *Malaysian Journal of Agriculture*, vol. 52 (1980) no. 4, p. 8.

15. *Malay Mail*, 13 March 1980; and 'War on Pests', *New Straits Times*, editorial, 14 March 1980.

16. *Star*, 17 December 1981.

17. Balasubramaniam *et al.*, 'Pesticide Legislation in Malaysia', p. 243.

18. *Star*, 14 June 1979; *New Straits Times*, 20 June 1979.

19. *Malay Mail*, 9 December 1981. The report itself is discussed later in this chapter.

20. Peter Ooi, Department of Agriculture, quoted in the *New Straits Times*, 5 March 1982.

21. A. Balasubramaniam, *Pesticide Pollution, Bull. Public Health Society*, vol. 8 (1974) pp. 27–32.

22. *New Straits Times*, 5 March 1982.

23. Sharom, op. cit., p. 8.

24. Cases of oil palm and cocoa pests declining following halting of spraying in the late 1950s and early 1960s are cited in Conway and Wood, op. cit., pp. 114–5.

25. *New Straits Times*, 5 March 1982; *Malay Mail*, 11 July 1979.

26. A. Yunus and G. S. Lim, 'A Problem in the Use of Insecticides in Paddy Fields in West Malaysia: A Case Study', *Malaysian Journal of Agriculture*, vol. 48 (1971) no. 2, p. 167.

27. A 15-member committee was established in May 1981 to look into the problem. For the background of the research at the Fisheries Research Institute, Penang, see also the *Star*, 16 March 1982, and *Malay Mail*, 23 January 1982. The question is also discussed in Yunus and Lim, op. cit.,

and in T. P. Moulton, 'The Effects of Various Insecticides (Especially Thiodan and BHC) on Fish in the Paddy Fields of West Malaysia', *Malaysian Journal of Agriculture*, vol. 49 (1973) pp. 247–8.

28. Yunus and Lim, op. cit., p. 167.
29. Information from industry sources given to the author in London, September 1979.
30. 'Nama dan Alamat Syarikat dengan Racun Perosak yang telah didaftar', *Acta Racun Makhluk Perosak 1974. Racun Perosak Yang Telah Berdaftar* (Kuala Lumpur: Lembaga Racun Makhluk Perosak, 1981) pp. i–xiii.
31. Balasubramaniam, 'Environmental Problems Arising from the Use of Pesticides', p. 23.
32. Statements by MACA chairman Udanis Mohamed Nor, *Malay Mail*, 13 March 1980; 'Agricidal', *Malay Mail*, editorial, 8 April 1981; 'Weed Out This Menace', *Malay Mail*, 7 April 1981.
33. Balasubramaniam, quoted in *Malay Mail*, 22 July 1981.
34. *New Straits Times*, 1 April 1981; *Malay Mail*, 31 March 1981.
35. R. de B. Ashworth, *Report on a Visit to Consider the Need for a Pesticides Approval Scheme* (Harpenden, Herts.: Ministry of Agriculture, Fisheries and Food, 1970).
36. D. S. Papworth, *Report to the Government of Malaysia. Pesticide Control and Legislation in Malaysia*, FAO Regular Program Document No. RAFE 11 (Bangkok, 1972) para. 6.1.
37. Balasubramaniam, in *Malay Mail*, 6 August 1981.
38. 'Watch It', *New Straits Times*, editorial, 18 July 1981.
39. '"Eco" Balance', *Malay Mail*, editorial, 5 June 1980; and the article by B. Wain in the *Asian Wall Street Journal*, 18 October 1980. Criticism of the Fourth Malaysia Plan centred on the lack of prominence given environmental matters (EPSM, press release, 21 April 1981). See also 'The Malaysian Environment: Ten Years After Stockholm', *Alam Sekitar*, vol. 7 (1982) no. 1.
40. EPSM, press release, 21 June 1979.
41. *Alam Sekitar*, vol. 6 (1981) no. 1, p. 1.
42. *Pesticide Problems in a Developing Country – A Case Study of Malaysia* (Penang: Sahabat Alam Malaysia, 1981). See also the SAM article 'Pesticides – Handle with More Care Please', *Sunday Star*, 6 December 1981; and G. Umakanthan, 'Beware this Scourge', *Malay Mail*, 9 December 1981.
43. Papworth, *Report to the Government of Malaysia*, para. 1.1.
44. Members included the Director of Health Services; the Directors of MARDI, RRIM, the Standards Institution of Malaysia, the Directors General of Chemistry and of Veterinary Services; the Director General of Forestry, West Malaysia; and the Directors of Agriculture, Sabah and Sarawak (*Laws of Malaysia. Act 149. Pesticides Act, 1974*, Part II, Section 3, pp. 10–11).
45. Papworth, *Report to the Government of Malaysia*, paras 1.1–1.3.
46. *New Straits Times*, 24 October 1978.
47. The charge was not usually made openly by government and other officials. This particular criticism was voiced by an unnamed academic

and was later challenged by the Consumers' Association of Penang, which with the closely related SAM tended to be among the main targets for such attacks (*Malay Mail*, 17 and 22 July 1981).

48. In 1981 EPSM criticised powers being sought in relation to registration, including the creation of a category of 'political societies' and related developments restricting opportunities for appeals to courts (*Alam Sekitar*, vol. 6 (1981) no. 2, p. 7); but this question went beyond the environmental area.

49. Papworth, *Report to the Government of Malaysia*, para. 5.2.

50. Ibid., Recommendation 6.24.

51. *New Straits Times*, 23 July 1981.

52. Earlier instruments were the Poisons Ordinance, 1938; enactments of several statutes before the 1950s which had implications for pesticide use; the Poisons Ordinance, 1952, which listed particularly toxic compounds to be barred entry into the country; and specific measures of 1949 and 1953, respectively, dealing with sodium arsenite and hydrogen cyanide. Some provisions for the control of pesticide residues in food were included in the Food and Drugs Ordinance, 1952. Early in the 1970s it was evident that this fragmented picture was an inadequate control mechanism because of ineffective enforcement and the restricted range of chemicals specified. On the origins of the changes, see Balasubramaniam *et al.*, 'Pesticide Legislation in Malaysia', p. 244.

53. Ibid., p. 248.

54. *Pesticides Act, 1974*, Part III, Sections 7 (2), 7 (3), 8 (1) and 8 (2). On the procedures being used in the registration process see also the statement by Dr Balasubramaniam, *Malay Mail*, 6 August 1981.

55. *Pesticides Act, 1974*, Sections 9 (1) and 10 (1).

56. Ibid., Section 20 (1). Procedures for application for a licence to manufacture are set out in Sections 15–20.

57. *Guidelines on Registration, Labelling and Classification of Pesticides* (Kuala Lumpur: Department of Agriculture, 1st edn 1976, 2nd edn 1980); and Balasubramaniam, *et al.*, 'Pesticide Legislation in Malaysia', pp. 245–6.

58. Balasubramaniam, *et al.*, 'Pesticide Legislation in Malaysia', p. 249.

59. *New Straits Times*, 22 July 1981, following the statement by Tan Sri Arshad Ayub, Secretary General of the Ministry of Agriculture. The list as of December 1981 is included in *Akta Racun Makhluk Perosak 1974. Racun Perosak Yang Telah Berdaftar* (Kuala Lumpur: Lembaga Racun Makhluk Perosak, 1981).

60. This was a major element in the charge of over-stringency of regulations being made by some manufacturers. See *Malay Mail*, 3 February 1981; and *New Straits Times*, 23 July 1981, for reactions to the eight-month grace period.

61. This is the *WHO Classification by Hazard*, adopted by the 28th World Health Assembly. See *Acta Racun Makhluk Perosak 1974. Garis-Garis Panduan Untuk Pendaftaran, Pelabelan Dan Pengkelasan Racun Perosak* (Kuala Lumpur: Lembaga Racun Makhluk Perosak, 1980) pp. i–ii.

62. Balasubramaniam *et al.*, 'Pesticide Legislation in Malaysia', p. 248.

63. After 20 May 1981, all advertisements of pesticides had to be submitted

to the Board for approval before being broadcast on Radio Malaysia or TV Malaysia; see *Akta Racun Makhluk Perosak 1974. Garis-Garis Panduan Untuk Permohonan Bagi Kelulusan Iklau Racun Perosak* (Kuala Lumpur: Lembaga Racun Makhluk Perosak, 1981).

64. *Malay Mail*, 13 February 1981; and *Akta Racun Makhluk Perosak 1974. Garis-Garis Panduan Untuk Permohonan Sesatu Permit Mengimport Racun Perosak Bagi Maksud-Maksud Pelajaran Atau Penyelidikan* (Kuala Lumpur: Lembaga Racun Makhluk Perosak, 1981).

65. *New Straits Times*, 18 May 1982.

66. *New Straits Times*, 21 December 1981. Pesticide residues in the blood serum of the general Malaysian population was also reported in one study to be much higher than that in the United States (see Dr Wong Kien Keong, Universiti Pertanian, reported in *Malay Mail*, 17 November 1980).

67. Regulatory change in the pesticides area was also affected by other developments; pesticide manufacturers thus welcomed the later change (in 1983) which led to much greater official protection of patents and industrial property rights generally.

CHAPTER 9

1. R. Aron, *The Industrial Society: Three Essays on Ideology and Development* (New York: Praeger, 1967) pp. 97–8.

2. E. V. Rieu (trans.), *Homer. The Odyssey*, (Harmondsworth: Penguin, 1946) p. 115.

3. Z. Futehally, 'Conservation in a World of Rising Expectations', in IUCN, *Proc. 11th General Assembly* (IUCN, 1972) p. 250.

4. *Pears' Shilling Cyclopaedia* (1911) p. 747.

5. See for example G. S. Lim, K. L. Heong, and A. C. Ooi, 'Constraints to Integrated Pest Control in Malaysia', in *Proc. Conf. on Future Trends of Integrated Pest Management, Bellagio, 1980* (Paris: IOBC, 1981) pp. 61–6.

6. Expenditures on food subsidies represented less than 1 per cent of government expenditures in 1970, and more than 10 per cent during the second half of the 1970s. See H. Alderman, J. von Braun, and S. A. Sakr, *Egypt's Food Subsidy and Rationing System: A Description* (Washington, DC: International Food Policy Research Institute, 1982) p. 9.

7. See for example *The Fragile Web: The International Agricultural Research System* (Ottawa: IDRC, 1983) pp. 11–23; and *United Kingdom Memorandum to the Development Assistance Committee of the OECD* (London: Overseas Development Administration, 1982) pp. 16–17.

8. See the comments by S. Wortman of the International Agricultural Development Service in 'How are we going to feed this world?' *Farm Chemicals* (International edn) Sept. 1979, p. 94.

9. *Manchester Guardian Weekly*, 15 July 1984.

10. J. Trauberman, 'Statutory Reform of "Toxic Torts": Relieving Legal,

Scientific and Economic Burdens on the Chemical Victim', *Harvard Economic Law Review*, vol. 7 (1983) no. 2.

11. Or, more accurately, companies have membership in national associations, which in turn may be members of GIFAP, the main industry grouping in the area.

12. C. Cockerill, 'Agricultural Pesticides: The Urgent Need for Harmonization of International Regulation', *California Western International Law Journal*, vol. 9 (1979) no. 1, pp. 111–38.

13. John Woodward, quoted by A. Holmes, *Principles of Physical Geology*, 2nd edn (London: Thomas Nelson, 1965) p. 1250.

Index